HOW THE
Brain
Influences
Behavior

HOW THE
Brain
Influences
Behavior

Management Strategies
for Every Classroom

David A. Sousa

CORWIN PRESS

A SAGE Company

For information:

Corwin Press

A SAGE Company

2455 Teller Road

Thousand Oaks, California 91320

www.corwinpress.com

SAGE Ltd.

1 Oliver's Yard

55 City Road

London EC1Y 1SP

United Kingdom

SAGE India Pvt. Ltd.

B 1/I 1 Mohan Cooperative Industrial Area

Mathura Road, New Delhi 110 044

India

SAGE Asia-Pacific Pte. Ltd.

33 Pekin Street #02-01

Far East Square

Singapore 048763

Printed in the United States of America.

Library of Congress Cataloging-in-Publication Data

Sousa, David A.

How the brain influences behavior: management strategies for every classroom / David A. Sousa.

p. cm.

Includes bibliographical references and index.

ISBN 978-1-4129-5869-1 (cloth)

ISBN 978-1-4129-5870-7 (pbk.)

1. Classroom management. 2. Problem children—Behavior modification. 3. Brain. I. Title.

LB3013.S628 2009

371.102′4—dc22   2008017847

This book is printed on acid-free paper.

08   09   10   11   12   10 9 8 7 6 5 4 3 2 1

Acquisitions Editor:	Allyson P. Sharp
Editorial Assistant:	David Andrew Gray
Production Editor:	Cassandra Margaret Seibel
Typesetter:	C&M Digitals (P) Ltd.
Proofreader:	Susan Schon
Cover Designer:	Tracy Miller
Graphic Designer:	Anthony Paular

Contents

ABOUT THE AUTHOR ix

ACKNOWLEDGMENTS xi

INTRODUCTION 1
Are Behavior Problems on the Rise? 1
   Can Neuroscience Help? 1
About This Book 3
   Questions This Book Will Answer 4
   Chapter Contents 4
   Other Helpful Tools 6

CHAPTER 1 — Handling Social Misbehavior 7
The Social and Emotional Brain 7
   Emotional Processing 8
   Pathways of Emotional Signals 13
   What Leads to Social Misbehavior? 15
   The Teacher Is the Key 17
Interventions for Handling Social Misbehavior 18
   Dealing With Social Anxieties 18
   Using Social Stories to Modify Behavior 20
   A Case Study: Using a Social Story for a Verbally Aggressive Student 22
   A Social Story for Angry Students 26
Summary 29

CHAPTER 2 — Dealing With Impulsive Behavior 31
What Leads to Impulsivity and Violent Behavior 31
   Genetic Variations 31
   Prenatal Exposure to Cocaine 32
   Cerebral Lesions 33
   An Important Word About Testosterone 34
   Ignorance of Rules of Behavior 35
Some Strategies for Controlling Impulsive Behavior 35
   Cognitive and Cognitive-Behavioral Interventions 35
   Putting Impulsive Problem Behavior in a Social Context 38

Using Picture Books to Curb Impulsive Anger or Anxiety   38

Other Suggested Strategies   42

Summary   43

CHAPTER 3 — Teaching Self-Control Through Self-Verbalization   **45**

Examining Self-Control   45

What Is Self-Control?   45

Are Children Learning Self-Control?   46

Brain Structures for Self-Control   46

Do Mirror Neurons Play a Role in Self-Control?   47

Losing Self-Control   48

Helping Students Regain Self-Control   50

Verbal Self-Control of Aggressive, Defiant, or Other Behavior   51

The Power of Self-Talk   51

The ZIPPER Strategy   52

"Say No and Walk Away" to Resist Peer Pressure   56

Self-Control Through Self-Talk and Self-Monitoring   57

The Nature of Attention   57

Self-Monitoring for Other Problem Behaviors   64

Self-Control Through Self-Rating of Emotional Intensity   65

The Anger Thermometer   65

Summary   66

CHAPTER 4 — Managing the Behavior of Boys   **67**

Why a Concern With Boys?   67

Gender Differences in Behavior   68

Genetic and Environmental Factors   68

Impact of Biology   69

Some Research Findings on Behavioral Differences   72

Using Research-Based Strategies   73

Movement-Based Instruction and Classroom Management   73

Boy-Friendly Instruction and Discipline   77

The Responsibility Strategy   81

And What About Girls?   87

The Rise of Cyberbullying   88

Bullying Versus Cyberbullying   88

Dealing With Cyberbullying   90

Summary   91

CHAPTER 5 — Building Positive Relationships With Troubled Students   **93**

Relationships and Research   93

Insights From Neuroscience   94

Some Research Findings   95

Developing Teacher-Student Relationships 98
The Importance of Positive Relationships With and For Students 98
Reaching Unreachable Students With Dialogue Journals 100
The Lunch Bunch: An Educator's Idea 104
Managing Serious Behavior Problems Through Adult Mentoring 105
Summary 114

CHAPTER 6 — Using Peer Relationships to Modify Behavior 115
Examining Peer Relationships 115
Dealing With Peer Influence: A Two-Edged Sword 116
The Desire to Be Liked 118
Peer-Mediated Behavior Management Strategies 119
Peer-Mediated Anger Management 119
Factors to Consider in Peer Mediation 120
Peer Confrontation to Curb Misbehavior 124
The Mystery Motivator/Mystery Character Intervention to Decrease
Inappropriate Behavior 129
Group Contingency Interventions 131
Summary 135

CHAPTER 7 — Managing Oppositional Behavior 137
What Is Oppositional Behavior? 137
Causes of Oppositional Behavior 137
Students With Oppositional Behavior in the Classroom 139
Teacher Knowledge of Oppositional Behavior 140
Teacher Frustration and Countercontrol 141
Defiant Students: Explosions Waiting to Happen 144
Avoiding Triggers for Misbehavior in the Classroom 147
Teaching Students to Relax 149
Other Strategies 154
What About Oppositional Defiant Disorder? (ODD) 155
Development of ODD 156
Treatment of ODD 156
Summary 157

CHAPTER 8 — Developing Positive Self-Esteem 159
The Nature of Self-Esteem 159
The Power of Self-Esteem 160
Research on Self-Esteem 161
Guidelines for Building Self-Esteem 164
Building a New Perspective on the Troubled Student:
The Strength-Based Assessment 165
What Is Strength-Based Assessment? 165

Motivation and Attribution Retraining   168
   Motivation Research and Attribution Theory   168
   The "Shine My Light" Strategy   174
Summary   178

CHAPTER 9 — Putting it All Together   179
Educational Climate: Are We Happy Here?   179
   What is Classroom Climate?   179
   The Biology of Happiness   180
Successful Behavior Management in the Classroom   183
   Assessing Classroom Climate   184
Classroom Management and Cultural Diversity   188
   Guidelines for Managing Diverse Classes   189
Positive Behavioral Supports in the Classroom   191
   What Are Positive Behavioral Supports?   191
   The Functional Assessment of Behavior   193
   The Behavioral Improvement Plan   193
   Multitiered Interventions and the Student Support Team   195
Summary   202
Conclusion   203

APPENDIX   205

GLOSSARY   223

REFERENCES   227

RESOURCES   241

INDEX   247

About the Author

 **David A. Sousa, EdD,** is an international educational consultant and author. He has presented at national conventions of educational organizations and has conducted workshops on brain research and science education in hundreds of school districts and at colleges and universities across the United States, Canada, Europe, Asia, and Australia.

Dr. Sousa has a bachelor of science degree in chemistry from Massachusetts State College at Bridgewater, a master of arts in teaching degree in science from Harvard University, and a doctorate from Rutgers University. He has taught high school science, served as a K–12 director of science, and was superintendent of the New Providence, New Jersey, public schools. He has been an adjunct professor of education at Seton Hall University, and a visiting lecturer at Rutgers University. He was president of the National Staff Development Council in 1992.

Dr. Sousa has edited science books and published numerous books and articles in leading educational journals. He has received awards from professional associations and school districts for his commitment and contributions to research, staff development, and science education. He is a member of the Cognitive Neuroscience Society, and he has appeared on the NBC *Today* show and on National Public Radio to discuss his work with schools using brain research.

Human behavior flows from
three main sources:
desire, emotion, and knowledge.

—Plato
The Republic

Acknowledgments

Corwin Press gratefully acknowledges the contributions of the following individuals:

Carolyn Chapman
International Consultant and Author
Creative Learning Connection, Inc.
Thomson, GA

Mary K. Edmunds
Teacher NBCT
Detroit School of Arts
Detroit, MI

Maurice Elias
Professor of Psychology, Director of Developing Safe and Civil Schools
Rutgers University
New Brunswick, NJ

Ken Garwick
Consultant
KC Consulting
Manhattan, KS

Toby J. Karten
Graduate Instructor, Author, Staff Developer
College of New Jersey, Gratz College
Marlboro, NJ

Allen Mendler
Educational Consultant and Corwin Press Author
Educational training in behavior management and
    motivation through the Teacher Learning Center.
Rochester, NY

Sylvia Rockwell
SPED Professor and Corwin Press Author
St. Leo University
Palm Harbor, FL

Stephen D. Shepperd
Principal
Sunnyside Elementary School
Kellogg, ID

Carol A. Tomlinson
Professor of Educational Leadership, Foundations, and Policy
Bestselling Corwin Press Author
University of Virginia
Charlottesville, VA

Introduction

Teachers today face many challenges. Not only must they present curriculum content in a meaningful way, but they are also expected to be drug, family, and guidance counselors, health care workers, as well as technology users and monitors. At the same time, they must check for weapons, maintain a safe and positive classroom climate, and deal with disruptive behavior. This last responsibility is demanding a greater portion of teacher time as the number of students with consistent behavioral problems appears to be growing.

The good news is that, despite the public perception, the number of threats and physical attacks against public and private school teachers, as well as the number of fights between students, have actually been declining significantly over the past 10 years. However, the number of disciplinary actions taken by schools in response to less serious behavioral offenses has increased over the same period of time. Whether this increase is the result of more behavioral problems or just more vigilant enforcement of stricter school policies is not clear. What is clear is that teachers report more incidents of disruptive classroom behavior than in the past (Dinkes, Cataldi, Kena, & Baum, 2006).

Can Neuroscience Help?

Trying to figure out what is happening in the brains of students with behavior problems can be frustrating and exhausting. Until recently, science could tell us little about the causes of inappropriate behaviors and even less about ways to address them successfully. For hundreds of years, observing human behavior was the only method researchers had to study how the brain worked. Through these observations, psychologists made educated guesses about which brain systems processed a stimulus and which systems directed the response. However, technology to detect the brain's electric and magnetic waves and, more recently, the development of brain imaging devices have added significantly to our understanding of how the brain controls behavior.

Types of Brain Imaging

Many people today are aware of brain imaging but may not be familiar with nature of the technology. Here is a brief review of the various techniques for looking inside the living brain. The

1

imaging technologies fall into two major categories: those that look at brain *structure* and those that look at brain *function*. When aimed at the brain, computerized axial tomography (CAT or CT) and magnetic resonance imaging (MRI) are very useful diagnostic tools that produce computer images of the brain's internal structure. For example, they can detect tumors, malformations, and the damage caused by cerebral hemorrhages.

Different technologies, however, are required to look at how the brain works. An alphabet soup describes the four most common procedures that can be used to isolate and identify the areas of the brain where distinct levels of activity are occurring. The scanning technologies for looking at brain function mentioned in this book are the following:

- Electroencephalography (EEG)
- Magnetoencephalography (MEG)
- Positron Emission Tomography (PET)
- Functional Magnetic Resonance Imaging (fMRI)

Here is a brief explanation of how each one works:

Electroencephalography (EEG) and Magnetoencephalography (MEG). These two techniques are helpful in determining how quickly something occurs in the brain. To do that, they measure electrical and magnetic activity occurring in the brain during mental processing. In an EEG, anywhere from 19 to 128 electrodes are attached to various positions on the scalp with a conductive gel so electrical signals can be recorded in a computer. In a MEG, about 100 magnetic detectors are placed around the head to record magnetic activity. EEGs and MEGs can record changes in brain activity that occur as rapidly as one millisecond (one-thousandth of a second). When a group of neurons responds to a specific event, they activate and their electrical and magnetic activity can be detected above the noise of the nonactivated neurons. EEG and MEG do not expose the subject to radiation and are not considered hazardous.

Positron Emission Tomography (PET). The first technology to observe brain functions, this technique involves injecting the subject with a radioactive solution that circulates to the brain. Brain regions of higher activity accumulate more of the radiation, which is picked up by a ring of detectors around the subject's head. A computer displays the concentration of radiation as a picture of blood flow in a cross-sectional slice of the brain regions that are aligned with the detectors. The picture is in color, with the more active areas in reds and yellows, the quieter areas in blues and greens. Two major drawbacks to PET scans are the invasive nature of the injection and the use of radioactive materials. Consequently, this technique is not used with typical children because the radioactive risk is too high.

Functional Magnetic Resonance Imaging (fMRI). This newer technology is rapidly replacing PET scans because it is painless, noninvasive, and does not use radiation. The technology helps to pinpoint the brain areas of greater and lesser activity. Its operation is based on the fact that when any part of the brain becomes more active, the need for oxygen and nutrients increases.

Oxygen is carried to the brain cells by hemoglobin. Hemoglobin contains iron, which is magnetic. The fMRI uses a large magnet to compare the amount of oxygenated hemoglobin entering brain cells with the amount of deoxygenated hemoglobin leaving the cells. The computer colors in the brain regions receiving more oxygenated blood and these colors will identify the activated brain region to within one centimeter (less than a half-inch).

Research Into Practice

The nature of the difficulties facing students with behavior problems vary from maintaining focus, controlling impulses, and building self-esteem to establishing relationships with peers and adults. Now, as a result of imaging and other technologies, neuroscientists can gain new knowledge about the brain's structure and functions. Some of this research is already revealing clues to help guide the decisions and practices of educators working with students who have behavior issues.

Students with behavior problems comprise such a heterogeneous group that no one strategy, technique, or intervention can address all their needs. Today, more than ever, neuroscientists, psychologists, computer experts, and educators are working together in a common crusade to improve our understanding of the learning process. Some of the research findings are challenging long-held beliefs about the cause, progress, and treatment of specific behavior problems. Educators in both general and special education should be aware of this research so that they can decide what implications the findings have for their practice.

ABOUT THIS BOOK

Numerous texts about the neuroscience of behavior are available as well as books on strategies for dealing with problem students. This book is unusual because it combines the two. It explores the neuroscience of behavior and then suggest ways that the scientific findings can be translated into effective strategies to manage misbehavior in the classroom.

Thanks to newer imaging devices, psychologists who explore how the brain works (now called neuropsychologists) have been able to detect which areas of the brain are involved in various emotional, cognitive, and social behaviors. Although much of this research has little impact on typical classroom operations, some of it does. What we are doing in this book is examining those areas of research that can help educators understand more about their students' emotional and social behavior in schools and classrooms, and how to deal with them.

> This book is unusual because it explores the neuroscience of behavior and then suggests ways that the scientific findings can be translated into effective strategies to manage misbehavior in the classroom.

As the amount of attention given to brain research grows, misinformation and inaccurate extrapolations of research findings also grow. What we have attempted to do here is select strategies that are compatible with, or can be induced from, the experimental evidence. The suggested interventions are drawn from clinical research that is consistent with the current findings in neuroscience. Nonetheless, more research is needed to confirm the link between those interventions and brain mechanisms.

Even with all that has been discovered in the last decade, there is a lot about the brain that we still do not know. It is important to remember that what we believe today about brain function is subject to change as our understanding and discoveries continue to evolve.

Questions This Book Will Answer

This book will answer questions such as these:

- How do the brain's emotional and rational areas develop?
- How does a young brain make social and emotional decisions?
- How does the rate of brain development explain the erratic behavior of adolescents?
- What leads to impulsivity and violent behavior?
- What leads to social misbehavior?
- What type of data collection can help teachers manage misbehavior?
- How can teachers use self-talk to effectively control misbehavior?
- Why are boys more likely to misbehave than girls and what can teachers do about it?
- How can teachers use movement during instruction to curb misbehavior?
- What impact can music have on behavior control?
- How do teachers build positive relationships with students with behavior problems?
- Do adult mentoring programs really work?
- Can teachers use peer influence to curb misbehavior rather than encourage it?
- What is oppositional behavior and how do teachers deal with it?
- How important is raising student self-esteem and what precautions are there?
- To what degree do school and classroom climates affect student behavior?

Chapter Contents

One of the more difficult decisions authors have to make is how to divide their material into chapters. It is often an arbitrary choice that decides what goes in which chapter, and that is the case here. Behavior, after all, is very complex. It results from the interaction of mental and physical systems operating in changing social and emotional environments. Many of the factors involved in determining behavior can influence each other, so separating them into chapters is not easy. As a result, a few of the suggested strategies show up in several chapters because they address multiple factors.

Chapter 1. Handling Social Misbehavior. This chapter begins with a discussion of how the emotional and rational areas of the human brain develop. It examines the processing of emotional information and how the brain decides on the appropriate response. Factors affecting social behavior are also explored and several strategies are offered that can help teachers control social misbehavior, especially in younger students.

Chapter 2. Dealing With Impulsive Behavior. Numerous research studies have focused on the potential causes of impulsive behavior. In this chapter, we explore those causes and discuss cognitive and cognitive-behavioral strategies that have been successful in controlling impulsivity and anger.

Chapter 3. Teaching Self-Control Through Self-Verbalization. The discovery of mirror neurons has helped to explain a variety of human behavioral responses. Here we discuss how mirror neurons play a role in self-control as well as the means by which an individual can lose and regain self-control. Some strategies are discussed that show how self-verbalization and self-monitoring can be used to help a student regain self-control when needed.

Chapter 4. Managing the Behavior of Boys. Although it is no secret that boys misbehave more often than girls, this chapter explains why that is so. It discloses the different genetic and environmental factors involved in male and female development and how these differences affect behavior. Numerous suggestions are presented to help teachers design classroom instruction and management activities that are more likely to curb misbehavior among boys at all grade levels. Some suggestions for adapting the strategies to manage girls' misbehavior are also discussed.

Chapter 5. Building Positive Relationships With Troubled Students. Humans, of course, are social animals, but exactly how do social bonds form? Developments in a new research field called social cognitive neuroscience are revealing some intriguing insights on how adolescents form relationships with their peers, their parents, and other adults. Students with behavior problems often have difficulty forming meaningful relationships. In this chapter we discuss the important research components and look at several approaches that can build constructive relationships between adults and students who have behavioral problems.

Chapter 6. Using Peer Relationships to Modify Behavior. Continuing our discussion of relationship-building, this chapter focuses on using peer influence to modify student misbehavior. Most students want to be liked and often act out just get their peers' attention. After discussing the neuroscience research in this area, we suggest ways that teachers can use the power of peer relationships to curb other students' outbursts rather than encourage it.

Chapter 7. Managing Oppositional Behavior. Students with oppositional behaviors can be successful in the regular classroom setting. When outbursts do occur, however, what can the teacher do to manage the behavior without upsetting other classmates and losing valuable instructional time? This chapter discusses the symptoms and causes of oppositional behavior and suggests some strategies that help teachers manage these students successfully in the classroom. It also includes a brief discussion of Oppositional Defiant Disorder (ODD).

Chapter 8. Developing Positive Self-Esteem. Although high self-esteem does not guarantee success in school, low self-esteem often results in poor academic achievement and social interaction. Here we explore the nature of self-esteem and look at recent research on how self-esteem affects an individual's responses to environmental challenges. We give some cautions about self-esteem, but also offer some useful suggestions on how teachers can help students raise their self-esteem by building on their strengths.

Chapter 9. Putting It All Together. The sum total of the interactions we discuss in all the previous chapters describe the school and classroom climate. In this chapter we explore the all-encompassing concept of climate and explain its enormous influence on student and teacher behavior. Because of its importance, we offer suggestions on how to assess classroom climate, how to manage diverse classrooms, and strategies for supporting positive behavior. The chapter also includes information on how positive behavioral supports, including the functional behavioral assessment and behavior improvement plan, can help teachers deal with recurring misbehavior.

Other Helpful Tools

Case Studies. In most chapters we include case studies that describe how a particular strategy or intervention was actually used with misbehaving students. We often include the actual dialogue between teachers and students in order to suggest how the teacher might introduce a particular intervention. Although the case studies are true, all names have been changed to protect privacy.

Appendix. Throughout the book we give examples of forms, worksheets, and checklists that are useful to implement a particular strategy. For the reader's convenience, these examples have been combined as reproducible black-line masters in the Appendix.

Glossary. We have included a glossary of terms used in the book to describe neuroscientific and psychological research.

References. Many of the citations in this extensive section are the original research reports published in peer-reviewed scientific and medical journals. These references will be particularly helpful for researchers and for those who would like more specific information on how the research studies were conducted.

Resources. This section offers some valuable Internet sites that will help teachers at all grade levels find many additional research studies and strategies for dealing with troubled youth.

The information presented here was current at the time of publication and we believe that it will assist teachers in dealing with students' problem behaviors. However, as scientists continue to explore the inner workings of the brain, they will likely discover more about the neural mechanisms governing emotional and social behaviors. These discoveries should help educators and parents understand more about the nature of human behavior and why persistent misbehaviors emerge. Stay tuned!

Handling Social
Misbehavior

THE SOCIAL AND EMOTIONAL BRAIN

"I was so angry, I couldn't think straight!" "He got me so mad, I nearly hit him!" Both of these statements make it clear that emotions were running high. Human beings have been interacting with emotions for thousands of years, but understanding where they come from and how they direct our behavior is still not fully understood. Nevertheless, thanks to the development of brain imaging techniques, researchers have made substantial progress in discovering the underlying neural networks that encourage and inhibit certain behaviors. After all, we are not just information processing machines. We are also motivated, social, and emotional beings who are constantly interacting with our environment. Schools and classrooms are particularly demanding environments because so many different personalities gather together in a confined area where they are expected to interact according to established rules of accepted emotional and social behavior.

> Schools and classrooms are demanding environments because so many different personalities gather together in a confined area where they are expected to interact according to established rules of accepted emotional and social behavior.

So what is happening inside the brain of students who display socially unacceptable behavior? Are these just temporary responses to a particular situation or are they symptoms of an underlying disorder? Do we immediately refer the student for mental evaluation or try a classroom intervention that may improve the behavior? These are difficult questions. But before we can answer them, we need to review some of what scientists know about how emotions are processed in the brain. The purpose here is not to make educators into neuroscientists. But the more teachers know about how the emotional brain works, the more likely they are to choose instructional strategies that will lead to appropriate student behavior and successful student achievement.

Emotional Processing

Long before the advent of brain imaging technology, researchers in the 1950s suggested that the structures responsible for processing emotions were located in the mid-brain, an area that Paul MacLean (1952) described as the *limbic system* (Figure 1.1). His work was very influential and the term "limbic system" persisted and continues to show up in modern texts on the brain. However, current research does not support the notion that the limbic system is the only area where emotions are processed, or that all the structures in the limbic system are dedicated to emotions. Brain imaging shows that the frontal lobe and other regions are also activated when emotions are processed, and limbic structures such as the hippocampus are involved in nonemotional processes, such as memory. In light of these newer discoveries, the trend now is to refer to this location as the "limbic area," as we have in Figure 1.1.

MacLean also described the *frontal lobe* (lying just behind the forehead) as the area where thinking occurs. We now know that the frontal lobe comprises the rational and executive control center of the brain, processing higher-order thinking and directing problem solving. In addition, one of its most important functions is to use cognitive processing to monitor and control the emotions generated by limbic structures. In this role, the frontal lobe is supposed to keep us from doing things when we are angry that we would regret later, and from taking unnecessary risks just to indulge emotional curiosity or please others.

Development of the Brain's Emotional and Rational Areas

Among other things, human survival depends on the family unit, where emotional bonds increase the chances of producing children and raising them to be productive adults. The human brain has learned over thousands of years that survival and emotional messages must have high priority when it filters through all the incoming signals from the body's senses. So it is no surprise that studies of human brain growth show that the emotional (and biologically older) regions develop faster and mature much earlier than the frontal lobes (Paus, 2005; Steinberg, 2005). Figure 1.2 shows the approximate percent development of the brain's limbic area and frontal lobes from birth through the age of 24 years. The limbic area is fully mature around the age of 10 to 12 years, but the frontal lobes mature closer to 22 to 24 years of age. Consequently, the emotional system is more likely to win the tug-of-war for control of behavior during the preadolescent years.

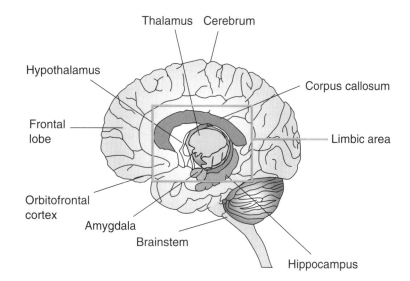

Figure 1.1 A cross section of the human brain showing major structures and highlighting the limbic area buried deep within the brain.

What does this mean in a classroom of preadolescents? Emotional messages guide their behavior, including directing their attention to a learning situation. Specifically, emotion drives attention and attention drives learning. But even more important to understand is that emotional attention comes *before* cognitive recognition. For instance, you see a snake in the garden and within a few seconds your palms are sweating, your breathing is labored, and your blood pressure is rising—all this before you know whether the snake is even alive. That's your limbic area acting without input from the cognitive parts of the brain (frontal lobe). Thus, the brain is responding emotionally to a situation that could be potentially life-threatening without the benefit of cognitive functions, such as thinking, reasoning, and consciousness (Damasio, 2003).

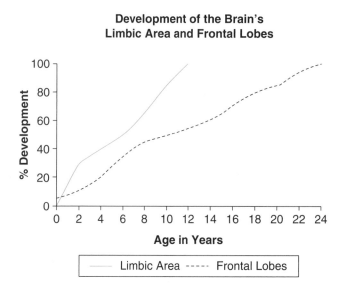

Figure 1.2 Based on recent studies, this chart suggests the possible degree of development of the brain's limbic area and frontal lobes.

Source: Adapted from Paus, 2005, and Steinberg, 2005.

Preadolescents are likely to respond emotionally to a situation much faster than rationally. Obviously, this emotional predominance can easily get them into trouble. If two students bump into each other in the school corridor, one of them may just as likely respond with a retaliatory punch than with a "sorry." On the positive side, this emotional focus can have an advantage when introducing a lesson. Getting the students' attention for a lesson will be more successful when they make an emotional link to the day's learning objective. Starting a lesson with "Today we are going to study fractions" will not capture their focus anywhere near as fast as asking whether they would rather have one-third, one-fourth, or one-sixth of a pizza. Whenever a teacher attaches a positive emotion to the lesson, it not only gets attention but it also helps the students to see real-life applications.

The Orbitofrontal Cortex: The Decision Maker

As investigations into emotions have become more extensive, it is clear that emotions are a complex behavior that cannot be assigned to a single neural system. Instead, different neural systems are likely to be activated, depending on the emotional task or situation. These systems might involve regions that are primarily specialized for emotional processing as well as regions that serve other purposes. However, two brain areas whose prime function appears to be processing emotions are the *orbitofrontal cortex* and the *amygdala* (Gazzaniga, Ivry, & Mangun, 2002).

The orbitofrontal cortex is at the base of the frontal lobe and rests on the upper wall of the orbit above the eyes (Figure 1.1). Research of this brain area indicates that it regulates our abilities to evaluate, inhibit, and act on social and emotional information. Exactly how this regulating effect works is still not fully understood, but imaging studies continue to provide clues. Brain scans reveal that a neural braking mechanism is activated for a few milliseconds (a millisecond is 1/1,000th of a second) when adults are asked to make a decision based mainly on an emotional stimulus. The braking signal is sent to a region near the thalamus (see Figure 1.1) which stops motor movement. A third brain region initiates the plan to halt or continue a response. The signals among these brain areas travel very fast because they are directly connected to each other. In this process, putting on the brakes may provide just enough time for the individual to make a more rational and less emotional decision (Aron, Behrens, Smith, Frank, & Poldrack, 2007). However, the less mature the regulating mechanisms are, the less effective this braking process can be. As a result, the abilities regulated by the systems in the orbitofrontal cortex essentially form the decisions we make regarding our social and emotional behavior.

The brain's frontal cortex activates a braking mechanism that halts movement for a few milliseconds to allow an individual to decide what action to take in response to an emotional stimulus.

Social Decision Making. One way in which we make decisions is to analyze incoming and internal information within a social context and then decide what action to take. For example, we might be so upset by something that we just want to shout out a cry of disgust. But if at that moment we are riding on a packed bus or walking through a crowded shopping mall, the social context (Will these people think I'm insane?) inhibits us from doing so. In schools, students often refrain from doing what they really want

Social context is a powerful inhibitor or encourager of behavior.

for fear of what their peers will think of their behavior. For instance, some students regrettably do not perform to their potential in school because they fear that their peers will think of them as nerds or teacher's pets and thus ostracize them from their social group. On the other hand, students sometimes perform risky behaviors (e.g., underage drinking, reckless driving) just to get their peers' attention. Social context, therefore, is a powerful inhibitor or encourager of behavior.

People with damage to the orbitofrontal region have difficulty inhibiting inappropriate social behavior, such as unprovoked aggressiveness, and have problems in making social decisions. Also, although they fully understand the purposes of physical objects around them, they often use them in socially inappropriate ways. For example, a student with this deficit knows well that a pencil is for writing, but may be using it to repeatedly poke others.

Emotional Decision Making. Because social cues often give us emotional feedback, how we act in a social context cannot easily be separated from how we evaluate and act on emotional information. Nonetheless, experimental evidence suggests that the orbitofrontal cortex evaluates the type of emotional response that is appropriate for a particular situation. Sometimes, this means modifying what would normally be an automatic response. For example, think of a toddler eyeing a plate of chocolate chip cookies. If the child is not allowed to have one, the frustration could well cause the child to throw a fit and physically display anger by kicking and screaming. His brain's frontal lobes have not developed sufficiently to moderate the impulse. Thus the child readily shares his emotions with everyone around him. Now an older child in the same situation might feel like throwing a fit but his frontal cortex has developed further and moderates the impulses. Head injury, abuse, alcoholism, and other traumatic events can interfere with the brain's ability to moderate emotions, resulting in a more primitive level of behavior inconsistent with the child's age.

Here's another example. We generally laugh out loud at a really funny joke. But doing so, say, at a lecture or in church would not be the emotionally appropriate action. Thus, the orbitofrontal cortex quickly evaluates the social situation and overrides the typical response of loud laughter (Rolls, 1999). To perform this function successfully, the orbitofrontal cortex has to rely on learned information from other brain structures. One of those structures that interacts with the orbitofrontal cortex is the amygdala.

The Amygdala: A Gateway for Emotional Learning

The amygdala (Greek for "almond," because of its shape and size) is located in the limbic area just in front of the hippocampus, one in each of the brain's two hemispheres (Figure 1.1). Figure 1.3 shows the location of the amygdala on each side of the brain. Numerous studies have indicated that the amygdala is important for emotional learning and memory. These learnings can be related to implicit emotional learning, explicit memory, social responses, and vigilance. Let's briefly explain each of these.

Implicit Emotional Learning. Suppose a student lives in a neighborhood where gang shootings are not unusual. The sound of gunfire produces fear in the student. If the student hears a car backfire in the school parking lot, that same fear reaction will occur. That's because the student's amygdala has associated a neutral stimulus (car backfiring) with a fearful event (a gun shot). This implicit learning has resulted in what is called *fear conditioning.* Someone coming upon a snarling dog would have a similar reaction. Information from the visual processing system would activate the amygdala which would immediately send signals to the brain stem to increase heart rate and blood pressure as well as to the frontal lobe to decide what action to take.

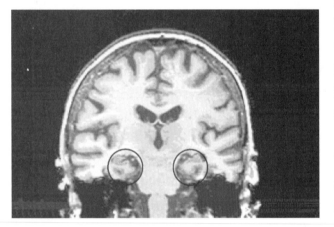

Figure 1.3 The circles show the location of the amygdala in the brain's left and right hemispheres.

Explicit Emotional Learning and Memory. The amygdala interacts with other memory components, particularly its neighbor, the *hippocampus* (Figure 1.1). The hippocampus (Greek for "sea horse," because of its shape) is situated in the limbic area just behind the amygdala in each of the brain's hemispheres. It is an integral part of the brain's memory systems and thought to be mainly involved in encoding cognitive and spatial information into long-term memory.

Information stored in long-term memory can activate the amygdala and cause a fear response to a situation even though the individual has not encountered that exact situation in the past. For example, imagine John, a middle-school student, walking to school and seeing another student coming toward him. As the other student draws near, John gets nervous and fearful and crosses to the other side of the street. What caused this response? It could very well be that John heard from one of his friends that the other student is a bully who gets into fights without provocation. Now, John has had no bad experiences with the bully, but learned about his aggressiveness explicitly from a friend, and that information was stored through the hippocampal memory system.

It is unlikely that John experienced fear when he was told the information. However, when he saw the bully walking toward him, the memory of the information alerted the amygdala, which provoked the fear response. This type of emotional learning, whereby we avoid or fear a situation because of what we are told rather than because of our own experience, is common in humans.

Of course, we remember some emotional experiences because they gave us good feelings: our first kiss, the pride we felt at graduation, our wedding day. The amygdala's interaction with the hippocampal memory system ensures that we remember things that are emotionally important for a long time, while also remembering those situations that can be threatening.

Teachers can use this information to enhance the impact of their teaching. Whenever a teacher can identify a strong emotional tie-in to the lesson content, and explicitly address that emotional connection while teaching, the content is likely to be recalled much longer and with greater clarity by most students. For

> *Whenever a teacher can identify a strong emotional tie-in to the lesson content, that content is likely to be recalled much longer and with greater clarity by most students.*

example, when teaching about the era of segregation in a U.S. History class, the teacher might want to begin by saying to the students, "Anyone wearing white tennis shoes has to sit in the back of the class today, and you cannot eat in the cafeteria at lunch! Please move to the back of the class now!" The teacher would then move those students. Next the teacher inquires how those statements and their forced move to the back made them feel. Finally, the teacher explains that some citizens of the United States were treated in such a poor fashion because of the color of their skin. It is likely that this example generates strong emotions in many readers, and therefore will be remembered much longer.

Social Responses. Although the role of the amygdala in social processing is limited, it does seem to be important in evaluating facial and vocal expressions. Brain imaging studies indicate that the amygdala on the left side of the brain responds more to voice information, and the amygdala on the right side is more involved processing facial expressions. These studies further demonstrate that the amygdala shows activation with different types of emotional expressions, such as happy or angry (Johnstone, van Reekum, Oakes, & Davidson, 2006). However, the activation is particularly intense when responding to fearful facial expressions. This response extends also to evaluating other social judgments about faces, such as deciding from a facial expression whether or not a person in a picture seems approachable or trustworthy (Adolphs, Tranel, & Denburg, 2000).

Such sensitivity to facial and emotional expressions is important for teachers to remember. No matter what we say to students, if the amygdala's assessment of our facial expressions and emotional demeanor contradicts our words, then they will probably not believe us. As a consequence, the teacher-student trust relationship is eroded.

Vigilance. It has long been thought that the amygdala not only processes an emotional stimulus, but also causes the emotional *response* to that stimulus. However, more recent research indicates that the amygdala's role seems to be to process emotional information and to *alert* other brain regions that should be sensitive to this information. Apparently, the amygdala increases the vigilance of other cerebral systems so that they can respond to the situation, if necessary (Anderson & Phelps, 2002).

Pathways of Emotional Signals

The *thalamus* is a limbic area structure that receives all incoming sensory impulses (except smell) and directs them to other parts of the brain for further processing. Incoming sensory

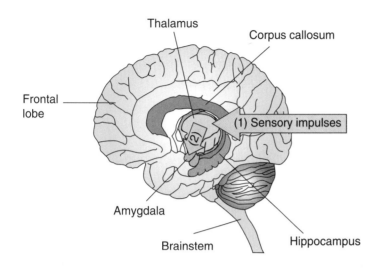

Figure 1.4 In the thalamic pathway, sensory impulses (1) travel to the thalamus where they are routed directly to the amygdala (2).

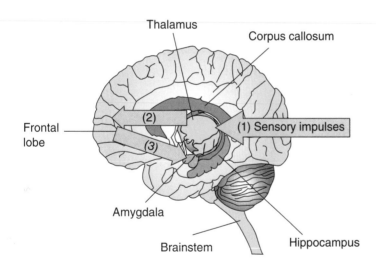

Figure 1.5 In the cortical pathway, sensory impulses (1) are routed first to the frontal lobe (2) for cognitive processing and then on to the amygdala (3).

information to the thalamus that has an emotional component can take two different routes to the amygdala. The quick route (called the *thalamic pathway*) sends the signals directly from the thalamus to the amygdala, as shown in Figure 1.4. The second possibility (called the *cortical pathway*) is for the thalamus to direct the signals first to the frontal lobe for cognitive processing and then to the amygdala, as shown in Figure 1.5.

The time it takes for signals to travel along the two pathways is different. For example, it takes sound signals about 12 milliseconds to travel the thalamic pathway and about twice as long to travel the cortical pathway. Which pathway the signals take could mean the difference between life and death. If the sound from an approaching car blasting its horn travels along the thalamic pathway, it will probably be fast enough to get you to jump out of the way even though you are not sure what is coming. Only later does your frontal lobe provide the explanation of what happened. Survival is the first priority; the explanation can wait.

Disturbances or deficits in this dual pathway system can explain some abnormal social behaviors. Social anxiety disorders, for example, can result whenever a certain action, such as walking into a crowd, is associated with fear. If this activity always takes the faster thalamic pathway, there is no opportunity for the frontal lobe to reassure you that there is no need for fear. Without that input, a phobia develops that cannot be easily moderated later through rational discussion. This probably explains why psychotherapy alone is seldom successful in treating many phobias and anxiety disorders (Restak, 2000;

Schneier, 2003). Treatments now often combine medication with psychotherapy. The principal medications used for anxiety disorders are antidepressants, antianxiety drugs, and beta-blockers to control some of the physical symptoms. Alternative therapies, such as diet modification, eye movement desensitization and reprocessing, and relaxation techniques have also been successful with some individuals. With proper treatment, many people with anxiety disorders can lead normal, fulfilling lives.

What Leads to Social Misbehavior?

Sociologists have examined for decades the various factors that influence how people behave in social situations. Children, of course, often behave quite differently from adults in similar situations, largely because their social skills are still developing. Further, as we discussed earlier, their frontal lobe's executive control system is immature and not yet fully capable of constraining excessive emotional responses.

The neurobiology of social behavior and misbehavior is not well understood. However, the new field of social neuroscience is emerging and some exciting avenues of research are being explored. The goal is to understand social behavior from the perspective of the brain. By using brain-imaging techniques and studies of people with brain injuries, researchers hope to decipher how neural pathways control attitudes, stereotypes, emotions and other socially motivated phenomena.

As exciting as brain imaging is, it does have its limits. People in a scanner cannot move very much and they do not usually interact directly with other people. The signals, by themselves, do not indicate a specific behavior. But these brain signals must be linked with behavior to have psychological meaning. Furthermore, the results of imaging studies must be associated with findings in other related areas, such as lesion studies, animal studies, and studies involving pharmaceuticals. With this approach in mind, research teams have begun examining areas of social behavior such as *stereotyping* and *attitudes*.

Stereotyping. In earlier studies, social psychologists have found that the brain automatically places people and objects into categories such as "familiar" and "foreign," and "good" and "bad." This categorization then biases an individual's feelings and reactions toward those people and objects. Not surprisingly, neuroscientists used imaging technology to focus on the amygdala to put together a possible neural pathway that might lead to stereotyping. One question they asked was "Does this brain structure consider people of different races as emotionally important?" They discovered that the amygdala is especially active at the sight of any unfamiliar face. However, once it has seen these faces several times, it stops emphasizing faces of people of the same race and only emphasizes more the sight of faces of a different race. Thus, the amygdala in whites is more active when they look at black faces, and in blacks it is more active when they look at white faces. This increased activity in the amygdala *could* evoke a fear response and subconsciously strengthen stereotypes about people of different races (Hart et al., 2000).

These results do not mean that there is a brain module for racial categories. It is more probably the result of environmental experiences during our development as a species. Our early ancestors did not get around very much and thus had no opportunity to encounter people who looked different from themselves. When they did encounter others, their brain circuits classified them as to whether they were likely to be an ally or an enemy.

Furthermore, the increased amygdala activity does not mean the response is unchangeable. New experiences change the brain. A follow-up imaging study revealed that the response of the amygdala to same-race versus other-race faces was altered by familiarity and learning (Phelps et al., 2000). In other words, just because we see the representation of a behavior in the brain does not lessen the importance of learning on generating or changing that behavior (Kurzban, Tooby, & Cosmides, 2001; Phelps & Thomas, 2003).

Attitudes. Researchers have long thought that an individual can change attitude after some amount of conscious reprocessing of information. Cognitive dissonance theory, for example, predicts that people change their attitudes after consciously realizing that there is a conflict between their core beliefs and their attitudes. Studies have used patients with amnesia to examine pathways that might be involved in changing attitudes. The researchers found that people with amnesia show an even bigger tendency to change their attitudes when shown a conflict between their attitudes and their beliefs than do people without amnesia. Cognitive dissonance theory would not have predicted this result because people with amnesia cannot remember long enough to realize consciously that a conflict exists (Ochsner & Lieberman, 2001).

However, when you think about it from the perspective of the brain, this finding does make sense. The brain consists of many automatic processes that respond unconsciously to the context of any situation facing the individual. When people with amnesia are told that their attitude conflicts with their core beliefs, their brain automatically changes the attitude to coincide with the beliefs. The only difference is that these individuals do not have access to the conscious processes, such as pride, that might stop them from going through with the change.

The implications of these findings can be applied to schools. Students with social and emotional problems often have distorted and negative attitudes and stereotypes about their family, school, peers, or even themselves. These attitudes and stereotypes may indeed be in conflict with their core beliefs, but they have not had the opportunity to do the cognitive reflection necessary to recognize that this conflict exists. Interventions, therefore, that help students reflect on their misbehavior and on the degree to which that misbehavior is directed by their attitudes and stereotypes are likely to be successful.

This cognitive reflection on one's awareness of and ability to manage one's emotions in a healthy and productive manner is known as *emotional intelligence.* Redenbach (2004) suggests that teaching emotional intelligence involves heightening the students' awareness of their feelings and the connection between their feelings and their actions. This instruction focuses on showing students the powerful choices they make when deciding how to act on their emotions. The result is an increase in the students' ability to manage their emotions successfully in a variety of situations.

With this approach, teachers help students to become experts in the five steps to emotional intelligence: self-awareness, mood management, motivation, empathy, and social skills. Accomplishing this requires the students to gain the ability to do the following:

- Accurately perceive, appraise, and express emotion
- Access or generate feelings on demand when they can facilitate understanding of themselves or another person
- Understand emotions and the knowledge that derives from them
- Regulate emotions to promote emotional and intellectual growth

The important point to be made here is that regardless of the basic cause of social misbehavior, most individuals can *learn* to moderate their behavior through appropriate interventions. Obviously, the sooner these interventions occur, the better. Numerous studies have shown that middle school students who display disruptive and antisocial behavior are at high risk for achieving poorly in high school and becoming dropouts (Battin-Pearson et al., 2000; Newcomb et al., 2002). But there is good news. The research studies also show that if interventions in elementary and middle schools can reduce forms of disruptive and antisocial behavior, then the students' chances for academic success in high school increase significantly (Fleming et al., 2005). These preventive interventions work with elementary

> *Regardless of the basic cause of social misbehavior, most individuals can learn to moderate their behavior through appropriate interventions.*

and middle school students to develop healthy peer relationships and avoid the influence of peers engaged in problem behaviors. Research studies have found programs such as the *Life Skills Training Program* (Botvin & Griffin, 2004), *Project Alert* (Ellickson, McCaffrey, Ghosh-Dastidar, & Longshore, 2003), and *All Stars* (McNeal, Hansen, Harrington, & Giles, 2004) to be effective.

The Teacher Is the Key

Once again, the classroom teacher becomes a key person in deciding how to deal with students who display inappropriate social and emotional behavior. We know from studies that elementary teachers regard certain social and self-control skills as essential for the students' success in their classroom. In one study, more than 125 elementary teachers identified the following seven social skills as being pivotal for student success in their classroom (Lane, Givner, & Pierson, 2004):

- Following directions
- Attending to instructions
- Controlling temper with peers

- Controlling temper with adults
- Getting along with people
- Responding appropriately when hit
- Using free time acceptably

Elementary teachers (and probably many of their colleagues in secondary schools) value skills that promote harmony in the classroom and want to minimize assertive behaviors that could be challenging or disruptive. Teachers, of course, are not diagnosticians or therapists, but they are keen observers. They can certainly recognize when a student's behavioral problems persist and escalate, and they can decide what options to choose. One of those options is to try with interventions that research studies support as effective in controlling student behavior. Here are few of those interventions aimed at controlling social misbehavior.

INTERVENTIONS FOR HANDLING SOCIAL MISBEHAVIOR

We have already seen that social misbehavior can arise for a number of reasons. Handling such misbehavior requires careful assessment of the situation to determine which interventions are likely to be most effective. Here are a few suggestions that include dealing with interventions that target social anxieties as well as those that use social stories to curb undesirable social behavior.

Dealing With Social Anxieties

Researchers in social neuroscience offer suggestions for dealing with students who have social anxieties because these are often an indication of potential misbehavior in social situations. The following suggestions are from the schoolpsychiatry.org Web site of the Department of Psychiatry at Massachusetts General Hospital (copyright MGH, 2006), and are included here with permission. With modifications, these interventions are appropriate for students at all grade levels. See the **Resources** section for more information about the material available from this source.

- **Using puppets with primary students.** Allow socially anxious children to practice social encounters—such as initiating, sustaining, and concluding a conversation—with puppets. You may need a script for some students. For example, "Hi, I'm Bunny the Rabbit. What's your name? I like to eat carrots. What do you like to eat? Where do you like to play? I have to go now. Thanks for talking with me. Goodbye."
- **Watching social encounters.** Some preadolescents and adolescents have little understanding of what to do in a social encounter. Ask the student to watch videos that include social encounters and to identify what others did to be comfortable. What did the video characters

do with their eyes? How did they move their hands and feet while talking to others? How did the others react? And how did the student feel while observing the character?

- **Helping the resistant contributor.** Some students speak off-task freely but resist speaking about the lesson topic for fear of making mistakes in front of their peers. Allow these students to observe several other students before attempting a task. They should observe how other students start speaking, how long they speak, where they look, and how they stop. Then have the reluctant student speak to a group of three or four familiar peers before presenting to the whole class.

- **Sitting with familiar or preferred peers.** Identify peers that the student feels safe sitting close to and place some students into close proximity. Guide the student about how to talk to peers about assignments, such as "How many assignments do we have? When are they due? Where do we start?"

- **Identifying a student helper.** Matching a reluctant or overbearing student with a specific peer or peers can often help that student demonstrate acceptable behavior and participate in class. If the student does not know an answer when called on, allow the student to select a "lifeline." This is a peer whom the student believes will know the correct answer. If the student uses a lifeline, do not accept the answer until the student using the lifeline states whether the lifeline's answer is correct.

- **Sharing feelings.** Adults and peers are often so busy dealing with a student's social misbehavior that they rarely stop and have a face-to-face talk about what is going on. Identify specific times when the student can share feelings with you or another staff person or peer.

- **Rehearsing social skills.** Some socially misbehaving students simply need practice in what constitutes *acceptable* behavior. In a small group facilitated by a counselor, ask the students to review and role play how to make and keep friends. Give students homework to practice the social skills in other settings, such as the classroom, playground, and at home. Then pick frequent or familiar social situations—such as establishing rules in playground games, buying groceries, ordering at a restaurant, asking others to play soccer—and allow the student to role play with other students.

- **Practicing self-monitoring.** Identify and practice steps for the student to self-monitor appropriate peer interactions. For example, "Am I letting other people talk, too? Are we taking turns? Am I learning something from this conversation?"

- **Examining the evidence of negative conclusions.** If the student says, "I can't go to gym class because everyone will laugh at me," ask the student, "What happened the last time you went to gym class? Did any good things happen last time?" Or the student might say, "I don't like coming to school because people make fun of me." Ask the student, "What do students do when they arrive at school? Which students are glad to see you?"

- **Identifying automatic negative thoughts.** The student says, "I act out to get other students' attention because I'm no fun. No one wants to be around (or play with) me." Ask the student, "What happened that made you think this?" or "What causes you to think this?"

Using Social Stories to Modify Behavior

Because of the impressive influence of peers on most students, teachers should consider using behavioral strategies that employ both the power of the social context to modify problem behaviors, as well as teach tactics to curb emotional outbursts. This approach is useful for both general and special education teachers.

The use of social stories—sometimes referred to as *comic strip conversations*—addresses both of these factors, and has received considerable research support (Agosta, Graetz, Mastropieri, & Scruggs, 2004; Haggerty, Black, & Smith, 2005; Parsons, 2006; Rogers & Myles, 2001). A social story is a brief story that presents a problem behavior and various potential consequences of that behavior in a social context. Social stories may teach various techniques for curbing anger or managing stress, as well as present alternative behaviors. In using this technique, a brief story—in most cases only five to 10 sentences—is written that shows some of all of the following elements:

- The occurrence of a problem behavior
- The social results of that problem behavior, and/or an alternative behavior or tactic appropriate for the situation
- A strategy for achieving behavioral change
- A reinforcement for changing to more appropriate behavior
- The positive social impact of more appropriate behavior

Why Social Stories Work

As we noted earlier in this chapter, the brain must not only monitor how its owner reacts to external situations when alone, but must also interpret the intentions and responses of others in a social context. Are they friend or foe? Will I learn from them or need to teach them? Do I want their approval or not? Do I care about them? Do they care about me?

These are very complicated notions for a young and immature frontal cortex to process. Jumbled or incomplete processing can lead to inappropriate social responses. Social stories focus the individual's attention on how one's responses affect the behavior of others. An individual's responses, for example, can cause others to accept or reject that individual. Careful construction of the social story can help a student's brain recognize the cause-and-effect nature of social responses. This process may result in more appropriate responses in future social situations.

Preparing Social Stories

Social stories are generally written in the first person in order to emphasize to the students that the social story applies directly to them. Diagrams or line drawings, similar to a comic strip, may be used to create a pictorial representation of the story for students who have difficulty in reading (Jaime & Knowlton, 2007). In other cases, rather than drawings or pictures, actual photographs of the target student may be used in the social story (Haggerty, Black, & Smith, 2005).

An example of a simple comic strip social story for an elementary student is shown in Figure 1.6. In this instance, a student has been talking loudly in the hallway. The teacher has told the student privately that not talking will earn the class two extra minutes of recess. It is important that the

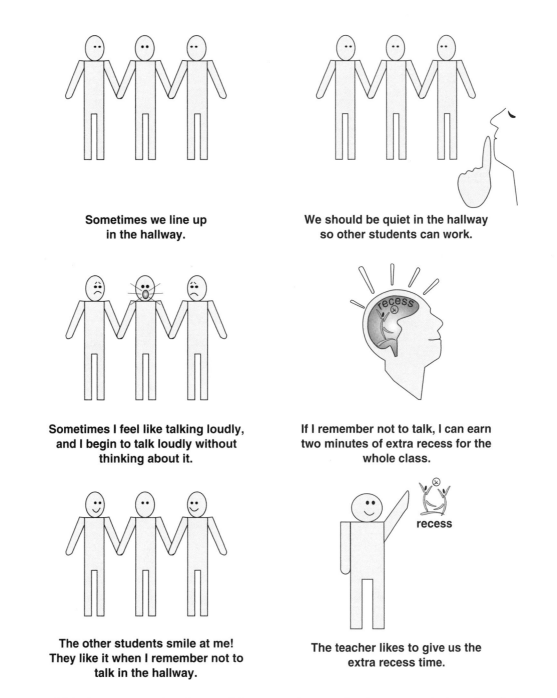

Sometimes we line up in the hallway.

We should be quiet in the hallway so other students can work.

Sometimes I feel like talking loudly, and I begin to talk loudly without thinking about it.

If I remember not to talk, I can earn two minutes of extra recess for the whole class.

recess

The other students smile at me! They like it when I remember not to talk in the hallway.

The teacher likes to give us the extra recess time.

Figure 1.6   This is an example of a social story using comic characters designed to help a student understand that it is important to keep quiet in the hallway.

teacher **not** tell the class that the student's talking will deny them extra recess time as this may cause resentment and rejection. On the other hand, knowing that the student's quiet behavior has **earned** extra recess time may increase the student's acceptance by peers.

A Case Study: Using a Social Story for a Verbally Aggressive Student

Jason's Cursing Behavior

Jason was a second-grade student who often cursed at other students, and this was disruptive in the general education classroom. He had previously been identified as a student with behavioral disorders, and while he was served in a resource room for one period per day, he spent the remainder of his school day in the second grade general education class. The general education teacher, Mr. Anson, consulted with the school psychologist, Ms. Utnay, and they decided to initiate a social story intervention for Jason.

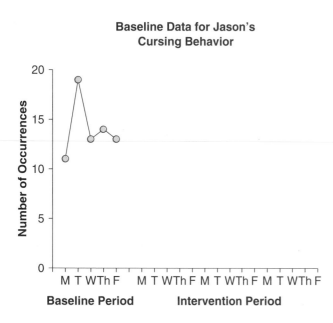

Baseline Data for Jason's Cursing Behavior

Because most of Jason's misbehavior seemed to occur after lunch, Mr. Anson began a simple count of the occurrences of cursing behavior during that time period each day. He counted each occurrence as one example of cursing, even if Jason used multiple words or sentences in that particular instance. Over a period of five days, it was determined that in the period from the end of lunch until Jason went to the afternoon bus, he cursed at other students an average of 14 times daily. It was also clear that most of Jason's cursing was impulsive. Some of these instances led to more serious behavior problems and often resulted in fights with other students. The chart in Figure 1.7 shows the baseline data obtained by Mr. Anson. (Note: Throughout this book you will see data collection charts like the one in Figure 1.7. They allow teachers an objective means of determining whether a particular intervention has been successful. See the Appendix for a black-line master of a data chart.)

Figure 1.7 On this chart, the teacher has recorded the baseline data for Jason's swearing behavior during the week before the intervention.

Creating the Social Story

Starting the Intervention. After baseline data were collected, Mr. Anson and Ms. Utnay began the social story intervention. Ms. Utnay took the lead when the two educators met and talked with

Jason about his cursing behavior. The dialogue below presents part of that initial discussion. Note how the psychologist used the idea of starring in a comic strip to hook Jason into participating.

Ms. Utnay: Jason, Mr. Anson and I wanted to talk with you about an idea we had. Do you remember last week when you had to go to the Principal's office for cursing at Tomika? You got mad at Tomika, and cursed at her during the science lesson. Remember that?

Jason: Yeah, I do.

Ms. Utnay: It wasn't very much fun was it.

Jason: The principal called my Mom, and she kept me from playing outside last Saturday. I was not happy about that, that's for sure!

Ms. Utnay: Well that doesn't sound like much fun at all. Do you remember why you said you cursed at Tomika?

Jason: I just got mad, I guess.

Ms. Utnay: Yes, you told Mr. Anson that you just got mad for no reason and cursed. At other times, you just seem to get mad for no reason, don't you?

Jason: Yeah. I don't know why, but I do.

Ms. Utnay: Well, maybe we can help. Mr. Anson and I have an idea that might help remind you not to curse at other students when you get frustrated. Would you be willing to try something with us?

Jason: What's that?

Ms. Utnay: We want to make a comic strip that can help to remind you not to curse at others. Do you like comic strips?

Jason: Yeah, sure.

Ms. Utnay: Let me tell you the best part. This comic strip will have one star: You! Would you like to star in your own comic strip?

Jason: Yeah! I could show my friends.

Ms. Utnay: You could. You could show your Mom, too, and get her to read it with you. Also, we think it would help to remind you not to curse at others when you get mad. That way you won't get punished.

Jason: OK.

Ms. Utnay: Now to get started, we want to take some pictures of you because you will be the star, and we will need you to act a bit for those pictures. Can you act for those pictures? Can you do that?

Jason: Sure, I can do that. Sounds like fun.

Ms. Utnay: It will be fun. But remember that we are doing this to help you remember not to curse at your friends in the class. That's the important thing here. OK?

Jason: OK.

Preparing the Comic Strip. It was explained to Jason that he would need to pretend for some of the pictures that would be used in the comic strip. In some cases, pictures may be made from actual photos taken during the regular class session, but for pictures involving anger, or severe behaviors, we recommend having the student act out the scene. For Jason's intervention, the sentences shown in Figure 1.8 were prepared as captions for each picture. For older students, these brief sentences may be expanded to three to five sentences for each picture. Note that several appropriate behaviors are suggested as alternatives to the inappropriate behavior of cursing at other students. Also, note the emphasis on the social consequences of Jason's inappropriate behavior.

After the pictures were taken for each sentence in the social story, Jason helped make his own comic strip by pairing the sentences and pictures together. This provided an opportunity for Mr. Anson to discuss these specific feelings and behaviors with Jason, as he prepared the comic strip. In those conversations, Mr. Anson repeatedly stressed that we all sometimes feel anger or get

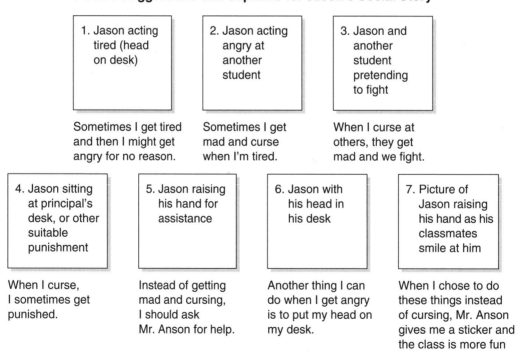

Picture Suggestions and Captions for Jason's Social Story

1. Jason acting tired (head on desk)	2. Jason acting angry at another student	3. Jason and another student pretending to fight
Sometimes I get tired and then I might get angry for no reason.	Sometimes I get mad and curse when I'm tired.	When I curse at others, they get mad and we fight.

4. Jason sitting at principal's desk, or other suitable punishment	5. Jason raising his hand for assistance	6. Jason with his head in his desk	7. Picture of Jason raising his hand as his classmates smile at him
When I curse, I sometimes get punished.	Instead of getting mad and cursing, I should ask Mr. Anson for help.	Another thing I can do when I get angry is to put my head on my desk.	When I chose to do these things instead of cursing, Mr. Anson gives me a sticker and the class is more fun

Figure 1.8   Here are suggestions for pictures and captions for Jason's social story designed to reduce his cursing behavior.

our feelings hurt, but that it is important to avoid responding instantly by doing something that leads to punishment. Thus, the very act of preparing for this intervention provides opportunities for Mr. Anson to discuss impulsive behavior with Jason.

> *Using social stories provides a mechanism for the teacher and student to work together to curb disruptive behavior.*

Several distinct elements may be included in a social story, depending upon the needs of the student. One critical factor in creation of the social story is the general order of the caption sentences. They initially identify the behavioral problem and perhaps the feelings that underlie the problem. Next, the positive and negative consequences are presented. In some cases, alternative behaviors might be suggested for the student, as was done in this example, while in other cases, various self-management strategies might be emphasized (see the following example). Note also that the reinforcement for appropriate behavior ("Mr. Anson gives me a sticker!") is emphasized in the social story (Figure 1.8).

Intervening With a Social Story

Once the social story book has been developed, the intervention can proceed. Each day for the next 3 weeks, Mr. Anson read the comic strip to Jason immediately after Jason returned from lunch. This was intended to remind Jason that he should use one of the alternative behaviors rather than cursing at others if he felt himself getting angry. Also, each day after reading the story with Jason, Mr. Anson encouraged Jason to raise his hand when he felt himself getting angry, so that Mr. Anson could walk over to Jason and help him relax. Occasionally, when Mr. Anson saw Jason becoming upset, he would walk over to Jason's desk and ask him quietly if he needed to rest his head for just a minute. In most cases, Jason said yes, and after one minute Mr. Anson could remind him (again, discretely) to lift his head and rejoin the class. One subtle advantage in using social stories is that this tactic makes the teacher an ally of the target student by providing a mechanism for them to work together to curb disruptive behavior.

In some cases when time allowed, after Mr. Anson invited Jason to lift his head, he would also ask Jason to come to the teacher's desk and quietly read the social story together. Again, this offered an opportunity for Mr. Anson to point out that Jason could control his own behavior in a way that did not result in Jason receiving punishment. Those discussions also emphasized the positive alternatives for misbehavior. Finally, at the end of each day during the intervention, Mr. Anson made time to talk briefly with Jason about his behavior. When possible and appropriate, Mr. Anson praised Jason for behavioral improvement and pointed out that he had received many stickers for good work that day.

As can be seen in Figure 1.9, Jason's cursing behavior did decrease significantly over that three-week intervention period. Although cursing was not totally eliminated, it was reduced to a much more

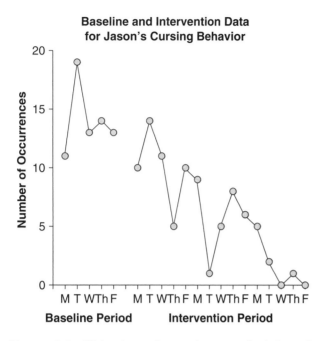

Baseline and Intervention Data for Jason's Cursing Behavior

Figure 1.9 This chart shows the record of Jason's cursing behavior over the three-week period during the intervention. Although the cursing behavior was not eliminated, it was significantly reduced.

manageable level by this intervention. For many students with significant behavior problems, reducing the number of such behaviors, rather than eliminating them altogether, is a much more realistic goal, and does serve to significantly enhance the atmosphere in the general education classroom.

A Social Story for Angry Students

Haggerty, Black, and Smith (2005) reported on a social story intervention that included a component for reducing stress and anger on the part of a six-year-old student with a learning disability. Kirk was described as a student of multiethnic descent who exhibited dyslexia and several other behavioral problems. He functioned in the average range on various IQ assessments, but was angry, inattentive, socially immature, and very anxious.

In implementing the social story tactic for Kirk, the teachers chose to include an emphasis on anger reduction, and they employed a self-statement intervention for that. Thus, this social story actually presented several tactics for self-management of anger. When Kirk felt angry or stressed, he was told to say, "Out with the bad," with each exhale, and "In with the good," with each inhaled breath. This is one form of relaxation that can result in curbing social misbehavior and reducing stress and anger. Kirk's social story book included a total of 8 captions, and given his reading level, the captions were typically several sentences long. Those sentences are shown in Figure 1.10, and in his social story book, each sentence was accompanied by a picture showing Kirk doing the described activity.

In the picture captions, one can see two distinct tactics for curbing impulsive anger ("In with the glad, out with the mad" and "counting to ten" to calm down). Pizzas were counted rather than merely "counting to ten," because inserting the word pizza provided a natural rhythm for that calming process (captions 4, 5, and 6 in Figure 1.10). Thus, Kirk was provided with two strategies for managing his impulsive behavior.

In addition to providing relaxation strategies, this social story also emphasized the social benefits of curbing one's anger (captions 6, 7, and 8 in Figure 1.10). This strategy—perhaps even some version of this same social story—can be used with many angry and defiant students. Teachers seeking new tactics for these challenging kids would do well to consider using this social story intervention.

Picture Suggestions and Captions for Kirk's Social Story

1. Picture shows Kirk angry

Hi! My name is Kirk. Sometimes I get mad. When I get mad, I feel tense. I look like this. I don't like to be mad. So I'm learning how to calm myself.

2. Picture shows Kirk breathing in

When I feel tense, I calm myself by breathing in deeply. Then I say, "In with the glad." It feels good when I do this. I like doing this. My teachers and friends like it, too.

3. Picture shows Kirk breathing out

The next thing I do is breathe out and say, "Out with the mad." I push the mad out. This is fun. I like doing this. I do this three times. It makes me feel less tense.

4. Picture shows four slices of pizza, numbered 1 through 4

Then I count to ten pizzas. I start with 1 pizza, 2 pizzas, 3 pizzas, 4 pizzas. This is fun. I feel better already.

5. Picture shows five slices of pizza, numbered 5 through 9

Then 5 pizzas, 6 pizzas, 7 pizzas, 8 pizzas, 9 pizzas. Wow! I feel good.

6. Picture shows Kirk smiling and holding up 10 fingers

Ten pizzas. Yes, I did it! I feel so good. I am happy and my teacher is happy. My friends are happy, too. I like feeling this way. I like feeling calm.

7. Picture shows Kirk smiling

I'm glad I learned to stop being mad. I feel so calm. I feel happy. I like taking care of myself. My teachers and friends like it, too.

8. Picture shows Kirk and teacher sitting, smiling; teacher's arm around Kirk

My teacher is very proud of me. She says I stop being mad very well. She tells my friends what a good job I do. I like my new skill.

Figure 1.10   These are picture and caption suggestions for Kirk's social story to reduce his stress and anger.

Guidelines for Developing Social Stories

The following are additional points that teachers should consider when developing a social story intervention (Agosta, Graetz, Mastropieri, & Scruggs, 2004; Jaime & Knowlton, 2007).

- **Write in the Third Person.** Writing the social story in the first person may make the story too intimate for some shy students. For those students, some researchers have recommended writing the social story in the third person.
- **Use the Present Tense.** Use verbs in the present tense in the social story because this makes the problem and the solutions seem more immediate to the student.
- **Emphasize the Positive.** The captions in the social stories generally emphasize what students should do and not what they should not do.
- **Maintain Respect.** The captions always use language that is respectful of all students and, in particular, the student with the behavioral problem. Stressing the distinction between the student and the misbehavior is critical, and the social stories give students the sense that they can control their own behavior.

Effectiveness of Social Stories

The social stories intervention has been successfully used with different types of students who display various behavioral problems, and research has repeatedly demonstrated the effectiveness of this intervention. Most of the research has been conducted using students with autism as subjects (Agosta et al., 2004; Parsons, 2006). However, other research has implemented this tactic for students with Asperger Syndrome (Rogers & Myles, 2001) or students with dyslexia and oppositional behavior (Haggerty, Black, & Smith, 2005). Further, this research has shown social stories to be effective for students in the primary grades through high school.

Notice in the previous examples of the social stories interventions the continuing emphasis on relationships with both teachers and students. The importance of these relationships for most students provides a potent basis for this intervention. Even students who say and act as if they do not care what their peers or teachers think, often really do care. Using these relationships as a hook to involve students in interventions to curb their own behavioral problems can be beneficial and productive (Stipek, 2006).

One caution is in order. Older students with more mild disabilities, such as learning disabilities or mild behavioral problems, may find this comic strip tactic to be juvenile, and thus may not wish to participate. However, others across the school age range may enjoy having a social story book made about them. Like all strategies, the teacher determines the student's general maturity and interest in participation prior to implementing this tactic.

There are several sources of social stories on the Internet, such as the Gray Center for Social Learning and Understanding. See the **Resources** section for more information about this center.

SUMMARY

Social behavior is greatly influenced by how the brain develops and organizes and interprets information from its environment. Emotional responses to one's environment are normal and their excesses are kept under control by the brain's executive control system. But given its strong genetic directive to keep its owner alive, the immature brain can sometimes misinterpret harmless social situations as threatening and overreact with an inappropriate response. If there are few or no consequences resulting from this misbehavior, then it is likely to continue. Faced with this situation, there are some interventions, such as social stories and others, that teachers can use to effectively moderate social misbehavior.

Dealing With Impulsive Behavior

WHAT LEADS TO IMPULSIVITY AND VIOLENT BEHAVIOR?

For hundreds of years, researchers have been trying to understand why people resort to impulsive and violent behavior with little or no provocation. Much of this research has centered around the social and economic factors that are often associated with increased aggression, such as drugs and alcohol, violence in the home, and poverty. Some children who are the victims or observers of domestic violence are at higher risk for solving their own confrontations with violence. However, these factors do not explain why some adolescents from perfectly normal home environments and with adequate financial means are also impulsive and violent.

Genetic Variations

A possible explanation for impulsive behavior may have been found in a 2006 study. Researchers discovered a variation in a gene located on the X-chromosome (one of the sex chromosomes, the other being Y) that is responsible for controlling the production of an enzyme known as monoamine oxydase-A (MAOA). This enzyme is directly involved in breaking down serotonin and dopamine, which are mood-regulating neurotransmitters (Meyer-Lindenberg et al., 2006). It seems that individuals with this gene variation produce less MAOA. As a result, concentrations of serotonin and dopamine fluctuate widely. A previous study had already shown a link between increased serotonin levels during early brain development with violence and the variant gene (Caspi et al., 2002).

The abnormal levels of serotonin and dopamine influence how the brain gets wired during the child's development. Using brain imaging, the researchers found that among their 97 participants, those with this variant gene tended to have

- a reduction of about eight percent in the size of emotion-related brain structures
- a hyperactive amygdala, and
- underactive impulse control circuitry in the frontal lobe.

The findings were much more prominent in males than in females. This was no surprise because the variant gene being studied is located on the X chromosome. Females have two X chromosomes, so they are protected if the healthy chromosome can inhibit or moderate the effects of the variant gene on the other chromosome. Males, on the other hand, possess only one X chromosome, so they suffer the full consequences of any variation on that chromosome (see Figure 2.1). No doubt multiple factors contribute to violent behavior, but these findings suggest that individuals, especially males, with this gene variation may be predisposed to impulsive violence.

Not all researchers fully agree with this explanation of reduced MAOA production. Although some studies have had similar findings (Beaver et al., 2007; Foley et al., 2007), others have not been able to find a *direct* link between MAOA variants and impulsive behavior (Haberstick et al., 2005; Young et al., 2006).

Other studies have found potential genetic links to impulsivity not related to MAOA production. The genetic variations do seem to affect how dopamine acts in the limbic area. In one study, the researchers found a high correlation between these gene variants and impulsivity among 195 male subjects (Eisenberg et al., 2007). The research in this area continues.

Prenatal Exposure to Cocaine

Several studies have shown that children who have had prenatal exposure to cocaine are significantly more likely to have problems with attention and impulse control by age five (Mayes, 2002; Savage, Brodsky, Malmud, Giannetta, & Hurt, 2005). No one knows for sure how cocaine affects the brain in a developing fetus. But the outcomes seem to indicate that the functions most likely affected include impulse control, emotional regulation, and short-term memory (Bendersky, Gambini, Lastella, Bennett, & Lewis, 2003).

These exposed children are at high risk of developing significant behavioral problems when the cognitive demands increase during their early school years. The probability of aggressive behavior becomes even greater if these exposed children are male and are raised in a high-risk family environment (Bendersky, Bennett, & Lewis, 2006). It is possible, of course, that these

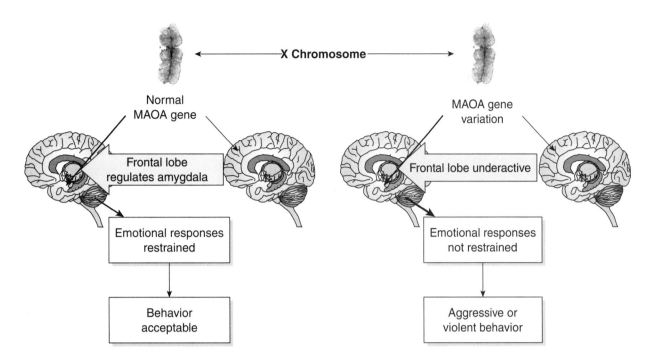

Figure 2.1   The left side of the diagram illustrates what happens when the X chromosome has the normal MAOA gene, resulting in typical brain growth. The cognitive processes of the frontal lobe regulate the emotional responses of the amygdala and the individual's response to a strong emotional stimulus is restrained and acceptable. The right side illustrates the situation when the variant gene alters the concentration of MAOA, affecting normal brain growth. The underactive frontal lobe provides little restraint and the emotional responses are likely to be aggressive or violent.

Source: Adapted from Meyer-Lindenberg et al., 2006.

effects may not persist as the child enters adolescence, a period when the frontal lobe continues to mature.

Cerebral Lesions

We discussed in Chapter 1 the role of the orbitofrontal cortex in making rational decisions (Figure 2.2). Studies have found that individuals with lesions in this area of the cortex often display impulsive behavior. The exact mechanism by which the lesion impedes the orbitofrontal cortex's functions is not known. However, the effect is a failure to inhibit inappropriate behavioral responses, even when the individual knows that negative consequences may result (Torregrossa, Quinn, & Taylor, 2008).

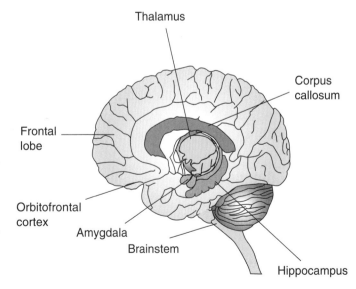

Figure 2.2   Individuals with lesions in the orbitofrontal cortex often display impulsivity.

An Important Word About Testosterone

Testosterone is a hormone that signals the body to build muscle and make red blood cells. It also serves to prepare the body to respond to competition and to challenges to one's status. Levels of testosterone in males and females remain low until puberty. Around the age of nine, the concentration rises sharply in males but gradually in females. By late adolescence, males are producing from 10 to 20 times more testosterone than females. Some researchers suggest that these high levels explain why males tend to be more prone to violence and more sexually assertive than females.

"That kid was really mad. His testosterone must have spilled over!" People often assume that the male hormone testosterone is closely connected to violence. Actually, recent research indicates that there is only a weak link between testosterone and aggression (Book, Starzyk, & Quinsey, 2001; Johnson et al., 2006). Furthermore, if you define aggression as simple physical violence, the link all but disappears. The nature of the link between testosterone and behavior does not appear to be a biological cause-and-effect mechanism. It is better described as a bi-directional relationship that is highly dependent on individual differences, prior experience, and the inclination for a specific behavior. Thus, testosterone is not a mechanism that *causes* or creates behavior. Instead, testosterone increases the likelihood that certain behaviors will be expressed if the inclination for that behavior already exists and the expression of that behavior is consistent with the social demands of a particular situation. Social situations (e.g., those that produce stress) permit, stimulate, suppress, or set the stage for the expression of specific testosterone-related behaviors (Booth, Granger, Mazur, & Kivlighan, 2006).

Effect of the Parent-Child Relationship

In a study of 654 normally developing youths, ages seven to 17, the expression of testosterone-related behavior was dependent on the quality of parent-child relationships. When parent-child relations were poor, sons with high testosterone levels were more likely to engage in antisocial and impulsive behavior, while sons with low testosterone levels were more likely to display symptoms of depression. But different results were found with daughters. When daughter-mother relations were poor, daughters with low testosterone levels were more likely to express risky and antisocial behavior. When father-daughter relations were poor, daughters with low testosterone levels were more likely to be depressed. Apparently, testosterone's relationship with risky behavior and depression was linked to the quality of parent-child relationships. As the quality of the parent-child relationship increased, testosterone-related adjustment problems are less evident.

> There is only a weak link between testosterone and aggression. The parent-child relationship has a far greater impact.

Interestingly, unlike the sons' testosterone, the daughters' testosterone was negatively related to risky behavior (Booth et al., 2003).

Several studies have found that male prisoners, actors, athletes, and blue-collar workers tend to have higher levels of testosterone than intellectuals, clerks, and managers. However, one must ask if this correlation represents a cause, or is this result merely an effect of the environment that these men were in. In other words, does being a violent criminal raise a man's level of testosterone or are high-testosterone men more prone to becoming violent criminals? No one knows the definitive answer, but the research evidence indicates that testosterone is the result of violence as much as it is the cause (Dabbs & Dabbs, 2000).

Ignorance of Rules of Behavior

For some children, persistent impulsive behavior has nothing to do with genetic variations, prenatal drug exposure, cerebral lesions, or testosterone. Behavior is learned, and the rules of appropriate behavior must be taught. Furthermore, they must be taught thoroughly so that the developing frontal lobe can build the knowledge base that will help it exercise restraint on impulsive emotional responses. This in-depth teaching typically takes place through parent-child interactions where appropriate behavior is rewarded and inappropriate behavior is admonished.

In reality, the nature of modern family life has decreased these interactions. Whether it is because of over-scheduling of children's time, internal family problems, or some other reason, children are not spending enough quality time with their parents to learn the family's moral principles and ethic, including what behavior is acceptable or unacceptable both inside and outside the home. As a result, these children come to school with little or no realization that their impulsive behavior is not consistent with the school's expectations. With appropriate instruction at school and at home, these children will eventually exhibit typical rather than atypical behavior.

SOME STRATEGIES FOR CONTROLLING IMPULSIVE BEHAVIOR

Cognitive and Cognitive-Behavioral Interventions

Numerous strategies can be found in the literature that are designed to deal with a student's impulsive behavior. Many of them rely on cognitive and cognitive-behavioral interventions that provide students with the tools necessary to control their own behavior. Essentially, these interventions are an attempt to get students to retrain their brain to use the cortical pathway more often than the thalamic pathway when they make decisions affecting their behavior (see Figures 1.4 and 1.5).

Cognitive-Based Interventions

Specific cognitive-based interventions include (Mennuti, Freeman, & Christner, 2006) the following:

- **Self-instruction or inner speech.** The goal here is to train individuals to make self-statements that will strengthen their self-control when faced with a problem situation. It involves talking oneself through defining the problem, approaching the problem, focusing attention, selecting an answer, and evaluating the outcome. See Chapter 3 for an in-depth discussion of this approach.

- **Social problem solving.** Closely tied to self-instruction, this intervention centers around the purposeful planning and organization of thoughts and behaviors to solve problems. The stages include recognizing that a problem exists, generating possible solutions, weighing the consequences of each possible solution, identifying obstacles, and implementing the preferred solution. An evaluation step may also be added.

- **Attribution retraining.** Because impulsive students do not take the time to understand the thoughts and feelings of others, they often misinterpret intentions and attribute hostile intent to peers who are not aggressive. Thus, this intervention encourages students to step outside of themselves and to look objectively at the situation. Then they are told about how other people feel and can be affected by their behavior. See Chapter 8 for a further discussion of attribute retraining.

- **Stress reduction.** This approach incorporates some of the methods used in the above interventions. The focus is on helping the student recognize feelings of anger and frustration when they arise, interpret situations accurately when this occurs, cope effectively with these feelings, and solve the problem situation.

Cognitive-Behavioral Interventions

Although cognitive-based interventions are effective with students who have mild impulsive behaviors, they may not be successful with students with more assertive impulsivity. Adding a behavioral component to the intervention often leads to greater success. This may be because a purposeful change in behavior requires greater communication between the decision-making and behavior control areas of the brain's frontal lobe and the emotion-regulating mechanisms of the limbic region (see Figures 1.4 and 1.5). The increased cross-talk between these two centers involves the more rational cortical pathways, thereby reducing unregulated impulsive responses.

Numerous studies attest to the effectiveness of cognitive-behavioral interventions in reducing aggressiveness and impulsivity (Lochman, Lampron, Gemmer, Harris, & Wyckoff, 2006). Some types of cognitive-behavioral interventions include (Mennuti et al., 2006) the following:

- **Self-management.** This approach focuses on teaching students to monitor, record, analyze, and reinforce their own behavior. Students rate the target behavior and compare their scores with those of the teacher. If the scores match, the students obtain a reward (positive reinforcement). The students are in complete control of the positive reinforcers they obtain because they are responsible for being aware of their behavior and for providing accurate scores.

- **Self-reinforcement.** A variation of self-management, but in this intervention, the students choose the reward based on their behavior rather than the reward being selected by the teacher.
- **Correspondence training.** This approach aims to improve the correspondence between what students say about their behavior and what they actually do. The students are taught to accurately report past behavior and they are rewarded for the truthful correspondence between their words and actions.

A Case Study: Using Self-Management to Increase Lisa's Completion of Assignments

Let's take a look at an example of applying one of these interventions in the primary classroom. The following case study is adapted from Mennuti et al. (2006). It demonstrates how a self-management intervention can be used to encourage a first-grade student to complete more of her assigned class work. Lisa is a first grader who demonstrated a low rate of academic engagement and a high rate of off-task behaviors. These problems were particularly evident during mathematics lessons and, as a result, Lisa consistently failed to complete her assigned tasks in this subject. Mathematics instruction often consisted of small-group work at five learning centers that focused on different levels of mathematics skills. No reward system was in place for successfully finishing assignments at the centers.

Starting the Intervention. Students were usually given five assignment sheets to complete (one for each center) within a 50-minute period. Lisa's teacher developed and implemented a self-management process that would increase Lisa's engagement with her work at each center. A sheet of laminated chart paper in the shape of a pie was cut so that five internal slices were removed, leaving the round pie crust. A Velcro strip was placed under each slice and five strips arranged equally around the pie crust.

Over three days, Lisa was taught how to use the pie chart. The teacher explained that each slice represented one worksheet for each mathematics period. As each period ended, Lisa was to take her pie to the teacher and decide if she had met the goal she set at the beginning of the period. If so, she could choose a prize from the toy chest that the teacher used as part of her classroom management plan.

Lisa would work with the teacher to set her goal for each day. During the first week, the goal was one worksheet. This amount would increase by one worksheet per week until her goal reached five. The pie would then be phased out and the rewards given less frequently until Lisa needed to complete all five worksheets on all five school days before she could get a prize.

Results. Lisa successfully met her goal of one worksheet per class period on the first three days of the intervention. On the fourth day, her goal was increased to two worksheets per class period, and she successfully completed that task over four days. As Lisa continued to complete more of the worksheets, the teacher began phasing out of the pie chart and rewards after four weeks. Although a slight decrease in work completion was noted when the reward was first removed, Lisa's performance returned to its previous rate as time went on. By the end of the seventh week of the intervention, Lisa was consistently completing five worksheets per class with 95 to 100 percent accuracy. Clearly this intervention was successful in increasing Lisa's work output.

This is just one example of how a cognitive-behavioral intervention can be used to redirect off-task behaviors to productive learning.

Putting Impulsive Problem Behavior In a Social Context

Constantly talking or interrupting others, shoving, fighting, consistent belligerence, and swearing are some examples of significant behavior problems that students display. Students with significant behavioral problems often exhibit these problems impulsively, perhaps when they are angry, emotionally injured, or merely anxious about some real or perceived threat. Regardless of the reason, impulsive emotional outbursts can be disruptive in the classroom, and teachers need strategies that will help students see the negative impact of their impulsive behavior on those around them and on their relationships with others in the classroom. Because human behavior frequently takes place in a social context, behaviors that significantly affect—either positively or negatively—a student's well-being are frequently undertaken in a social context, such as the home, the playground, or the classroom. Within this social context for behavior, impulsive misbehavior can be more readily managed when students

- See the potentially negative consequences of their misbehavior in that context, because most students care deeply about their relationships with their peers and teachers (Bender, 2003; Stipek, 2006), and
- Understand alternative strategies that effectively reduce impulsive behavior.

Using Picture Books to Curb Impulsive Anger or Anxiety

The use of picture book stories has been shown to be an effective technique to teach impulse control and management of emotions such as anger and aggression (Patton, Jolivett, & Ramsey, 2006; Zambo, 2007). Similar to the social stories strategy described in Chapter 1, using picture books that feature characters who display extreme emotions allows teachers to explore and discuss anger, anxiety, fear, or other emotions with students who demonstrate behavioral problems. Instead of using line drawings or photographs of students with behavioral problems, picture books present different characters in emotional situations and suggest how various emotional outbursts may have a negative impact on those characters. These books also allow teachers to select particular emotional responses that they would like to explore with specific students. For example, see *Hands Are Not for Hitting* (Agassi, 2000) and *Words Are Not for Hurting* (Verdick & Heinlen, 2004).

Advantages of Picture Books

The picture book concept has roots in the longstanding tradition of *bibliotherapy*—the use of books and stories for therapeutic sessions with troubled students (Zambo, 2007). Although teachers are not therapists, they nevertheless are often required to assist students in understanding and regulating their emotions in schools and classrooms. Students can often relate to the character's feelings in picture books and then talk more openly about their own emotions. This approach provides students with a constructive option for managing their impulsive behavior.

> Picture books provide students with a constructive option for managing their impulsive behavior.

Another advantage of using picture books involves the distancing of the emotions from the target student. The emotional characters in these picture books provide students the freedom to talk about negative emotions that they might not otherwise discuss directly with a teacher. For example, when a student reads about, or witnesses pictures of, a character who has difficulty managing anger, that student is more likely to talk about anger with the teacher because it is not the student's anger, it is that of a character in the picture book. Furthermore, the picture books allow for isolation of particular emotions for different children. For example, the picture book that one might use with an enraged, aggressive second grader would present different characters and situations from the picture book used with clingy or attention-seeking students in grade five.

A Case Study: Lukay's Picture Book

Let's look at an example. Lukay transferred into Mr. Timmons' third-grade class in a small rural school about two months after the school year began. Because the school was fairly small, many of the second-grade students had attended both first and second grade together in the same class, and thus those students knew each other fairly well. Lukay, on the other hand, had moved often in his young life, and he demonstrated some behavioral problems, such as impulsivity, or anger at other students or at himself. He often misbehaved immediately after he failed in an academic task. Mr. Timmons became concerned one day when Lukay got angry after not receiving a high grade on a spelling quiz. Lukay stated, "I hate it that I'm so stupid!" He then threw his notebook across the floor. Although neither self-hatred nor suicide is typical of young children, a statement such as this is reason for concern, so Mr. Timmons decided to use picture books to explore Lukay's emotional state.

The picture book, *When Sophie Gets Angry—Really, Really, Angry* (Bang, 1999), shows a child named Sophie experiencing anger with her sister and losing control. Sophie is pictured kicking, screaming, and threatening to "Smash the world to smithereens!" The text presents pictures of these emotional states and emphasizes the facial expressions that characterize such impulsive and destructive behavior. These pictures can be greatly beneficial to students with special needs who may not be able to read the text. However, the text also describes the heightened emotional states by using words like "explode," "smash," and "roar" printed in large letters and sometimes printed in bright colors. One of the illustrations in this particular book includes dragon-like fire coming from Sophie's mouth.

Using this material and similar books, Mr. Timmons planned a series of reading and instructional sessions to help Lukay learn about his emotions and how to manage them. Mr. Timmons first completed an ABC log (Antecedent, Behavior, Consequences) as shown in Figure 2.3, in which he noted all of the impulsive emotional outbursts shown by Lukay over a five-day period. That provided information which Mr. Timmons could use as a baseline count of Lukay's displays of anger. An ABC log such as this often proves to be a very useful tool in helping teachers catalogue behavioral problems for later discussion with parents, administrators, or other professionals. Every teacher should consider regularly documenting behavioral problems in this fashion, or with some similar note-taking system.

ABC Log of Lukay's Anger Behavior			
<u>Day/Date</u>	<u>Antecedent</u>	<u>Behavior</u>	<u>Consequence</u>
Monday 9/17/07	Spelling test returned. His grade was 82.	"I hate that I'm so stupid." Tossed book on floor.	I talked with Lukay. Reported this to guidance office.
Tuesday 9/18/07	I told students to line up for recess. I asked Lukay to answer a question in class.	"I don't have any friends to play with! I hate school!" Lukay said, "This is stupid!"	Made certain Lukay was included in softball. I ignored response and called on another student
Wednesday 9/19/07	No emotional outbursts noted today.	A good day for Lukay.	
Thursday 9/20/07	Students told in math to find a math partner. Later same day: When told a pop quiz was coming.	"I hate this! Nobody likes me!" Lukay screamed, "Why all these f_____ tests?"	I talked with Lukay. I took Lukay to office and requested help.
Friday 9/21/07	Just before final spelling test	Lukay screamed, "I don't want to do that damn test!"	Decided to initiate intervention.

Figure 2.3   This log records a student's emotional outbreaks over a five-day period. See the Appendix for a black-line master of this form.

After the five-day baseline, Mr. Timmons began using the picture book as the reading materials for Lukay. Of course, in general education classes, it is possible to use the picture books for whole-class lessons when discussing impulsive behavior. In those instances, teachers would discuss the emotional issues in a particular picture book with the entire class, and then work briefly one-to-one with the student targeted for the intervention. However, in this example, Mr. Timmons chose to use the picture book exclusively with Lukay, working from 10 to 15 minutes each day for the next 10 days. When he worked with Lukay, Mr. Timmons either gave the other students written work or he asked a cooperating special education teacher to teach the class.

On any given day, Mr. Timmons would use the picture book, or others that addressed impulsive emotional behaviors (see Zambo, 2007, for recommendations). He and Lukay would read several pages from the book, and after reading each page, he asked Lukay to help him interpret the pictures in the book. Lukay was thus interpreting facial expressions and developing ideas about why the characters might feel particular emotions. Also, whenever negative consequences followed impulsive misbehavior, Mr. Timmons repeatedly pointed out that not thinking before one acts often has negative results.

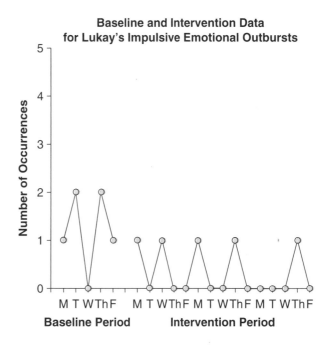

After only two days, Lukay began to talk a little about himself, usually saying things like, "I sometimes feel that angry," or "It makes me mad when I don't do well on tests, too!" Of course, in each instance, Mr. Timmons pointed out that everybody feels angry from time to time, but that a person must learn to express anger without being mean to anyone else.

In some cases, teachers may wish to indicate that they are actually keeping data on a student's impulsive outbursts. For many students, actually seeing the count of their impulsive behavior decrease over time can be rewarding. However, in this instance, Mr. Timmons decided not to share the data with Lukay because it might damage the rapport that he was trying to establish. In order to know that this picture book intervention worked over time, he kept a daily count of the number of impulsive behaviors Lukay displayed. The data in Figure 2.4 clearly indicate that using picture books decreased the number of impulsive behaviors demonstrated by Lukay from a total of six in the baseline week to only one outburst during the third week of intervention.

Figure 2.4 This chart records the number of emotional outbursts displayed by the student during both the baseline week and during the three weeks of intervention.

Other Suggested Strategies

Researchers studying impulsivity offer suggestions to teachers for dealing with students whose impulsive behavior disrupts class and school activities. The following suggestions are from the schoolpsychiatry.org Web site of the Department of Psychiatry at Massachusetts General Hospital (copyright MGH, 2006), and are included here with permission. See the **Resources** section for more information about the material available from this source.

> *Getting the student to pause through counting or writing may give the brain the few seconds it needs to dampen impulsive emotional responses.*

With modifications, these suggestions are appropriate for students at all grade levels. Note that several of them rely on having the student pause before responding, such as by counting or writing. Those few seconds may be just enough to give the brain's frontal lobe a chance to assess the learning situation cognitively and to dampen impulsive emotional responses.

- **Identifying what "ready to learn" looks like.** Some impulsive students do not know the meaning of being ready to learn. Help the student understand the characteristics of a student who is ready to learn: for example, looking at the teacher, raising a hand, watching to see who the teacher is calling on, and checking one's answer against that of the called-on student.

- **Establishing a waiting routine.** Develop with the student a multi-step plan for waiting, such as: "Count to five, then raise your hand and look the teacher in the eyes."

- **Writing before answering aloud.** For students who impulsively blurt out answers, establish a routine whereby the student writes out the answers before saying them aloud.

- **Signaling when transitions are coming.** Prepare the student for transitions in class activities, clarifying the appropriate and expected behaviors. For example, "Finish your work, put all the materials where they belong, and line up putting your hands in your pockets (or some other age-appropriate action)."

- **Transitioning apart from the group.** If a student's impulsivity includes antisocial behavior, identify options for the student to leave the classroom a few minutes before or after peers to, for example, go to the gym or get on the school bus.

- **Posting classroom and school expectations.** Our purpose here is to get the frontal lobe to learn thoroughly the expected behaviors. So signs around the classroom that clearly remind students of behavior expectations inside and outside the classroom serve as cognitive reinforcers.

- **Focusing on the expected behavior.** When inappropriate impulsive behavior occurs, clarify what you want the student to do rather than describing the misbehavior. Ask the student to say aloud the expected behavior, privately to you. This approach once again causes the student's brain to rehearse and relearn the appropriate response.

- **Examining impulsive acts.** Work with the student to examine impulsive acts and then discuss practicing thinking before acting. Use children's and adolescent literature to explore the causes of impulsive behavior and the resulting consequences. Where appropriate, explain how the young brain develops and that emotional responses tend to come first. This explanation does not provide an excuse for unacceptable behavior but alerts the student as to why it is so important to pause and reflect before acting. Doing otherwise may result in negative consequences.

- **Making consequences clear.** When a student's impulsive behavior persists, shift the conversation to student choices and consequences. Including consequences allows the brain's frontal lobe to understand what will happen if its restraint over impulsivity fails. For example, you might say: "You can decide whether to complete this task right now. If you choose not to complete this task now, the likely consequences will include more homework tonight, or staying in to finish during recess/after school."

SUMMARY

Impulsive behavior may result from a number of causes, including genetic predispositions, prenatal exposure to cocaine and other drugs, and cerebral lesions. It may also result from just not knowing how to behave in different environments. Numerous strategies are available to teachers to deal with impulsive students. They include cognitive and cognitive-behavioral interventions, picture books, and other approaches designed to help students learn thoroughly what is acceptable behavior as well as the consequences of unacceptable impulsive behavior.

Teaching Self-Control Through Self-Verbalization

EXAMINING SELF-CONTROL

Seeing a child throw a temper tantrum in a shopping mall reminds us that the capacity to willfully control our actions is not innate. Rather, it emerges gradually during a child's development. Self-control, then, is one of the more obvious indicators of social maturity. The child's tantrum is much more tolerated and understood than one thrown by an adult.

What Is Self-Control?

One of the most important skills that children must develop is self-control (also called self-regulation). Self-control refers to the internal mechanism that underlies the mindful, purposeful, and thoughtful behaviors of all children. It is the capacity to control one's impulses, both to stop doing something that is unnecessary (even if one wants to continue doing it), and to start doing something that is necessary (even if one does not want to do it). This ability to inhibit one response and to enact another on-demand is a skill used in thinking as well as social interactions. The child who does not have self-control at age 5 cannot follow the teacher's directions at age 6, and cannot plan how to solve a problem at age 7. The child without self-control of emotions at age 4 will not be able to control temper at age 5 and will have frequent negative peer interactions at age 7 (Boyd et al., 2005).

Self-control is necessary for positive social relations with others and for successful learning in school. To learn anything in a school setting, children must ignore those next to them who are fun to play with and concentrate on the teacher's lesson. Paying attention and remembering things on purpose are also part of self-control. The role of self-control in school success—from preschool and kindergarten to middle and high school—has been documented in research studies. Levels of self-control actually predict school success in first grade over and above children's cognitive skills and family background (Ravner & Knitzer, 2002). Children lacking emotional self-control are at higher risk for disciplinary problems and are less likely to make a successful transition from preschool to kindergarten (Huffman, Mehlinger, & Kerivan, 2001). Emotional self-control seems to play a part in child resiliency and later adjustment (Eisenberg et al., 2004). Children who did not learn self-control in preschool can turn into bullies with aggressive habits of interaction that are difficult to break in later years (Shonkoff & Phillips, 2000).

Are Children Learning Self-Control?

In some studies, as many as 32 percent of preschoolers in Head Start programs have behavioral problems (West, Denton, & Reaney, 2001). Kindergarten teachers report that many of their students are not socially or emotionally prepared for the challenges of school and estimate that 20 to 30 percent of all entering kindergartners have poor social skills. They enter unable to learn because they cannot pay attention, remember information, or function socially with other students. As a result, more children are hard to manage in the classroom because they cannot get along with each other, follow directions, or delay gratification. They often show aggression and belligerence in the classroom and on the playground. These missing social and emotional skills mean that teachers spend too much of their time reining in unmanageable children and too little time teaching. Without intervention, the result can be growing aggression, behavioral problems, and, for some, delinquency and crime through the school years and into adulthood (Boyd, Barnett, Bodrova, Leong, & Gomby, 2005).

BRAIN STRUCTURES FOR SELF-CONTROL

How does a developing child learn self-control and what can go wrong during the process? We noted in Chapter 1 that the brain's frontal lobe plays an important role in monitoring the limbic area in an effort to keep emotions under control. But we also discovered that the frontal lobe matures much more slowly than the limbic structures, leading to excessive displays of emotions during the preadolescent and adolescent years. The part of the frontal lobe that appears to be closely involved in monitoring emotions is called the *anterior cingulate* (see Figure 3.1).

Research studies using brain imaging and electroencephalography (EEG) indicate that the anterior cingulate is highly activated whenever an individual is attempting to resolve conflicting ideas or facing distress. Individuals in a classroom or any other social situation are rarely in complete agreement with each other. When disagreements arise, the brain is often in distress. But our ability to curb the distress and seek compromise is essential for social interaction and harmony. Distress prompts the amygdala to generate negative emotions that can escalate unless some mechanism intervenes to provide restraint. In this situation, the anterior cingulate reins in the amygdala, thereby tempering the expression of distress. Thus, the anterior cingulate allows for civil discussions and makes conflict resolution possible (Bush, Luu, & Posner, 2000; Goldberg, 2001).

As one would expect, similar studies with children show that their response time to controlling emotions and resolving conflicts is much slower than in adults. Furthermore, the response time increases as the child gets older (Davidson, Amso, Anderson, & Diamond, 2006; Yarkoni, Braver, Gray, & Green, 2005). This explains why children, whose anterior cingulate is still immature, often get caught up in their emotions and have difficulty understanding and resolving conflict.

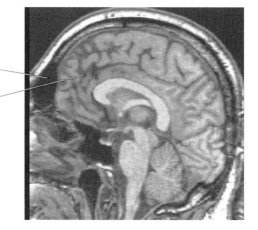

Figure 3.1   This brain scan image shows the location of the anterior cingulate in the frontal lobe. Activity in the cingulate is high when the brain is confronting conflict or in distress.

Do Mirror Neurons Play a Role in Self-Control?

What Are Mirror Neurons?

Apparently the old saying, "monkey see, monkey do" is truer than we would have guessed. Scientists using fMRI technology recently discovered clusters of neurons in the premotor cortex (the area in front of the motor cortex that plans movements) firing just before a person carries out a planned movement. Curiously, these neurons also fired when a person saw someone else perform the movement. For example, the firing pattern of these neurons that preceded the subject grasping a pencil, was identical to the pattern when the subject saw someone else do that. Thus, similar brain areas process both the *production* and *perception* of movement. Neuroscientists believe these mirror neurons may help an individual to decode the intentions and predict the behavior of others. If you see someone reach for a ball even though his hand is out of sight, your mirror neurons tell you that he is going to pick up the ball even before he does it (Fadiga, Craighero, & Olivier, 2005; Iacoboni et al., 2005).

People who say, "I feel your pain" may be accurately describing their feelings. Studies show that structures in the limbic area that activate during one's own pain also activate during empathy for another's pain. Mirror neurons allow us to re-create the experience of others within ourselves, and to understand others' emotions and to empathize. Seeing the look of disgust or joy on other people's faces cause mirror neurons to trigger similar emotions in us. We start to feel their actions and sensations as though we were doing them (Singer et al., 2004).

Mirror Neurons and Self-Control

Mirror neurons probably explain the mimicry we see in young children when they imitate our smile and many of our other movements. We all experience this phenomenon when we attempt to stifle a yawn after seeing someone else yawning. Neuroscientists believe that mirror neurons may explain a lot about mental behaviors that have remained a mystery. For instance, mirror neurons likely play a role in a toddler's ability to quickly develop articulate speech.

One of the most fundamental human social attributes is the ability to interact with others. As we said earlier, humans are not born with an innate set of rules of how to control their behavior, especially in situations involving conflict. This self-control must be learned. The discovery of mirror neurons may have revealed one of the biological mechanisms that explains how individuals learn to control their emotions and behavior in social settings. After all, the ability to understand the intentions of others is fundamental to determining your response and perhaps your survival. Is that person smiling because he is pleased to see me or because he is plotting something?

Children learn about the various responses they can make by watching what their parents, teachers, and others do in similar situations. Mirror neurons very likely coordinate the neurological mechanisms that record these responses. Later, the child imitates the response and is now on the road to developing self-control and social conditioning (Brass & Heyes, 2005; Meltzoff, 2007). The implication here is that teachers and parents need to remain rational and calm when interacting with children in situations involving conflict. When adults lose their temper and act irrationally, the child's brain is learning that such behavior is an acceptable choice for dealing with conflict.

> *When adults lose their temper and act irrationally, the child's brain is learning that such behavior is an acceptable choice for dealing with conflict.*

Clearly, learning self-control must begin early. Preschoolers must practice self-control if they are to develop finely-tuned skills. If children do not practice deliberate and purposeful behaviors, memory traces in the brain are not reinforced (the "use it or lose it" principle). So, if preschoolers do not practice self-control enough, the related brain areas will not be fully developed, and the end result may be adults who still act like they are in their "terrible twos."

Losing Self-Control

It is worth repeating that the rules for exhibiting self-control are not innate; they have to be learned. Surely, cerebral mechanisms like the anterior cingulate are available to process incoming information and generate responses, but it is up to the individual to learn and decide which type of response is appropriate for a particular situation. Sometimes the response seems appropriate to the individual, but is way out of line with what others expected.

It is also important to recognize whether a particular student's loss of control is a frequent occurrence. Remember that every one of us is capable of losing control when there is sufficient provocation. Fortunately, for most of us this does not happen often. For some students, however, losing emotional control is the norm rather than the exception. Why? A number of factors can explain why people regularly lose their self-control. Here are a few of them.

- **Childhood Environment.** What did the person learn about self-control as a child? Was the child taught the rules of behavior? How did the parents deal with their child's misbehavior? Was it quickly addressed or was it ignored? Were there any consequences for serious misbehavior? Was the child taught that certain behaviors might be overlooked at home but were not acceptable at school or in other public settings? What kind of self-control example did the parents set? Did they show restraint when provoked or did they fly into a rage? These are important questions because researchers today are concerned that students are spending much more time interacting with their technology than with their parents or other adults. Consequently, they are not being taught the rules of behavior or methods for self-control.

- **Age.** As we discussed in Chapter 1, the executive control system in the frontal lobe of children and adolescents is not sufficiently mature to fully moderate the limbic area's emotional responses. Younger people, then, overreact emotionally to minor provocations more than adults. Generally speaking, the younger the person, the greater the overreaction.

- **Stress.** When the body is under stress, a hormone called *cortisol* is released into the bloodstream. Belonging to the family of steroid compounds, cortisol alerts the brain so that it can focus on the cause of the stress and decide what to do about it. This alertness also prepares the body to defend itself in case the source of the stress could cause harm to the individual. Usually, the stressful situation is short-lived and body chemistry soon returns to normal. However, people under continual stress are in cortisol overload. They have a "short fuse" and can overreact quickly to a minor incident and lose emotional control. Some students may be under constant stress because of unsafe conditions at home (e.g., illegal drugs, domestic abuse, sleep deprivation), bullying at school, or unrealistic expectations.

- **Brain Deficits.** Among one of the less common causes of loss of self-control is a deficit in one or more of the cerebral mechanisms that are supposed to keep emotions in check. A congenital defect or later damage to the anterior cingulate or mirror neuron system, for example, could interfere with this area's ability to moderate excessive emotional responses. Also, imbalances in the concentrations of certain neurotransmitters in the brain can cause interruption of the nerve signals that would have prevented the loss of emotional control (Sousa, 2007).

Helping Students Regain Self-Control

Classroom Procedures and Strategies

Nearly all children and preadolescents lose control occasionally in the classroom. But the frequency of these instances can be increased or decreased by the procedures that teachers use during class time. Students whose attention is continuously focused on instruction and classroom activities are less likely to have self-control issues. Thus, attention-getting strategies are valuable tools for maintaining a productive learning experience. One effective strategy is *novelty.*

Using novelty does *not* mean that the teacher needs to be a stand-up comic or the classroom a three-ring circus. It simply means using a varied teaching approach that involves more student activity. Here are a few suggestions for incorporating novelty in your lessons (Sousa, 2006).

- **Humor.** There are many positive benefits that come from using humor (not teasing or sarcasm) in the classroom at *all* grade levels. Laughter provides more oxygen to fuel the brain and causes a surge of endorphins to flow into the blood, giving the student a feeling of euphoria. At the same time, laughter decreases stress and blood pressure, and relaxes muscle tension. Good-natured humor creates a positive classroom climate, increases retention and recall, and improves everyone's mental health. It also provides an effective discipline tool because it can be a way of reminding students of the rules of behavior without raising tension in the classroom.

- **Movement.** When we sit for more than twenty minutes, our blood pools in our seat and in our feet. By getting up and moving, we recirculate that blood. Within a minute, there is about 15 percent more blood in our brain. We do think better on our feet than on our seat! Students sit too much in classrooms, especially in secondary schools. After a time, they get fidgety and if no relief is in sight, they begin to lose control. Look for ways to get students up and moving, especially when they are verbally rehearsing what they have learned. See Chapter 4 for an in-depth discussion of movement during instruction.

- **Multi-Sensory Instruction.** Today's students have grown up in a multi-sensory environment. They are more likely to give attention if there are interesting, colorful visuals, and if they can walk around and talk about their learning.

- **Quiz Games.** Have students develop a quiz game or other similar activity to test each other on their knowledge of the concepts taught. This is a common strategy in elementary classrooms, but underutilized in secondary schools. Besides being fun, it has the added value of making students rehearse and understand the concepts in order to create the quiz questions and answers.

- **Music.** Although the research is inconclusive, there are some benefits of playing music in the classroom at certain times during the learning episode. For example, music can be an effective memory device when important facts are set to a familiar melody.

Novelty, of course, won't work all the time and with all students. Individuals with serious and persistent self-control issues resulting from brain deficits often need professional help to treat their condition. However, when most students lose their self-control, it is more likely the result of their age or lack of strategies at their command to moderate their emotional responses.

VERBAL SELF-CONTROL OF AGGRESSIVE, DEFIANT, OR OTHER BEHAVIOR

The Power of Self-Talk

One strategy that has been successful in moderating persistent emotional behavior is self-talk (also called *internal dialogue*). This approach has been shown to help people change undesirable behaviors into desirable ones. Research into the power of self-talk began in earnest in the late 1970s at Pennsylvania State University. Psychologist Michael Mahoney discovered that the most successful athletes were plagued by the same doubts and anxieties as their less successful peers. However, they compensated better by using self-talk to constantly encourage and motivate themselves, to reaffirm their beliefs in their abilities, and to visualize their movements for optimal performance (Mahoney, 1979). Numerous follow-up studies over the years, both in and outside sports, have consistently shown that self-talk improves an individual's performance, not only by enhancing desirable skills but also by limiting the effects of undesirable behaviors. In school settings, self-talk has also proved to be very successful (Purkey, 2000).

Many students with emotional and behavioral problems do not believe that they can exercise any control over their behavior. They often feel they are "victims" of their moods and emotions. For such students, teaching them verbal interventions involving self-instructional dialogue (or self-talk) for modifying their behavior can be empowering. Thus, verbal control of one's own behavior can be a critically important skill for students with behavior problems. Chapter 1, for instance, described a strategy that involved having a student use the phrase, "Out with the bad," with each exhale, and "In with the good," with each inhaled breath. This is one example of self-verbalizations that can be used to modify behavior.

Using self-verbalizations to control, modify, or prevent certain behaviors is supported by findings from cognitive behavioral research. This approach suggests there is a direct relationship between what students tell themselves about what should or should not be done and their behavior. By teaching students to use self-talk, teachers empower students to gain increasing control over their problem behaviors. Considerable research supports how well this tactic works with aggressive and highly disruptive students (Buron, & Curtis, 2003; Elias, 2004; Salend & Sylvestre, 2005; Smith, Lochman, & Daunic, 2005). Furthermore, this tactic becomes increasingly effective as the students' cognitive processing develops with age, making this an excellent approach for students from the lower grades through high school. This section presents several self-talk strategies that empower students to modify or control their own behavior.

The ZIPPER Strategy

The ZIPPER strategy uses the acronym ZIPPER to teach appropriate self-reflective behavior in emotionally charged situations (Smith, Siegel, O'Connor, & Thomas, 1994). Many students with behavior problems, when confronted with an emotionally charged situation, tend to display aggressive behavior, and for those students and adolescents, the ZIPPER strategy works well. The steps involved in this strategy are shown in Figure 3.2. Note the relationship between the acronym ZIPPER and what the student must do (i.e., "ZIP Your Mouth!"). Again, knowing what to say to oneself can empower students whose behavior has seemingly been totally out of control to modify their own reactions to potentially explosive situations.

The ZIPPER Strategy for Avoiding Conflict		
Z	Zip Your Mouth	Stop and take a deep breath!
I	Identify the Problem	What do I need? What is my problem?
P	Pause	Take a moment to calm down. Remove myself from the situation if I can.
P	Put Yourself in Charge	Take control of my actions.
E	Explore Choices	What can I do? Try and relax. I could forget about it.
R	Reset	Pick an option.

Figure 3.2   This chart summarizes the steps in the ZIPPER strategy that are effective in helping students avoid getting involved in conflict.

Source: Adapted from Smith et al., 1994.

A Case Study: Using the ZIPPER Strategy With Dustin

Many teachers have faced defiant or aggressive students in secondary classes, and this example is one intervention option for such a situation. Dustin was an aggressive student, who had previously been identified as a student with behavioral disorders. As soon as he entered the sixth grade he displayed aggressive tendencies and managed to provoke a fight during the first week of school. During that week, Mr. Trotter, the special education teacher, also noted that several times each day Dustin would get into some type of verbal altercation with other students. In some cases, the other students provoked the situation by calling Dustin "Killer Dustin," a name Dustin had earlier acquired by fighting in elementary school. When Dustin heard that term, he would curse at the other students, or walk over and hit them.

To plan an effective intervention, Mr. Trotter began a baseline count of Dustin's aggressive behaviors, and kept that count for two weeks. The data showed that Dustin had some type of verbal altercation in Mr. Trotter's resource class at least three times each day, with an average of 3.8 daily occurrences in that one class. The baseline data are shown in Figure 3.3. When asked about the problem, Dustin merely responded that the other student "called me a name, so I hit him!"

Teaching the ZIPPER Strategy

Mr. Trotter determined that Dustin needed a self-control strategy for cooling down and avoiding such altercations. Mr. Trotter decided to talk about the ongoing problem with Dustin early in the morning, and not immediately after Dustin was engaged in such counter-productive behavior. He called Dustin in for a meeting one morning prior to the first class. Here is the dialogue between Mr. Trotter and Dustin (this can be used as a training dialogue for this intervention).

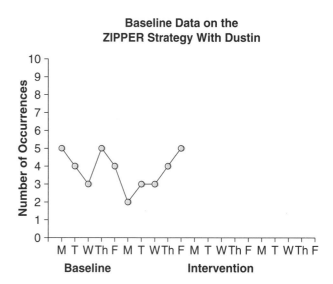

Figure 3.3 This baseline graph shows the number of aggressive behaviors displayed by Dustin during a two-week period.

Mr. Trotter: Dustin, you know you've been in trouble for getting into fights here repeatedly.

Dustin: Those bastards don't like me.

Mr. Trotter: That language is not acceptable in my class, and I'd ask that you not use it, but that's not what I want to talk about. I kept some notes on how many times you've been sent to the office, or missed the morning break because you had some words or hit someone. Want to see?

Dustin: OK. But this is not all my fault!

Mr. Trotter: (Mr. Trotter shows Dustin the baseline chart of his behavioral infractions, as shown in Figure 3.3) This chart shows that you've had about three incidents every day over the last two weeks.

Dustin: I told you, this is not all my fault. But I guess you're telling me this is not so good!

Mr. Trotter: You're right, not so good. If you are always in trouble, do you think the other guys will want to hang around with you?

Dustin: Some do!

Mr. Trotter: You're right, some do, but you could have many more friends, and maybe we can find a way for you to stay out of trouble, even if you get mad. Do you want to see a little trick that will help you do that? Nobody else knows about this, so it will be our private trick to help you stay out of trouble. OK? (Note how Mr. Trotter is using this "our private trick" idea to stir Dustin's interest.)

Dustin: What's this private trick about?

Mr. Trotter: The trick is simple: It's ZIPPER! That's all it is. The key to it is to remember ZIPPER and also to remember to use it. Think you can do that?

Dustin: It means zip my mouth, right?

Mr. Trotter: Yes, it does mean that, but it means more too. It's a way to help you zip your mouth and think before you let someone else make you angry. That way, you have power over your own anger and bad feelings. Want to try it? (Note here how Mr. Trotter is talking about "power" to lure Dustin to want to do the intervention.)

Dustin: I guess so.

Mr. Trotter: Here is a little chart I made for you. Don't let anyone else see this, and this idea will be only for you!

At that point, Mr. Trotter presented a page-size laminated chart of the ZIPPER strategy as shown in Figure 3.2. He discussed each step with Dustin and modeled the various actions in each step. This training emphasizes various role-play situations, similar to the situations that may have provoked Dustin previously. Also, modeling various actions for each of the steps is important, since that supports the student's understanding of the actions in that step. Mr. Trotter provided several practice examples as the dialogue continued.

Mr. Trotter: Let's see if you can do this now that you know the steps. Imagine that you come into class today and hear a couple of the other guys chuckle, and one mentions, "Here's Killer Dustin!" Isn't that what they call you that makes you mad?

Dustin: Yeah, that really gets to me. And I've told them not to call me that!

Mr. Trotter: Now that you know ZIPPER, what is the first thing you do? Do you curse or call them a name?

Dustin: No. I zip my mouth and think about what I want to happen and what my problem is. (Note that after training, Dustin should be able to either paraphrase or state explicitly what each step in the ZIPPER strategy is, as he did here.)

Mr. Trotter: Good, zipping your mouth when you're angry, and thinking before you speak is always a great idea. Next, think about what the problem is for that situation?

Dustin: Somebody called me something that I don't like, and I want them to stop!

Mr. Trotter: You're right. You want them to stop. So what's the next step in ZIPPER?

Dustin: Now I do the two Ps. I pause and then put myself in charge.

Mr. Trotter: Right, pause so that you don't react to others, and next, put yourself in charge! That always feels better, and that's what strong, successful guys do.

Dustin: Next, I explore my choices.

Mr. Trotter: Right, you explore choices. What are some of your choices when others call you a name? What could you do?

Dustin: I could just walk away or I could ask them not to call me that anymore.

Mr. Trotter: Either of those should work, as long as you ask them not to call you names without getting angry yourself. It might be wiser to just walk away. That might be your best choice because then you wouldn't get angry, and you'd be in charge. That way you won't be responding to them.

Of course, this script can be adapted for use with older high school students.

An Intervention Using ZIPPER

During the next two weeks, Dustin used the ZIPPER intervention. Each day, Mr. Trotter had Dustin bring the ZIPPER chart to his desk in the morning to review the steps. Mr. Trotter then reminded Dustin, quietly and privately, to do ZIPPER if other students began to bother him. Dustin started using the intervention when he felt himself getting angry. In fact, Dustin liked to turn and stare at Mr. Trotter whenever he began the ZIPPER tactic because he wanted Mr. Trotter to see that he had remembered to use it. When he did forget and had angry words with another student, Mr. Trotter offered a reminder. He would say in front of the other students, "Dustin, remember our secret idea?"

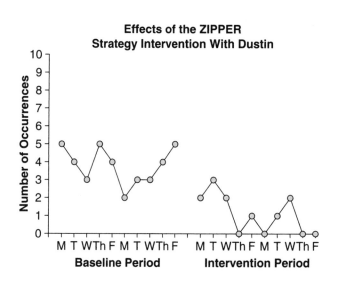

Figure 3.4   This chart shows that the ZIPPER strategy intervention resulted in Dustin displaying fewer aggressive behaviors than before the intervention.

That was usually enough to remind Dustin to begin ZIPPER, and Dustin liked the fact that all the other guys saw that he and Mr. Trotter shared a secret strategy.

The intervention data shown in Figure 3.4 revealed that during the next two weeks, Dustin developed much more control over his own reactive and aggressive behaviors. Actually, the instances of hitting were totally eliminated, and the only inappropriate behavior Dustin showed during the intervention was cursing in response to other students' provocations, a behavior that occurred much less frequently in Mr. Trotter's class.

The ZIPPER strategy involving self-talk as described here holds the potential to actually empower students who seemingly have no control over their anger. It is useful at all grade levels and should be a tool considered by teachers who deal with angry or defiant students. Furthermore, as a student's cognitive processes mature, this tactic becomes increasingly effective, making it particularly useful for middle and high school students. Note in the training dialogue that Mr. Trotter emphasized that this was Dustin's "private idea." This approach tends to build rapport between the teacher and the student with the behavior problem, as shown by Dustin's desire to have Mr. Trotter notice each time he employed the strategy.

"Say No and Walk Away" to Resist Peer Pressure

Aggression is not the only behavior problem that can be addressed by verbal self-talk. The cognitive-behavioral approaches that we discussed in Chapter 2 are effective for many problem behaviors. For example, a study found that self-talk can help students with disabilities resist peer pressure by employing a program that empowers students to "Just Say No and Walk Away!" (Collins, Hall, Rankin, & Branson, 1999). The researchers described a case study in which Rena was a 15-year-old student with moderate intellectual disabilities, mainly weaknesses in expressive and receptive language. That weakness made this intervention an interesting choice for her because one might believe that such limited language skills would reduce its effectiveness. Baseline data were taken in an integrated inclusion class where collaborating peers presented Rena with pressure situations for inappropriate actions (e.g., hanging out together instead of going to class). In the baseline phase, Rena yielded to that pressure six out of seven times over seven school days. At that point the intervention began. The training in the correct response (i.e., "Just say no and walk away") included the following:

- Definition and discussion of incorrect behavior
- Discussion of consequences of incorrect behavior
- Modeling of the correct response
- Multiple role-play examples in which a collaborating peer presented Rena with peer pressure to do something against the rules, and Rena was coached to perform the correct response of saying no and walking away within three seconds

The intervention data showed a drastic increase of the target response within only four days of beginning the intervention, indicating that this self-dialogue was highly effective in helping this adolescent resist peer pressure. In fact, for the last four days of the two-week intervention period, Rena was able to resist peer pressure each time one of the collaborating peers suggested an inappropriate behavior.

These results, like the other research on verbal self-control of inappropriate behaviors, suggest that this technique is highly effective (Salend & Sylvestre, 2005; Smith, Lochman, & Daunic, 2005). When faced with the opportunity to teach students with emotional disturbances in the general education classroom, teachers should consider employing this strategy because the benefits of fostering self-control are profound over the long term.

SELF-CONTROL THROUGH SELF-TALK AND SELF-MONITORING

The Nature of Attention

When the teacher's classroom strategies for getting and maintaining attention (such as the novelty ideas mentioned earlier) are not working for a particular student, a more structured and clinical intervention, such as self-talk, may be needed. Self-talk has been implemented to curb many inappropriate behaviors as well as increase appropriate behaviors. One of the earliest implementations of the self-talk strategy involved increasing attention (Hallahan, Lloyd, & Stoller, 1982; Konrad, Fowler, Walker, Test, & Wood, 2007; Mathes & Bender, 1996; Swaggart, 1988). Teachers often tell inattentive students to pay attention in class. However, in spite of the attention problems demonstrated by students today, only a few teachers actually have time to *teach* students exactly how to pay attention. Because paying attention came as a fairly natural ability for most teachers, many assume that

> *In spite of the attention problems demonstrated by students today, few teachers actually have time to teach students how to pay attention.*

students know how to pay attention. This is understandable because teachers are effective learners. In short, paying attention was not a problem for most teachers when they were students.

However, many students *do* have significant difficulty maintaining attention, and those students often do not realize that their inattention is a major problem. Further, they may not even realize exactly what "paying attention" really means (i.e., to logically follow the presentation or discussion and to bring themselves back to the task when their thoughts wander off the subject).

Let's take a moment to reflect on what paying attention means. First of all, few human beings can remain 100 percent focused on one task or issue for an extended time. All learners—students and adults—find that their minds wander off the subject and may fixate momentarily on unrelated thoughts. These wanderings are the result, in part, of the brain's natural interest in almost any new stimulus. A noise in the hallway, a plane flying overhead, a dropped textbook—these are all stimuli that can easily capture the brain's attention because they represent novelty (Sousa, 2006). Given that everyone is off-task for some percentage of time, effective learners learn how to mentally "check in" on the class discussion and on the academic task at hand. It is this "checking-in" process that is the essence of effective attention skills. They also learn how to screen out unimportant stimuli to rein in the brain's novelty-seeking tendencies.

This frequent refocusing on the learning task or discussion is the very skill that students with attention problems lack. Their inability to tune in often results in unusual or out-of-place comments—statements that have nothing to do with the ongoing lesson. Consequently, they often perform poorly on worksheet types of tasks in the classroom. Once attention mentally wanders outside the classroom, the student may find it difficult to complete the required tasks. This explains why a cognitive-behavioral strategy such as self-talk is so effective for this behavior problem, and research has consistently shown that self-monitoring using self-talk interventions work (Konrad et al., 2007).

The self-talk strategy teaches students to constantly use self-questioning to monitor their attention and other behaviors. Various terms have been used to describe this strategy, including self-monitoring, self-instruction, self-questioning, etc. Although the technique may be used to enhance both behaviors and specific, discrete academic skills, the focus in this context is on behavior.

How to Structure Self-Talk to Increase Attention

In order to implement this strategy to increase attention, you will need three things. Although this may seem like a lot of preparation for a teacher's busy schedule, each item can be easily made and the success of this approach for increasing attention is worth it.

1. Self-monitoring audiotape to use as a cue to self-question

2. Self-monitoring check sheet

3. Worksheet of academic tasks, i.e., any worksheet you would normally have the students complete for academic practice

In self-monitoring to enhance attention, an audiotape is used as the cue to make a student attend to the worksheet or other assigned task. This tape may be made using materials in the school or home. Obtain a small tape recorder and a blank audiotape, and sit down at a piano or with any musical instrument. Record a series of the same note or tone on the tape. The time between the tones should range between 10 and 90 seconds, and the tape should continue for a period of approximately 20 minutes, resulting in 20 to 25 tones on the tape. (Note: You might consider assigning the task of making this audiotape to a reliable student.)

In addition to this cuing tape, a self-monitoring check sheet is needed. This sheet reminds students of the self-questioning they should use to indicate if they were paying attention. The check sheet has a space for the student's name, the date, and lines on which students indicate if they were on or off task when the self-monitoring tone sounded on the audiotape. It also states the self-talk question that students are to ask themselves when they hear the tone. In this instance it is, "Was I paying attention?" Younger students who are not yet reading may benefit from pairing that question with a picture of a smiling face to indicate they were paying attention, or with a frowning face to indicate off-task behavior. A sample self-monitoring check sheet is shown in Figure 3.5.

Finally, the worksheet for the self-monitoring intervention involves a practice sheet of academic problems on which the student can achieve a minimum of 80 percent accuracy. In short, this intervention should be done with work that the student has already been taught, and on which further practice is needed. Students may engage in a variety of subject-matter activities, and these procedures may be used successfully while students work on arithmetic, handwriting, reading comprehension, and other academic tasks. Also, individualized computerized drill and practice activities (as long as they are not time-dependent activities) can be used when implementing a self-monitoring intervention. The content or type of instructional work really does not matter. The only restriction is that the student should not be in the initial learning stage on the content of the task.

Self-Monitoring Check Sheet

Name _____ Date _____ Period ____

Number of times I was paying attention today __

WAS I PAYING ATTENTION?

YES	NO
_____	_____
_____	_____
_____	_____
_____	_____
_____	_____
_____	_____
_____	_____
_____	_____
_____	_____
_____	_____
_____	_____
_____	_____
_____	_____
_____	_____

Figure 3.5 This is an example of a check sheet to help students monitor their attention. See the Appendix for a black-line master of this form.

Collecting Baseline Data on Attention

Begin this intervention by collecting some baseline data on how well the target student is initially paying attention. This can be done easily through a time sampling procedure, in which you observe the student every 10 seconds or so, and check for on-task or off-task behavior. To get the baseline data, assign about 15 minutes of individual practice work on various academic tasks each day for five days. During that practice period, work at a desk that allows a view of the eyes of the target student. During that time, observe the student's attention for 10 minutes. Specifically, check every ten seconds whether the student's eye contact is with the worksheet (on task) or elsewhere (off task). Use a simple observation record sheet containing columns for on-task and off-task behavior to collect these baseline data. A sample teacher observation sheet is found in Figure 3.6. At the end of the 10-minute period you will have 60 indicators, and you can easily compute the

**Teacher Observation Check Sheet
of Student On-Task Behavior**

Name _____ Date _____ Period ____

Percentage of on-task behavior _____
(On-task checks ÷ 60 = Percent of on-task time)

On task	Off task	On task	Off task	On task	Off task
____	____	____	____	____	____
____	____	____	____	____	____
____	____	____	____	____	____
____	____	____	____	____	____
____	____	____	____	____	____
____	____	____	____	____	____
____	____	____	____	____	____
____	____	____	____	____	____
____	____	____	____	____	____
____	____	____	____	____	____
____	____	____	____	____	____
____	____	____	____	____	____
____	____	____	____	____	____
____	____	____	____	____	____
____	____	____	____	____	____
____	____	____	____	____	____
____	____	____	____	____	____
____	____	____	____	____	____
____	____	____	____	____	____

Figure 3.6   This is an example of a check sheet to help teachers observe a student's on-task and off-task behaviors during an academic activity. See the Appendix for a black-line master of this form.

student's percentage of on-task time by simply dividing the number of on-task checks by 60.

Beginning the Intervention

Explain the process. Begin the intervention by introducing the self-monitoring procedure. Explain to the student that this process will help the student be more attentive in class and complete the class assignments more often. Be sure to note that being more attentive will help the student get class work done more quickly and therefore result in more free time in class. Mention, too, that part of the procedure includes students talking to themselves about increasing their attention. Then present the student with the self-monitoring check sheet, the cuing audiotape, the tape recorder, and a worksheet of problems to complete. Explain that the tape is to be played while the student completes the worksheet. In larger general education classes, you may use headphones, or perhaps have the student move to the back of the room for this work, to minimize distraction to others.

The student is taught how to use the tape recorder and begin completing the worksheet. Each time a tone is sounded, the student asks the question found on the self-monitoring sheet, "Was I paying attention?" The student answers that question by marking the check sheet either "yes" or "no" and then returns to the worksheet. Thus, the tone on the audiotape becomes the cue for the student to refocus on the worksheet task, and the check sheet provides a written record of when the student was paying attention. Over time, this practice in refocusing at frequent intervals results in the students *learning* to pay attention as well as creating a *habit* of attention. This procedure teaches a student how to pay attention.

Describe the attention/inattention behaviors. In the next step, describe to the student in detail the behaviors that are to be considered as paying attention and those that are not paying attention. For example, if the student is supposed to self-monitor while working on a mathematics assignment, explain that paying attention means that the student is seated at the desk with pencil in hand, looking at the mathematics paper, or consulting with you. Not paying attention during this task might be defined as talking to others, laughing, playing with another student, looking out the window, or walking around the room. Carefully tailor the description of off-task behaviors so that they closely resemble the kinds of off-task behaviors the student has previously demonstrated.

Model the process. It is important to model the use of the self-monitoring check sheet, as well as examples of attention and non-attention while having the student observe the teacher. Most students love to "grade the teacher" during this role-play of attention and inattention. Finally, ask the student to demonstrate the self-monitoring procedure under your supervision for two or three minutes. During this period, emphasize that each time a tone sounds, the student checks the appropriate line on the self-questioning check sheet and then returns immediately to continue with the worksheet of academic problems. On the first day of intervention, the training procedure takes about 15 to 20 minutes to complete. Hallahan, Lloyd, and Stoller (1982) provided a teaching script that can be used for much of this intervention training (see Figure 3.7).

For several days following the initial instruction in self-monitoring, briefly review with the student the examples of on- and off-task behavior and the check sheet recording procedures. After two to three days, using self-monitoring on one or two worksheets each day, the student should grasp the concept, and on succeeding days, will merely obtain the cuing tape along with a check sheet, and begin completing the worksheet with no additional instruction. Although you will need to work directly with the student on the first day of intervention, you will be free on subsequent days to observe the student's actual on-task behavior, using the same procedure and observation sheet previously described (10 minutes of observation, noting behavior every 10 seconds).

A Script for Teacher Introduction of Self-Monitoring

Johnny, you know how paying attention to your work has been a problem for you. You've heard teachers tell you, "Pay attention," "Get to work," "What are you supposed to be doing?" and things like that. Well, today we are going to start something that will help you help yourself pay attention better.

First, we need to make sure that you know what paying attention means. This is what I mean by paying attention. (Teacher models immediate and sustained attention to task.) And this is what I mean by not paying attention. (Teacher models inattentive behaviors, such as glancing around and playing with objects.) Now, you tell me if I was paying attention. (Teacher models attentive and inattentive behaviors and requires the student to categorize them.)

Okay, now let me show you what we're going to do. While you are working, this tape recorder will be turned on. Every once in a while, you will hear a little sound like this. (Teacher plays tone on tape.) And when you hear that sound, quietly ask yourself, "Was I paying attention?" If you answer "yes," put a check in this box. If you answer "no," put a check in this box. Then go right back to work. When you hear the sound again, ask yourself the question, answer it, mark your answer, and go back to work. Now, let me show you how it works. (Teacher models entire procedure.)

Now, Johnny, I bet you can do this. Tell me what you are going to do every time you hear a tone. Let's try it. I'll start the tape and you work on these papers. (Teacher observes the student's implementation of the entire procedure, praises the student for correctly using the procedure, and gradually withdraws.)

Figure 3.7 Here is an example of a possible script that a teacher can use to introduce a student to the self-monitoring process.

Source: Adapted from Hallahan et al., 1982.

One source of confusion involves the multiple recordings resulting from this intervention. Note that the teacher's time sampling observation of on-task behavior (every 10 seconds for 10 minutes each day) is the critical variable. This information is different from the student's self-recording of attention because the latter record is made at random intervals based on the sounds of the tones on the audiotape. Thus, these observations are not simultaneous, though both should occur during the same 10-minute worksheet activity. Research studies have shown that this procedure will be effective regardless of that slight difference in measurement (Mathes & Bender, 1996).

Weaning Procedures

Obviously, it is not in the student's best interest to become dependent on audiotape cues and self-monitoring check sheets for all schoolwork. After implementing the self-monitoring tactic described above for 10 to 15 days, begin to wean students from these cues. Hallahan, Lloyd, and Stoller (1982) have recommended a two-phase weaning procedure.

First Phase: Remove the tape recorder. Generally, after a minimum of 10 days using the worksheet, the check sheet, and the audiotape, the student's level of on-task behavior will have increased and teachers may begin the weaning process. When the student has reached a high level of attention using this procedure, remove the audiotape cue as a first weaning step. Here is a script you may use to explain the first weaning phase to the student (Hallahan et al., 1982).

You have been doing really good work on____ (mathematics, reading, etc.) lately, don't you think? You've been doing so well that I don't think you need to use the tape-recorded tones anymore. Today, whenever you think about it, ask yourself the question, "Was I paying attention?" and then mark your card. Do you have any questions?

Point out that the student should continue to self-monitor with the self-monitoring sheet. Thus, the student is still verbally checking, "Was I paying attention?" This phase lasts for a minimum of three to five days, as this time frame builds a strong habit of attention.

Phase Two: Remove the self-monitoring check sheet. After the student has shown the ability to self-monitor, remove the self-monitoring check sheet, using something like the following script.

You are really doing good work on____ (mathematics, reading, etc.) without using the tape-recorded tones, don't you think? You have been doing so well that I don't think you need to use the self-monitoring card anymore. I think you can do a really good job without using the tape-recorded tones or the self-monitoring card. Today, whenever you think about it, ask yourself the question, "Was I paying attention?" If the answer is "Yes," say to yourself, "Yes, good job." If the answer is "No," say to yourself, "No, I'd better start paying attention," and then get back to completing your worksheet. Do you have any questions? (Hallahan, Lloyd, & Stoller, 1982).

At this point, the student is doing self-monitoring without any external supports (i.e., no audiotape or check sheet), and studies have documented that most students with poor attention will have created the habit of using self-talk to increase their on-task time. Of course, in order to continue fostering that skill, each time you give a practice task (i.e., a worksheet assignment), the student is reminded to do self-monitoring.

Although this is a simple procedure to teach, it is sometimes difficult to decide when to start the second weaning phase. There are no set rules, and the recommendations for a specific number of days are merely guidelines. Of course, if during the initial 10 days of training and the weaning phases, the student's attention skills diminish, immediately restart the full procedure using both the audiotape and check sheet. Similarly, if the procedure works for several weeks after the last weaning phase but the student later shows signs of inattention, you will need to implement the entire procedure again.

A Self-Monitoring Example

Anton was an eighth-grade student with behavioral disorders who was receiving all of his education in general education classes. Ms. Tooney realized that Anton was not completing his work in mathematics by the end of the period even though he was capable of doing the work. Upon closer observation, Ms. Tooney realized that he was often staring out of the window and not focused on his work. She collected baseline data and then implemented the self-monitoring intervention. Figure 3.8 shows the baseline and intervention data from this self-monitoring project.

The baseline data show that Anton was indeed off task well over 50 percent of the time. This is consistent with research demonstrating that students with learning disabilities and behavioral disorders are on task generally between 35 and 45 percent of the time. However, as these data

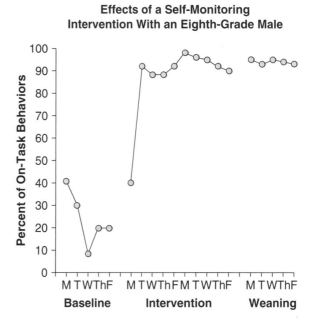

Figure 3.8 This graph shows one week of baseline data, two weeks of intervention data, and one week of weaning period data collected during a self-monitoring intervention project with an eighth-grade male student.

indicate, the 10-day self-talk intervention was effective for Anton. In the final week—the weaning phases of the intervention—his on-task time during seat work increased to over 85 percent. Results such as these are common in research studies on self-monitoring, indicating that this is one of the most effective interventions available for increasing attention behavior (Harlacher, Roberts, & Merrell, 2006; Mathes & Bender, 1996).

Self-Monitoring for Other Problem Behaviors

So far, we have discussed the self-monitoring procedure as it applies to enhancing attention. However, after the promising research findings on using self-monitoring to improve attention skills, researchers began to apply these same procedures to enhance behavior in other areas as well (Harlacher, Roberts, & Merrell, 2006; Kern & Dunlap, 1994). For instance, every teacher has been frustrated when an otherwise talented student simply forgets books, pencils, or other materials. Self-monitoring for class preparedness has been shown to be a highly effective variation of the application of self-monitoring. For that procedure, a tape recorder and audiotape are not needed. Rather, teachers need only create a self-recording sheet on which students indicate their class preparedness at the beginning of the period. A sample check sheet for a secondary student is shown in Figure 3.9.

Check Sheet of Class Preparedness Behavior

Name _____   Date _____

Check off (✓) each period in which you were prepared for each indicator. At the end of the day, compute the percentage of "yes" answers by dividing the number of checks by 30. Discuss this with your homeroom teacher the following morning.

Class Preparedness	**Classes/Subjects/Periods**					
	English	Math	Soc. Stud.	Science	Health	Techn.
1. I have my paper/pencils.	_____	_____	_____	_____	_____	_____
2. I have my textbook.	_____	_____	_____	_____	_____	_____
3. I have my homework.	_____	_____	_____	_____	_____	_____
4. I was in class when the bell rang.	_____	_____	_____	_____	_____	_____
5. I took my seat before class.	_____	_____	_____	_____	_____	_____
6. Other behavior to be monitored.	_____	_____	_____	_____	_____	_____

Figure 3.9   An example of a check sheet that students can use to self-monitor their class preparedness behaviors. See the Appendix for a black-line master.

The checklist can be modified for use with inattentive and chronically unprepared students, stressing whatever behaviors may be necessary. If the indicators do not capture the specific behavior or preparedness issues that need to be addressed for a particular student, teachers can easily adapt the check sheet by adding another column or different column labels. Research studies indicate that self-monitoring interventions of this nature are very effective for elementary, middle, and high school students (Snyder & Bambara, 1997).

It is also possible to have students self-monitor almost any type of inappropriate behavior, and use self-talk to gain control over those behaviors. For example, students may be taught to check off each time they blurt out an answer without raising their hand, each time they use obscene language, or each time they call another student a disrespectful name. Here, too, a large body of research has shown that having students self-monitor their own negative behaviors, and use self-dialogue to either avoid inappropriate behavior or substitute a more appropriate behavior for the situation, leads to a substantial decrease in inappropriate behaviors (Harlacher, Roberts, & Merrell, 2006).

SELF-CONTROL THROUGH SELF-RATING OF EMOTIONAL INTENSITY

Many children and adolescents with severe behavioral problems lack the ability to regulate the intensity of their emotions. Younger children may demonstrate such a lack of self-regulation by being impulsive, as we described in Chapter 2. Adolescents may demonstrate emotional or violent physical or verbal reactions to even the slightest perceived provocation. Thus, students who do not self-regulate the intensity of their emotional reactions can be difficult to manage in the classroom. Fortunately, the self-talk strategy lends itself well to the management of emotional intensity (Buron & Curtis, 2003; Elias, 2004; Jaime & Knowlton, 2007; Williams & Shellenberger, 1996).

Jaime and Knowlton (2007) suggested the use of rating scales that encourage students to monitor their emotions and emotional intensity. These rating scales typically involve having students who demonstrate self-regulation problems to self-rate the intensity of their emotions. Taking a moment to pause and complete such a self-monitoring of emotions can often mean the difference between an emotional explosion or just a momentary burst of anger that was managed so that it did not lead to inappropriate behavior. Typically these scales are set up to assess emotional intensity in just three, four, or five levels (Buron & Curtis, 2003; Williams & Shellenberger, 1996). By keeping these scales simple, the strategy can be used with students of varying disabilities, ranging in age from the lower elementary grades through high school (Jaime & Knowlton, 2007).

The Anger Thermometer

One example of a rating scale is the *anger thermometer,* recommended by Elias (2004). This procedure combines a rating scale and a graphic to assist in self-monitoring of emotional intensity. An adapted anger thermometer sheet is shown in Figure 3.10. As you can see, the highest intensity anger is scaled as "red hot" anger, and is depicted as the highest of the indicators on this five-level scale. Teachers can also add suggestions to this rating scale for what a student should do when feeling "red hot," such as going to talk with the teacher immediately or simply putting one's head on the desk for a brief timeout. Using this or similar self-rating scales assists students is regulating their emotional intensity. The intervention design described earlier for the self-monitoring of attention can easily be adapted to use the anger thermometer.

The Anger Thermometer

How angry am I? Circle one set of words that describe how you feel and what you can do about it. If possible, please suggest how the teacher might help.

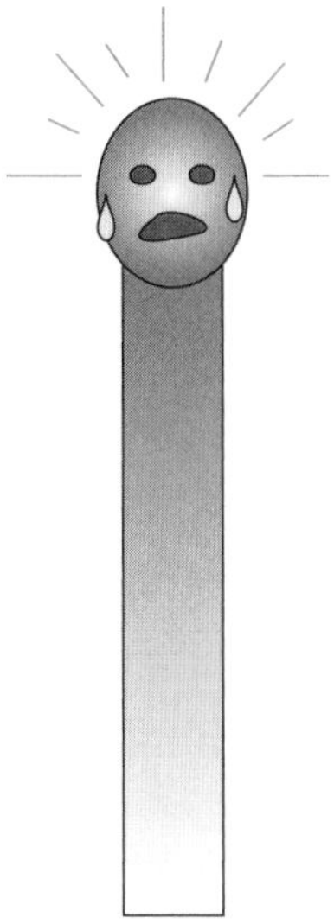

RED HOT! BURNING UP!

_____

_____

VERY HOT! TOUGH TO HANDLE!

_____

_____

Warm! Feeling some heat.

_____

_____

I noticed some anger.

_____

_____

Not really angry.

_____

_____

Figure 3.10 Here is an example of a check sheet that students can use to self-monitor their emotional intensity. See the Appendix for a black-line master of this.

Source: Adapted from Elias, 2004.

SUMMARY

Self-control is a learned behavior. Children begin to learn about self-control when their parents admonish them for temper tantrums and other displays of inappropriate behaviors whether at home or in public. Brain systems are in place to moderate excessive emotions, but these, too, need to develop and learn a variety of potential responses based on an individual's experiences. The lack of self-control is generally the result of insufficient exposure to situations where the individual learns what is socially acceptable emotional behavior. Self-talk is an effective approach for helping students regain control over their unacceptable behaviors. Instructional techniques based on self-talk, including the ZIPPER strategy, "Say No and Walk Away," and self-monitoring activities, have all shown to be effective in helping students with self-control problems.

Managing the
Behavior of Boys

WHY A CONCERN WITH BOYS?

Almost every veteran teacher will admit that boys present many more disciplinary challenges in the classroom than girls. Boys fall behind girls in literacy in the earliest years of school and never really catch up (Newkirk, 2006). As for behavior, many educators suspect that the misbehavior demonstrated so much more frequently by boys stems, in part, from academic deficits and perhaps even from the very instructional methods and materials used in the traditional classroom. For example, some educators have noted that young boys seem to require reading materials that are more oriented to "heroes and superheroes" using "superpowers," but few basal reading programs include stories of this nature. Perhaps boys have a distinct preference for these reading materials because their stories manifest clear distinctions between good and evil. In contrast, young girls seem to prefer reading materials that emphasize the more subtle aspects of relationships and friendships (King & Gurian, 2006; Tatum, 2006).

> Although the strategies suggested in this chapter are particularly effective for boys, they can be effective for girls as well.

For these reasons, many educators have begun to pay particular attention to the educational and disciplinary needs of males in the classroom. Consequently, in this chapter we will discuss some possible genetic, biological, and psychological reasons why boys misbehave in school more often than girls. We will also suggest some strategies that are particularly effective for handling boys' misbehavior, although these tactics are effective for girls as well.

GENDER DIFFERENCES IN BEHAVIOR

Genetic and Environmental Factors

For decades, the physical, emotional, social, and behavioral differences between males and females have fed the story lines of many a television comedy series. They have spawned a variety of parlor games, and generated some popular and undying myths. Yet buried in all this hype are a few scientific findings that shed light on why males and females often behave differently in the same situation.

Behavior is the result of genetic and environmental (social) factors. The genes that now underlie the behavior differences between males and females must have been selected because they improved the chances that an individual of that gender would survive and reproduce. If we accept the theories about the different roles that our male and female ancestors played, then it becomes possible to understand why their behavior and associated cognitive skills developed differently.

Development of the Male Brain

Males were the hunters, builders, and defenders of their tribes. Successful hunters needed to make weapons that would kill the prey before the prey killed the hunters. They had to be good trackers, throwers, and archers. They had to determine what kinds of materials would make a shelter waterproof and able to withstand strong winds. They also had to learn how to defend themselves against invading tribes seeking to expand their territory. Eventually, as communities grew larger, a social hierarchy had to be devised. Those individuals who were the most aggressive very likely became leaders. Aggression is an effective strategy for establishing social dominance and resolving social conflict. In short, males who were good at making weapons and tools, as well as aggressive and socially dominant, were more likely to survive and win the favor of females to mate.

Development of the Female Brain

Females stayed close to home and raised the children. Childcare is a challenging task. First, deciding why an infant is crying requires making educated guesses about what is wrong. The children of females who were good at this were more likely to survive. Females who created a community of friends could help each other watch and care for the other's children when necessary. Building friendships made for a more stable and watchful community where children could be safer and less likely to be attacked by ever-present predators. Making friends and keeping a partner, however, required that she be mindful of the feelings of others (especially her mate), be ready to compromise, and be a good listener. Such strategies reduced the chances of conflict and aggression within the family and community. In short, females who were good at empathizing, child-rearing, and working toward a community consensus were more likely to survive and reproduce.

Social Brain Has Changed Little

Modern day humans behave much like their ancestors. Although the social environment of Western societies has changed dramatically during the last 200 years, the social brain is essentially the same as it was thousands of years ago. Of course, the brain has *learned* and participated in these social changes, but how it emotionally *reacts* to them has hardly changed at all. Hurling an insult at someone provokes the same inflamed emotional response today as it did in our ancestors in the cave. Granted, the contemporary legal consequences might discourage a violent reaction in most of us, but the strong emotional feelings still emerge, nonetheless.

Impact of Biology

Along with genetic influences, biology plays a role in explaining the sex differences in behavior. Male babies typically have higher levels of the sex hormone testosterone in their blood than female babies. As we discussed in Chapter 2, a high level of testosterone does not in itself cause aggressive behavior, but it does increase the likelihood that certain misbehaviors will be expressed if the genetic inclinations are present and the situation provokes it (Booth, Granger, Mazur, & Kivlighan, 2006). On the other hand, research studies indicate that low levels of testosterone (common in females) lead to higher levels of language, better communication and social skills, and increased eye contact (Baron-Cohen, 2003). These advantages suggest that females are more likely than males to resolve conflict by resorting to face-to-face communication and talking the matter through.

Structural Differences in the Male and Female Brain

It is important to recognize that neither the male nor female brain is better or worse than the other. Their genetic composition has been selected to successfully support entirely different roles. In addition to initiating and monitoring biological processes, genes influence the growth and development of brain structures. Because the mix of genes is somewhat different in males than in females, it is no surprise that there are gender differences in the anatomies of several brain structures, some of which are believed to be associated with behavior. These brain regions include areas that have been associated with memory, social behavior, and emotional processing and response (see Table 4.1).

Table 4.1   Gender Differences in Brain Regions Thought to Be Associated With Behavior

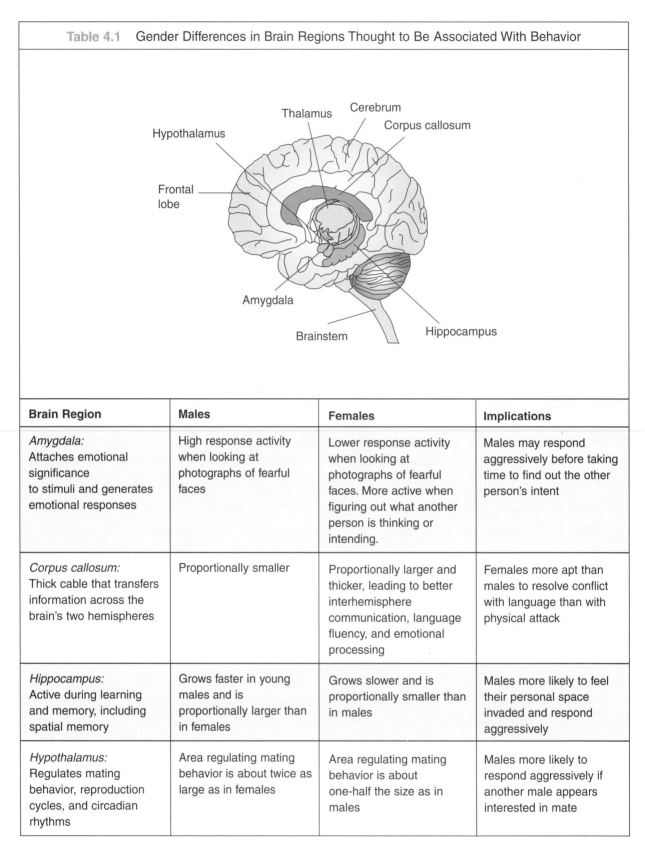

Brain Region	Males	Females	Implications
Amygdala: Attaches emotional significance to stimuli and generates emotional responses	High response activity when looking at photographs of fearful faces	Lower response activity when looking at photographs of fearful faces. More active when figuring out what another person is thinking or intending.	Males may respond aggressively before taking time to find out the other person's intent
Corpus callosum: Thick cable that transfers information across the brain's two hemispheres	Proportionally smaller	Proportionally larger and thicker, leading to better interhemisphere communication, language fluency, and emotional processing	Females more apt than males to resolve conflict with language than with physical attack
Hippocampus: Active during learning and memory, including spatial memory	Grows faster in young males and is proportionally larger than in females	Grows slower and is proportionally smaller than in males	Males more likely to feel their personal space invaded and respond aggressively
Hypothalamus: Regulates mating behavior, reproduction cycles, and circadian rhythms	Area regulating mating behavior is about twice as large as in females	Area regulating mating behavior is about one-half the size as in males	Males more likely to respond aggressively if another male appears interested in mate

Sources: Adapted from Baron-Cohen, 2003; Bishop & Wahlsten, 1997; Cahill, 2005; and Suzuki et al., 2005.

Amygdala. As we discussed in previous chapters, the amygdala is the brain's gateway to emotions. Brain scans indicate that the amygdala in male brains shows far greater activity than in female brains when looking at photographs of fearful faces. This response difference is probably linked, once again, to survival. The man was the family's defender. Seeing a fearful or hostile look on another's face could be the warning sign of brewing conflict. The quicker an individual's brain processed an emotional response to the face and generated a defensive posture, the more likely that individual would survive.

The female amygdala, however, shows higher activity (along with parts of the frontal lobe) than the male's when looking at photographs of eyes and trying to figure out what a person is thinking or intending to do. Thus, the female is more apt to plan her response to an emotional threat through communication and reason. Furthermore, the amygdala of both genders is rich in testosterone receptor cells. Because males generally have a much higher amount of testosterone than females, the male response to an emotional threat is more likely to be: act first, talk later. The opposite is true for females.

Corpus Callosum. Another structure to consider is the *corpus callosum,* a thick bundle of nerves that connects the brain's two hemispheres and allows information to flow between them. Although the female brain is typically about eight percent smaller than the male brain, the corpus callosum in women is proportionally larger than in men. The larger size is due to a greater number of nerve fibers connecting the hemispheres. Consequently, on tasks that would benefit from the rapid transfer of information between hemispheres, such as analyzing intent and communication, females should do better, and numerous studies have shown this to be the case (Bishop & Wahlsten, 1997; Cahill, 2005).

Hippocampus. We discussed in Chapter 1 the importance of the hippocampus in encoding information into long-term memory. It is particularly important in recording spatial memories, such as knowing your way around your home in the dark, or driving a specific route to work each day. It also influences an individual's personal space. Although the size of one's personal space varies among cultures (e.g., closer for Mediterranean cultures, further back for North Americans) there is a minimum distance in all cultures within which an individual feels threatened. In young males, the hippocampus grows faster than in young females (Suzuki et al., 2005). It seems then that young males establish their personal space sooner than females and are thus more likely to feel threatened and respond aggressively when others come too close.

Hypothalamus. Near the hippocampus is a small but important structure called the *hypothalamus.* This collection of nuclei work together to maintain the internal stability of the body's systems. Two areas of the hypothalamus, however, have clear differences in male and female brains: the *suprachiasmatic nucleus* and the *preoptic area.* The suprachiasmatic nucleus is important in regulating circadian rhythms (e.g., light-dark cycles for sleep) and reproduction cycles. The main difference between males and females in this nucleus is shape: spherical in males, elongated in females. Researchers are now trying to determine if the difference in shape influences the connections that this area makes with other areas of the brain.

The preoptic area is involved in mating behavior. In males, this area is more than twice as large as in women and contains twice as many cells. This size difference becomes apparent after a person is only four years old. Most young males, then, typically begin to demonstrate mating behaviors sooner and more intensely than young females of the same age. One of these behaviors is the aggressive response that arises if a male believes his current mating relationship is being threatened by another male's actions (Cahill, 2005).

Some Research Findings on Behavioral Differences

Evidence of this persistence in behavioral differences shows up in research studies. For example, to solve conflicts, boys are more likely to use *physical* aggression while girls are more likely to use *verbal* aggression (Calvete & Cardenoso, 2005). Girls tend to get better grades in school because they are more self-disciplined than their male peers. Throughout elementary, middle, and high school, girls earn higher grades than boys in all major subjects. However, girls do not outperform boys on achievement or IQ tests. Researchers suggest that this disparity may be because girls are more self-disciplined, and this advantage is more relevant to report card grades than to achievement or aptitude tests (Duckworth & Seligman, 2006).

Male and female teachers often display differences in their disciplinary approaches to male and female children. One study explored these differences, examining the connection between an educator's gender and method of disciplining urban, elementary school-aged children. Given surveys that contained eight behavioral scenarios (four scenarios with boys and four with girls), elementary school teachers were asked how they would react in order to discipline the student involved. Responses for each scenario were listed in random order and ranged from most assertive to least assertive disciplinary action.

> *Male and female teachers display differences in their disciplinary approaches to male and female children.*

Although there were many similarities between male and female teachers' discipline responses, male teachers were significantly more likely than female teachers to select a more aggressive disciplinary approach toward boys. Both male and female teachers chose more often to ignore the boys' misbehavior if no aggression was involved. Female teachers were slightly more consistent with their disciplinary responses for both boys and girls (Rodriguez, 2002). More findings from research are included in the following discussion of how to translate the research on gender differences in behavior into instructional and management strategies that work.

USING RESEARCH-BASED STRATEGIES

Research studies over the years support the notion that differences in certain brain structures in males and females lead to differences in behavior, including their responses in social situations. Because attending school is a major opportunity for social interaction, teachers need to understand these differences and be prepared to deal with them effectively. For the foreseeable future, we can assume that boys will continue to be the source of more behavior problems than girls. So let's move on to some research-based strategies that we suggest teachers consider when handling the misbehavior of boys. Remember, these strategies can also be adapted for use with misbehaving girls.

Movement-Based Instruction and Classroom Management

Importance of Movement In Learning

The emerging research on brain-compatible instruction has highlighted the importance of including instructional activities that include movement. Called *movement-based instruction,* this powerful classroom technique has been shown to encourage appropriate behavior because some students who may be hyperactive will have some of their need for movement addressed in the context of the lesson. Because physical movement has long been associated in the human brain with survival, brain imaging studies show that movement stimulates long-term memory and recall. Remember that time you were at your desk and your mind stopped working while you were trying to balance the checkbook, do a tax return, or plan a lesson? You took a break, and after a short walk you were able to return to the desk and complete the task. What happened during that brief walk? Moving activated long-term memory sites, allowing you to recall the information you needed for the task at hand.

Figure 4.1 explains what happened. When sitting for more than 30 minutes, blood begins to pool in your feet and in your seat, decreasing the amount of blood flowing through the brain. The arrows in the diagram on the left of Figure 4.1 show the frontal lobe accessing long-term memory sites to gather data for solving a cognitive task. When we get up and walk around, two beneficial things happen: First, the movement

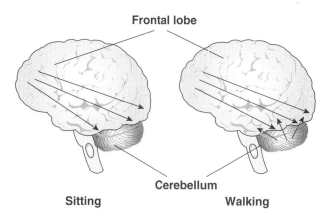

Figure 4.1 The arrows in the diagram on the left represent the frontal lobe accessing long term storage sites near the base of the brain. The diagram on the right shows how walking stimulates the cerebellum to activate additional long-term sites, thereby increasing the information available to solve a problem.

breaks up those pools and sends more oxygen-rich blood to the brain. Second, the cerebellum, which controls our walking is stimulated and it activates additional long-term storage sites. As a result, you now have more memory sites contributing information to help you solve the task at hand.

Most students enjoy movement-based learning activities because it is more natural to move than to stay still. Movement stimulates the flow of oxygen-rich blood and brain chemicals, such as noradrenaline and dopamine, that are natural motivators and serve to maximize cerebral energy levels. Thus, curriculum content that is associated with frequent movement will likely be learned and remembered for a much longer time than if presented in the traditional fashion whereby the teacher talks the sitting students through the content. What research is telling educators is that, whenever possible, content should be associated with repetitive movement (Bender, 2008; King & Gurian, 2006; Sousa, 2006; Tate, 2003).

Incorporating movement into a lesson does not have to be complicated. One simple example of movement-based learning for the upper elementary grades involves associating the parts of a business or personal letter with parts of the human body (Chapman, 2000). Note in the example pictured in Figure 4.2 how movement logically flows from the top of the human body to the legs, as the organization of the various components of a letter follow from top to bottom. This type of activity, repeated frequently during a two-week unit of instruction on letter forms can greatly enhance learning and retention.

Although teachers of younger students have used movement in their teaching for years, researchers are now advocating the use of movement across all grade levels, particularly to teach

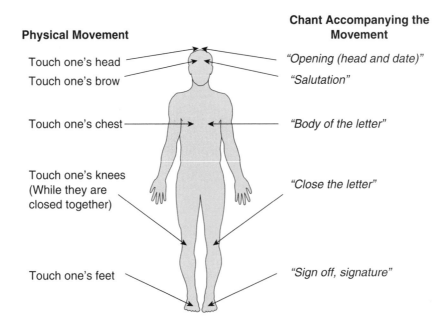

Figure 4.2   This diagram illustrates how easily movement can be incorporated into a lesson. Here, the students touch a part of their body while singing a chant that helps them associate the body part with the part of a business or personal letter.

Source: Adapted from Chapman, 2000.

content in the subject areas in secondary school. For example, imagining one's body superimposed on a map, and then associating various body parts with locations on the map can assist students in learning where the continents are on the globe, where individual states are located, or where various cities or rivers are within a single state (Chapman, 2000).

Many other examples of movement-based learning exist in the literature. Moving students along a large number-line on the floor assists in mathematical measurement activities or in operations with positive and negative integers (Tate, 2003). Arranging cards on the classroom floor that depict both the words and the punctuation for a sentence is much more interesting to students than teaching the same grammar and punctuation lesson merely using a worksheet. This "card on the floor" movement activity serves as both an effective instructional technique as well as an enhancement to class management for boys, since the male students are less bored than they would be sitting at a desk with a worksheet on the same content (King & Gurian, 2006).

Ways of Using Movement

There are two distinct ways to use movement for teaching content. In the previous examples, each student is acting independently (i.e., a student touching his/her body parts to represent parts of a letter). Another option is to ask several students to move together through a representation of the content, perhaps representing different roles. When this type of activity is repeated over time, students are more likely to learn and remember the content.

Given this overall emphasis on movement, teachers in the upper grade levels should consider using some movement-based learning activity during every learning episode. For example, making lines of 3, 5, and 7 students can be used to illustrate a bar graph, or semantic webs can be constructed with students holding a poster to represent their position on the web. However, rather than using several different movement activities each day during an instructional unit, teachers should develop a unified movement activity that represents the essence of the whole unit (see the "cell wall" example that follows). Merely adding different content to the same movement simplifies matters for the teacher yet enhances the instructional impact of that movement for the students.

> *Try not to let a learning episode go by without some type of movement-based activity!*

Again, the general guideline for teachers across all grade levels is simple: Try not to let a learning episode go by without some type of movement-based learning activity.

Movement-Based Instruction in a Lesson

With this emphasis on instructional movement in mind, we can now consider how to use movement in a lesson so that it not only serves as an instructional tool but controls undesirable behavior as well. For many male students with attention-deficit hyperactivity disorder (ADHD) or oppositional defiant disorder (ODD), distraction or hyperactivity are fundamental characteristics of their learning difficulties. This is not to suggest that young females do not display similar problems. However, many more males than females are identified as hyperactive and defiant, as research studies and most experienced teachers will confirm.

Across the grade levels, many of these male students cannot control their impulse to move. Consequently, these students will move around the classroom regardless of what the teacher does. These students do not move around because they are spiteful, evil, or meanspirited individuals who intentionally plan to disrupt the instructional activity. Rather, most of them move at inappropriate times in the classroom because everything in their mind and body is shouting: "You have to move right now!"

For teachers of these students, providing some movement options in the classroom is a must for survival, and building movement into the content-based teaching is the most efficient way to do that. It also has the added result of enhancing the effectiveness of one's teaching. Frequently using movement-based activities while learning content reduces the unscheduled moves of hyperactive male students because they will have some of their urge for movement met by the activity. Movement-based instruction is not only a very effective instructional strategy for young males, it is also an effective classroom management technique. Here are other examples.

Movement-Based Instruction in Biology: An Educator's Idea

Ms. Susan Jasper was teaching at Jackson County High School in a ninth/tenth grade biology class. The lesson was the first lesson focusing on cells and came the first day of a two-week instructional unit on that topic. Ms. Jasper was using a diagram on an overhead transparency that depicted a cell wall as a circle enclosing the cell. Both bacteria and food enzymes were represented by external arrows impacting on the cell wall, and while the cell wall kept the bacteria out, the food enzymes penetrated the wall. The diagram showed that the main functions of a cell wall are twofold: keep bacteria out and let food in.

Although the transparency showed this process graphically, the class seemed uninvolved with this lesson. Several students were getting physically restless and two were whispering in the back of the room. Suddenly, Ms. Jasper stopped talking about the overhead diagram and asked five male students to stand up and lock their elbows together in a circle to represent the cell wall. Ms. Jasper explained to the class that the cell wall was very strong—like those young men. That comment captured the interest of these males since they were being described as "strong" in front of their peers. Ms Jasper then asked a female student to pretend to be a bacterium, and told her to "Get into the cell!" Ms. Jasper explained that tickling above the waist was allowed, but no touching was allowed below the waist. The males in the cell wall were told to "Keep out the bacterium!" Ms. Jasper then shouted "Go!"

After a few moments of tickling and fun, Ms. Jasper shouted, "Freeze! What does a cell wall do with the bacterium?" The class answered loudly in unison, "Keeps it out!" Next, another female was selected as the food enzyme, and the males forming the cell wall were told to "Make her work for it, but then let this food enzyme in." Both the bacterium and food enzyme began to tickle the cell wall, and within a few seconds the food enzyme got into the center of the cell. Ms. Jasper again shouted "Freeze! What does a cell wall do with a food enzyme?" The class answered, "Let's it in."

In this simple example, Ms. Jasper cleverly used a sexual allusion to get the students' attention—a tactic that usually works with high school students, but is not always wise or appropriate. Still, it worked wonderfully in this case because Ms. Jasper knew which of these students would cooperate without letting the activity get out of control. She subsequently reported that, because the secondary students loved that movement-based example, she used it each day during the ten-day instructional unit. She added content throughout the unit to enhance the movement model of the cell. Within a few days, other types of cells (e.g., cells featuring a cell membrane rather than a cell wall) were discussed along with other internal structures, such as the nucleus.

Although this example reflects excellent teaching in a secondary class, it also represents a classroom management strategy. Whenever the students appeared bored or distracted during the two-week unit, Ms. Jasper introduced a movement-based activity related to the content that the students enjoyed and that quickly brought them back on task. Further, she reported that throughout the unit, she often asked, "How can we incorporate this new cell structure into our movement model?" Finally, the students enjoyed the movement so much that Ms. Jasper now develops at least one such movement example for each instructional unit she teaches. She also noted that every single student in the class knew the function of the cell wall—keep bacteria out and let food enzymes in.

Boy-Friendly Instruction and Discipline

The gender-based differences in the brains of boys and girls that we discussed earlier in this chapter suggest that some instructional tactics might be more appropriate for boys. For example, males seem to participate more in discussions when the literature they read has clear delineations of good and evil, heros and villains, or right and wrong. Boys tend to be more boisterous in the classroom than do girls, and this may be misinterpreted as "hyperactive" or even "behaviorally disturbed." Implementing instructional tactics that target these differences seems to result in making boys less disruptive in the classroom overall, and at least one school credits such "boy-friendly" teaching with closing a significant achievement gap between boys and girls in their elementary school (Allen, 2006; King & Gurian, 2006).

These brain-compatible classroom tactics have been featured in a wide variety of instructional methods books, and are generally being well received by educators today. Our point here is that, whenever possible, teachers should use techniques that capture the energy and attention of the males in their classes, in order to indirectly reduce disciplinary problems with those students. Although many instructional suggestions have been suggested, the following are directly related to the learning capabilities and difficulties of males.

Instructional Tactics to Motivate Males and Decrease Behavior Problems

Here are five suggestions based on the research literature for strategies and techniques that have been shown to motivate male students and decrease their misbehavior.

- **Use more visual representations.** Because the brains of males generally have more areas dedicated to spatial-mechanical functioning, using dynamic visual representations often results in increased attention, which will, in turn, result in less misbehavior.

- **Use dynamic, moving models.** Because the male optical and visual processing systems rely more heavily on cells that detect motion, using a physically moving example of a concept is likely to engage males in the learning task more so than static graphics. In many cases, computerized instructional packages can make traditional charts and graphs dynamic. For example, in biology class, rather than merely presenting a series of overhead transparencies depicting growth of a fetus over time, a computerized presentation would generate a video of a growing fetus.

- **Build learning activities around team competition.** Boys are naturally more aggressive than girls, and while overt aggression can sometimes cause problems, team competition can channel those aggressive tendencies toward productive learning experiences, and thereby reduce inappropriate aggression. Team competitions that involve running from one location to the next to identify a question for the team, can result in increased attention for young boys.

- **Use role play activities.** Because boys are less likely to be as highly attuned to various social situations as girls, providing learning opportunities that offer the option of acting out the learning content can be effective. Although girls also benefit from role play activities, boys are more likely to understand the social implications of the learning content in actual role play situations, certainly more so than when a teacher merely asks the boys to reflect on content.

- **Use music to enhance memory.** Although music can be used to facilitate memory for all students (consider the "ABC" song so frequently used to teach the alphabet), music coupled with movement may be particularly appropriate for young males. Here is a mathematics chant using the rhythm of "We will, we will rock you!" for teaching about circles (Bender, 2005).

> *This is circumference, all around the side.*
> *Next comes the radius, middle to the side.*
> *Next is diameter, all the way through!*
> *All of that's a circle, I'll show it to you.*

In using this chant, students can walk in lines into the various components mentioned above. For example, while chanting the first line, six to ten students march into an open space in the classroom, making a circle. While chanting the second line, three to four students enter the circle and form the radius. During the next line, six to eight students enter the circle again, forming the diameter. In this fashion, both music and movement are coupled to represent the components of the circle.

A Case Study: Using Music and Movement to Curb Inappropriate Behavior

Ms. Lovorn was teaching mathematics in her fourth-grade class and noted that each time she began the lesson, Eric would begin to misbehave. Sometimes he tossed his books on the floor, or he called other students names to provoke an argument. During the next few weeks, Ms. Lovorn noted that he was more likely to do so when the mathematics assignment involved multiplication and division. Subsequently, a few observations of Eric's mathematics skills confirmed that he had never mastered the times tables. Apparently, Eric was misbehaving whenever he was confronted with a mathematics problem requiring multiplication facts.

Almost every veteran teacher has encountered students whose misbehavior was caused by a deficit in prerequisite knowledge. These students are essentially using misbehavior to avoid work that they know they cannot do successfully. Although the times tables were included in the third-grade curriculum, Ms. Lovorn noted that several other students had not mastered the threes, fours, sixes, sevens, eights, and nines times tables. Apparently, the only times tables that all students had learned were the simpler ones: the ones, twos, fives, and tens. For that reason, Ms. Lovorn felt comfortable spending a brief time each day on the times tables with the entire class, but she also wanted to intervene to curb Eric's inappropriate behavior. She decided to combine these two needs into one plan.

Initially Ms. Lovorn collected some baseline data on Eric's misbehavior during mathematics. She found that over four days she had reprimanded him more than 30 times for his misbehavior during the daily 50-minute mathematics class. She then decided to use a music and movement-based intervention that the students would enjoy because it would be more interesting while enhancing the likelihood of remembering the content. At the same time, it would teach Eric his times tables and likely decrease his misbehavior. To focus on Eric, she made him the "Times Table Leader." His job was to lead the class in a chant of the multiplication facts known to the class while "slapping out" the times tables.

Initially the class focused on the three times table only. Each day, Eric was presented with a times table chart that represented all of the equations in the three times table set: $3 \times 1 = 3$, $3 \times 2 = 6$, and so forth through $3 \times 10 = 30$. Eric was taught to read the equations aloud while leading the class in reciting the times tables to the rhythm of "We will, we will rock you!" The class participated by calling out the times tables and slapping out that rhythm on their desks. During that one sentence, the students should be able to chant the first two equations. The next time they repeat the sentence, they chant the next two equations, and so on. Ms. Lovorn participated as the class chanted the equations using that rhythm, and each day the class recited the entire set several times before moving on into their other mathematics work. The entire recitation for any given day lasted only about two minutes. After two weeks, the class moved to the four times table for two weeks, and then to the sixes, and so on.

As they progressed through the times tables over the next several weeks, Ms. Lovorn noted that students at their desks doing other work appeared to be "slapping out" the rhythm and reciting times tables in order to find a multiplication fact that they needed. Ms. Lovorn told Eric and all the other class members that if they needed a multiplication fact for a times table set that they have *not* practiced using the rhythm, she would gladly provide the answer. However, if a student needed a multiplication fact for a set they had previously practiced, Ms. Lovorn would gladly "slap out" the times table with the student for that particular set. This provided her with opportunities to remind the class that while they may not have practiced the seven times table, they did know some of it because they had previously practiced the threes and fours, and that 7×3 was the same as 3×7, and 7×4 was the same as 4×7.

> *Using music and movement together helped this teacher redirect a student's chronic misbehavior to leading productive classroom activities.*

Many students in the class appeared to be learning their multiplication facts and were retaining that information for use in other work. However, the most impressive results were shown in Eric's behavior. Over a period of only five days, his behavior during mathematics instruction improved dramatically, and by the end of the project, his misbehavior was all but eliminated. As the data in Figure 4.3 show, his occurrences of misbehavior during mathematics were reduced to an average of less than one misbehavior per day in the last two weeks of the intervention period. Ms. Lovorn shared this intervention with the principal and school counselor, both of whom were impressed. However, the real payoff came when she shared this with Eric's parents at the next parent-teacher meeting. Eric's mother almost came to tears while saying quietly, "I'm so glad you've noted Eric's love for music, and used that to make him behave. Most of his other teachers could not figure out how to make him behave in class. Everyone in my family has always loved

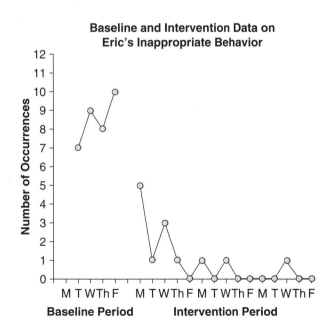

Figure 4.3 This chart shows frequency of Eric's misbehavior before (baseline) and after the music and movement intervention during his mathematics lessons.

music, and I know Eric does. He listens to his MP3 player for hours on end, and if music can help him behave better, all the better. Thank you for seeing that in him, and for caring."

Targeted interventions to improve behavior do require that the teacher take some extra time for planning, as Ms. Lovorn did in this example. The payoff includes more successful learning and a more enjoyable class. Sometimes, too, these interventions make a critically important difference in a student's life.

The Responsibility Strategy

Males frequently seek attention in the classroom in very inappropriate ways. Although females also need attention during their childhood and adolescent years, males seem to require more of their teacher's time. Unfortunately, some males get attention through oppositional or defiant misbehavior. From the perspective of the male student, attention for a negative behavior is still attention. Furthermore, during an episode of misbehavior, the offending student often captures the attention of his peers and, thus, feels empowered. At the same time, the teacher needs to address the student's misbehavior. This results in unfortunate situations where the student, through his misbehavior, has the attention of his peers and the teacher, and the lesson is at a standstill. Now the student is in a powerful position, and many oppositional students intentionally seek their recognition by creating and misbehaving in situations such as these.

In some cases, a cycle begins in which the only recognition these students receive stems from their own misbehavior, and given the desire of most young males to receive attention (some might say, "show off"), more misbehavior follows. One way to effectively counter this negative, self-feeding cycle is to provide positive attention for *appropriate* behaviors. Specifically, teachers should seek ways to empower male students by having them perform a classroom responsibility that the students will take seriously and be proud to do (Tournaki & Criscitiello, 2003).

The term "Responsibility Strategy" was first used by Bender (2003), though the idea is certainly not new. The essence of a responsibility strategy involves empowering male (or female) students by providing them a way to earn positive attention for necessary and appropriate behaviors. Through this strategy, students are encouraged to identify their unique contribution to the "society" of the classroom, and to meet those responsibilities to the teachers, the classmates, and the school, thus gaining the positive attention that they seek. Using these students for individual responsibilities allows them the opportunity to "show off" in an appropriate way, and, for many males, that is sufficient motivation to participate in a responsibility strategy intervention. Moreover, the tasks done by these students should be selected so that they assist the teacher and others in the class.

> *Responsibility strategies work because they give otherwise disconnected students opportunities to make meaningful contributions and to feel valued as a member of the school community.*

One critical factor in this behavioral intervention is to ensure that the task gives *meaningful* responsibility to the students—one which they wish to take and that allows them to receive positive attention. Such responsibilities not only fill the attention needs of the students, but also positively affect the students' relationships with the teacher and others in the classroom. If students who are aggressive, defiant, and oppositional can find ways to demonstrate their personal authority and power in productive ways, they will not need to demonstrate their power in disruptive ways.

Note that a responsibility strategy intervention is different from the more common "reinforcing appropriate behavior" strategy. In using responsibility strategies, the opportunity to perform the task should not be contingent upon appropriate behavior. Rather, the message the students need to glean from the responsibility strategy is that their responsibility is so essential for the class that they must do that task daily, even if they misbehave on any particular day. The intent here is to convince the students that (1) their task is essential, (2) their responsibility task is their contribution to the society of the class, and (3) they are meaningfully integrated into the class. Here are several examples.

Light Bulb Monitor: An Educator's Idea

Dr. Bob Brooks, who was principal of a locked-door school unit in a psychiatric hospital for difficult kids, often tells of a student who broke every light bulb he could reach within the school. All lights were fair game, and he really didn't care what disciplinary measures were used as punishment for breaking light bulbs, since he was going to break them anyway. He clearly derived a great deal of pleasure from this destructive and bizarre behavior.

To Dr. Brooks' credit, he reflected on that student's relationship to the class and the school in general. He decided to provide a positive behavioral opportunity and a responsibility for this student that was directly related to the student's interest in light bulbs. Dr. Brooks made that student the "Light Bulb Monitor" for the entire school. Dr. Brooks explained to the student that each day the student was expected to go from room to room and assure that every light bulb was working properly. If a light bulb was out, the student had the responsibility of reporting the problem to Dr. Brooks' office. Naturally, the student loved going into a room of his peers each morning, filled with his own sense of self-importance, and switching on the lights several times while the teacher checked attendance or attended to other business. His peers saw that he was given special privileges along with his unique responsibility. That peer recognition made a positive difference in this student's behavior. At the same time, this particular responsibility strategy ended the light-bulb-breaking incidents. More importantly, this student had assumed a responsibility, and was making a meaningful contribution to the school, perhaps for the first time in his life.

Reverse Role Peer Tutoring: Another Responsibility Strategy

Peer tutoring has long been shown to be an effective learning strategy. A variation described here involves role reversal and has been useful in curbing undesirable behavior. Reverse role peer tutoring is another example of providing a serious responsibility to students with behavioral problems. In reverse role peer tutoring, students with behavioral problems and other disabilities serve as tutors rather than tutees, and research over several decades has confirmed that this tactic will curb the inappropriate behavior of students with emotional problems (Maher, 1982, 1984; Tournaki & Criscitiello, 2003).

Charles Maher was among the first to develop this concept. He reported on several research studies in which adolescents with terrible behavior records were used as tutors for students with mental disabilities in lower grade levels. Initially, this tactic may seem frightening for an experienced educator. Imagine selecting a group of adolescent males who have been identified as violent or aggressive, and using them as tutors of younger students! In a very real sense, this took considerable courage because these aggressive adolescents could have victimized their younger tutees. Fortunately, the research results demonstrated just the opposite.

In several controlled studies, the behavior of the socially maladjusted students used as tutors improved dramatically, compared to another group of similar students who received only peer counseling (Maher, 1982; 1984). The number of disciplinary problems for the tutors went down, their attendance improved, and their tutoring even assisted them academically. Anecdotal notes across these studies suggested that the *responsibility* of tutoring seemed to be the deciding factor. By virtue of reverse role tutoring, these students with disabilities were seen as "leaders," a role they had rarely experienced.

Anecdotal reports on this intervention were particularly enlightening. These behavior-problem adolescents began to protect their tutees on the playground and began to relate to them as younger siblings. Clearly, reverse role tutoring gave these behavior-problem students a responsibility for others and established a meaningful connection that greatly improved their own behavior. Other studies that used students with behavior problems as tutors have had similar positive results (Lazerson, Foster, Brown, & Hummel, 1988; Tournaki & Criscitiello, 2003).

One key indicator in using a responsibility strategy is the frequency of the behavior problem. Many students act up from time to time, but when teachers or administrators have a student who demonstrates disciplinary problems frequently, one might conclude that punishment options are not working. For many male students who seem to be constantly in the principal's office for misbehavior, implementation of a responsibility strategy would be appropriate. The same is true for students who feel disconnected with the school environment or with others within that environment. In that case, the responsibility strategy is well worth considering (Blankenship & Bender, 2007).

> *Despite its atypical approach, reverse role peer tutoring has been shown to be an effective technique for curbing chronic misbehavior in students.*

This strategy should be used when teachers and administrators have exhausted all other options. In such cases, a specific set of responsibilities individually selected for the student may result in reconnecting the student emotionally to the school, establishing a basis for positive relationships, and improving behavior. The responsibility strategy is appropriate in situations where students are angry, aggressive, or oppositional. After the immediate behavioral concern is over, the teacher talks with the student about how the student can assist in the class, using his leadership skills.

Implementing a Responsibility Strategy

For students who are frequently in trouble, address an immediate behavioral disruption through other strategies because the responsibility strategy is a long-term intervention. Figure 4.4 shows the seven steps involved in implementing a responsibility strategy in your class.

Step 1. Disengage from the immediate behavior problem. Walker and Sylwester (1998) suggest that teachers disengage from the situation rather than escalate to a power struggle with the offending student. For example, inform the student in a soft voice that he (or she) will need to schedule a conference about the misbehavior. Then turn away from the student and attempt to get the other students to refocus on the class work at hand.

Step 2. Reflect on the misbehavior and gather baseline data. Next, reflect on the student's relationship with everyone in the class and school. Understanding the motivation of a student is important and one initial step for this intervention is reflecting on what actually motivates the student to misbehave. Ask yourself: "How have I invited this student to positively contribute to this class today?" This statement is phrased very carefully. Note the phrasing, "How have I invited . . .?" Has the student been *invited* to demonstrate his capabilities, talents, or leadership skills? Has he been directly and personally invited to present a positive contribution to the class?

In some cases, the answer is probably that the student has not been effectively invited to make an appropriate and meaningful contribution. This does not suggest ineffective teaching, a lack of caring, or a lack of attention to student needs. Rather, this simply reflects the reality that teachers often face: Attending to the diverse emotional and behavioral needs of 20 to 30 or more students in the class at the same time. Still, this brief reflection can motivate teachers to find ways to involve the student and to make him feel special by inviting him to contribute in a more appropriate way. Also, at this point, a baseline count of problem behaviors is begun. Generally, a minimum of five days of baseline data is recommended.

Step 1: Disengage from the immediate situation.

Step 2: Reflect on the misbehavior and gather baseline data.

Step 3: Select a contribution or responsibility.

Step 4: Consider the implications of the responsibility.

Step 5: Meet with the student to jointly choose a task.

Step 6: Discuss the responsibility with the student and principal.

Step 7: Monitor the student's behavior during the intervention.

Figure 4.4   These are the seven steps that teachers should take when implementing a responsibility strategy.

Step 3. Select a contribution or responsibility. Next, select a responsibility for the student, based on careful consideration of the student's interests, capabilities, and desires. You may wish to talk with the student about his interests. In some cases, particular misbehaviors can provide a clue to student interest, as in the case of the light bulb monitor we described earlier. Does the school need to take photographs for a particular event? Could you use someone to report gang graffiti? Might adjudicated delinquents, supervised by teachers, take some responsibility for notifying teachers about verbal fights on the playground? If planned appropriately, any of these tasks could represent an effective contribution to the school and a positive responsibility for troublesome students.

The actual task assigned for the responsibility is unimportant and almost any necessary task will serve the purpose. However, two things are critically important:

1. The student must feel that he is truly given an opportunity to contribute. In other words, the student must have impressive "bragging rights" along with the task.

2. The student must believe that the task is important to the class. He must be made to feel like he is a contributing partner in a task that he values.

Step 4. Consider the implications of the responsibility. In selecting the responsibility, consider the implications should the student choose to undertake the responsibility. This involves obvious issues such as the student's confidentiality, privacy, safety, and legal liability. For example, no student's responsibility should require that he leave the campus or get involved in physical altercations that have already begun between other students. The principal, because of training in school law and policy, should be contacted when considering responsibilities that involve students leaving the classroom. Also, supervision should always be available for any student completing his responsibility, particularly when the student is having a challenging day behaviorally.

In addition to routine supervision, remember that students may need to be more closely supervised the first few times they try out their responsibilities. In implementing the tutoring intervention described earlier, consider how and what type of training to offer the tutors. How much supervision will be necessary for those tutors, and what types of reinforcement can be offered to them? For example, do they get to leave the classroom a few minutes early to go to tutoring? Leaving the classroom takes place in front of peers and indicates a great deal of trust, thus providing substantial reinforcement, even for students with serious behavior problems. However, you should carefully consider implications of this type of responsibility in advance.

Step 5. Meet with the student to jointly choose a task. After gathering the baseline data, meet with the student and discuss the responsibility strategy options. The student should be allowed to choose which option he would like as his contribution to the class. Again, the student must feel that the task is important and that choosing it is critical to his ownership of this responsibility. Thus, you should present several choices and be prepared for a discussion which may generate others. After the discussion, you and the student select a responsibility task. The student writes a one-paragraph agreement, including a description of the task and specific statements about how it is to be done. Both you and the student sign the agreement.

Step 6. Discuss the responsibility with the student and the principal. If the student's responsibility involves duties outside of class, the intervention is discussed with the school administrator. Involving the student in this discussion will highlight the importance of the task for the student as well as inform the principal as to why the student is doing tasks around campus.

Step 7. Monitor the student's behavior during the intervention. With baseline data already collected, it is now necessary to collect data on the student's behavior during the intervention period. The data will provide an assessment of how well the responsibility strategy worked.

Why Give a Student This Responsibility?

Some teachers may question the wisdom of providing a responsibility for students who are known to frequently misbehave. Is it realistic to hope that students with a history of misbehavior will take any responsibility seriously? Surprisingly, the research cited earlier suggests that even students with fairly severe behavioral problems will take some responsibilities seriously, although the manner in which students are approached with the responsibility is crucial. If a responsibility or task is unilaterally announced to students with behavior problems, they will probably not participate willingly or actively. However, thorough reflection on the individual student and on potential responsibilities, coupled with an invitation to contribute, results in most students with behavioral problems taking and fulfilling their responsibilities seriously.

Most teachers remember being helpers around the class when they were students in school. Tasks such as dusting erasers, cleaning the blackboard or dry-erase board for teachers, and doing other classroom jobs often result in fond memories. These teachers might also remember how special, and how important and involved, those mundane tasks made them feel. Students with behavior problems in our classes today have rarely performed those jobs, because those tasks were usually reserved as privileges or rewards for good behavior. Perhaps this is one reason why the research has shown this responsibility tactic to be so effective, even with hard-core students with serious behavior problems. For some students, this might be just the ticket to turn negative behavior into positive behavior, and thereby improve the student's relationship with the teacher and with others in the class and school.

> *Research studies confirm that even students with serious behavioral problems can take and fulfill their responsibilities seriously.*

The Class Production Assistant: An Educator's Idea

Here is another example of a responsibility strategy related by Wendy Williams, a teacher at Taylor Elementary School, in Lawrenceville, Georgia.

My student, Shanta, has mild autism as well as certain overt behavior problems. Wherever he was in school, he always seemed to get into trouble. He would draw on everything within reach, turn off the CD player while I was using it during the lesson, and touch all of the levers and buttons on the school bus. Clearly, Shanta was fascinated by electronics and he loved to draw, but his behavior was inappropriate.

I decided to try several things with him to curb these behaviors. First, I made him the "Class Production Assistant" during circle time in my room. During that time, I typically play easy-listening music on the CD player and either read a story or discuss one of the lessons with the class. The musical selections I use are fairly long, and when a song ended, I made it Shanta's job to turn off the CD player. I explained to him that he would need to stop turning off the player unless the song ended, but that he could touch that button when the music stopped. As my production assistant, he gets to sit beside me in the circle, with the CD player between us, and he now automatically turns it off each time he is supposed to.

In addition, I made a personal file folder for Shanta with lots of drawing paper for him to use in his drawing. I used paper that included space for a drawing and some lines at the bottom for writing a description of the picture. Now, each day Shanta is supposed to "make book pictures" for me, and each time he draws a picture, we put it in Shanta's "picture book" (the picture book is a three-ring binder that holds all of Shanta's former pages). We call the picture book, "Shanta's Picture Book."

Finally, I showed him how to clean the room with a spray cleaner and rag (mostly cleaning the dry-erase boards in the class), and each time he gets those clean, he is offered five minutes for one of his preferred activities. He usually chooses to draw more for the picture book. He will also pick up any trash on the floor around the room because he knows he will get the reward at the end. I've let him know that these things are very important for our whole class and that no one else has the right to earn time for their preferred activity by cleaning the room. These strategies worked for Shanta, and he has gone from being very disruptive to being a real sweetie. Now I really enjoy having him in the class.

Giving responsibility to misbehaving boys may seem odd, but there are many situations where this approach can be successful.

And What About Girls?

We made clear at the beginning of this chapter that many of the strategies used here could be readily adapted for use with girls who misbehave. We also explained that a girl's brain is different in some ways from a boy's brain, especially in the early development of communication skills. Consequently, girls are more likely to settle disputes verbally rather than physically. It takes a lot to provoke most females to physically attack another female. But when the anger level gets to the breaking point, the confrontation can be extremely vicious and result in serious injury.

Disciplining girls will probably be more effective when the approach takes into account gender differences. When using strategies to address misbehavior in girls, including those in this chapter, consider adapting them with the following thoughts in mind:

- **Talk it over.** Girls' language and communication skills develop faster than boys. They also have more brain regions involved in language processing and are very good at it. As a result, they are more apt to talk about what provoked them to misbehave. Encourage them to discuss whether they understand the consequences of their actions and what would be appropriate steps to take to curb that behavior in the future.

- **Focus on feelings.** We noted earlier in this chapter that female brains are more attuned to how others feel and are better at empathizing. Ask the girl to think about how her misbehavior made others feel, and how she would feel if the misbehavior were directed toward her.

- **Shift to perception.** After talking about her feelings, shift to discussing how others perceive her. Females are more sensitive than males to what others think about them. Describe how her misbehavior may negatively affect what other students think of her.

- **Use delayed gratification.** Females are better than males at yielding to delayed gratification. Discussing a potential future reward may be enough to moderate or eliminate her misbehavior.

When educators have a deep understanding of how boys' and girls' brains differ, they can make more informed decisions about which strategies are likely to be effective for dealing with misbehavior.

THE RISE OF CYBERBULLYING

It may seem odd at first glance to include this topic here. But put simply, boys are more apt to be school bullies than girls. And bullying of all types is becoming a major and persistent problem in schools. Much has been written about bullying in recent years and many Internet resources are available to help teachers, administrators, and parents deal with the issue. Our purpose here is not to deal much with traditional bullying. Rather, we want to raise awareness of how technology has raised bullying to a new and insidious level and to suggest some actions that schools can take to prevent it.

Bullying Versus Cyberbullying

Educators have been concerned with bullying for a long time. But a new threat has emerged in recent years as an increasing number of students gain access to cell phones, personal digital assistants (PDAs), and the Internet. This threat, called *cyberbullying,* is the intentional and repeated harm inflicted on someone through electronic devices. Believing they are anonymous, cyberbullies engage in cruel and harmful actions that embarrass and demean fellow students without fear of discovery or facing the consequences for their behavior. Some students have committed suicide because they could not take the harassment any longer. Because the problem occurs in the hidden online world, its effects can be similar to, but also different from, traditional bullying. Table 4.2 compares traditional bullying with cyberbullying.

Bullying is often categorized as direct and indirect. Common forms of direct cyberbullying include denigration, exclusion, harassment, and masquerading. Denigration occurs most frequently by students against school employees, usually teachers and administrators. Angry students may establish a Web site to ridicule their victim and post harmful, untrue, or cruel statements. The primary purpose is to damage the victim's reputation. Online exclusion occurs when victims are rejected by their peer group and omitted from technological communications with the group. A victim of harassment may receive persistent hurtful or offensive messages through various forms

Table 4.2	Comparison of Traditional Bullying With Cyberbullying	
	Traditional Bullying	**Cyberbullying**
Description	Can be categorized as direct or indirect. Direct bullying is more physical than indirect and includes shoving, hitting, verbally threatening, tripping, and stabbing. Both direct and indirect bullying include spreading rumors, blackmailing, and excluding from a group.	Can be both direct and indirect. Flaming is an indirect form that consists of an argument between two people that includes rude and vulgar language, threats, and insults. Direct forms include denigration, excluding, and harassment.
Extent of problem	Nearly one-half of middle/junior high school students report being victims of traditional bullying.	About one-fourth of middle/junior high school students report being victims of cyberbullying.
Gender differences	Male bullies are likely to engage in direct bullying, while female bullies are likely to engage in indirect bullying.	Males are more likely to be cyberbullies than females, although the gap is much narrower than in traditional bullying. Female cyberbully victims are more likely to inform adults than their male counterparts.
Identification	The bully intentionally and repeatedly harms individuals or groups through power, age, and physical strength. Identifying the bully is usually easy.	The cyberbully may hide in anonymity, making identification more difficult. This anonymity also raises the fear factor.
Effect on victims	Victims experience academic, personal, and social problems, including withdrawal and depression.	Victims often withdraw from school activities, and become ill, depressed, and suicidal.

Sources: Chibbaro, 2007; Crawford, 2002; Li, 2006; Quiroz, Arnette, & Stephens, 2006; and Willard, 2006.

of technology. Masquerading is pretending to be someone else and sending material that makes that person look bad or puts that person in danger.

Cyberbullies who are often overlooked are the "social climber bullies." These bullies are upper social class students who bully within the context of the "in-crowd," teasing those who want to be part of the in-crowd (the wannabes) and insulting those who are excluded from the in-crowd (the losers). They are overlooked because they are looked upon with favor by teachers and administrators. Furthermore, the losers and the wannabes don't report the cyberbullying to school personnel because to do so would bring retaliation to the losers and ruin the wannabes chances of gaining their desired social status (Willard, 2006). Cyberbullying victims, in general, are often reluctant to tell adults because they fear the bullying will become more intense and they worry that the adults will take away their access to the communications technology.

Dealing With Cyberbullying

Schools must develop strategies for preventing and intervening in cyberbullying that should include the following (Beale & Hall, 2007; Chibbaro, 2007; Harris & Petrie, 2003; Ribble & Bailey, 2006; Willard, 2006):

- There should be a clear, updated written policy stating that all forms of cyberspace harassment, both during and after school hours, will not be tolerated. Many schools have adopted an Accepted Use Policy (AUP). Some secondary schools have integrated a short curriculum unit that teaches students about how to use technology appropriately. Components include etiquette, responsibility, rights, safety, and security. The instruction is designed to make the students technologically literate and give them an understanding of proper use through guided practice and modeling.

- A range of punishments should be in place for cyberbullies, including loss of computer privileges, detention, suspension, and expulsion. In some areas, law enforcement authorities may need to be notified.

- Students should have a means of reporting cyberbullying anonymously.

- School personnel should carry out awareness campaigns to alert teachers, students, and parents about cyberbullying. Because cyberbullying frequently occurs away from school, parents should be reminded to monitor their child's online activities. The Center for Safe and Responsible Internet Use has published a parents' guide to cyberbullying and cyber threats. See the **Resources** section for more information on this site.

- Ask the local police department if they have cyber experts who can speak to parents and students about proper Internet use.

- Conduct professional development workshops so that teachers and administrators can be trained in the nature of cyberbullying and its effects, how to respond if it is detected, and how to report it.

- Student training should include learning how to identify cyberbullying at school and away from school, providing students methods of reporting it, and discussing school policy.
- Increase supervision of school areas where cyberbullying is likely to occur.
- Counseling and support programs should be in place for both the victim and the cyberbully. Victims could be offered training in developing a more positive self-concept, increasing assertiveness skills, reducing social isolation, and practicing behaviors that will reduce the risk of further victimization. Bullies could be counseled and trained in improving their self-concept, recognizing the legal and personal consequences of cyberbullying, increasing social problem-solving, developing anger management skills, and increasing the ability to empathize with their victims.

Despite the convenience of communications technology, its misuse by students creates new challenges for teachers, administrators, and parents. Cyberbullying is on the increase. Thus, school personnel must take all the necessary steps to design and implement prevention and intervention programs that protect students from the negative effects of cyberbullying.

SUMMARY

Differences in biology and brain structures between the two genders lead to differences in their behavior. These differences become apparent in social environments such as schools. Females tend to be more socially aware, communicative, and likely to resolve conflict through language rather than physical aggression. Males, on the other hand, tend to be more physically aggressive, mobile, and protective of their personal space than females. When teachers understand the nature of these gender differences, they can select strategies that are more likely to be successful in curbing the misbehaviors of males in the classroom.

Thus, by using movement (perhaps coupled with music or chants), appropriate reading materials emphasizing clear hero roles, and responsibility tactics that allow students opportunities to "show off" for good behavior, teachers can reach the young males in their classes and, at the same time, make the class a much more enjoyable place for all.

The threat of cyberbullying is real, and schools need to develop programs to curb and eliminate its negative effects on the school community.

Chapter 5

Building Positive Relationships With Troubled Students

RELATIONSHIPS AND RESEARCH

Teachers seem to be faced today with troubled students more than ever. Family problems at home, the temptation of alcohol and drugs, the stresses of puberty, the demands of interactive technology, and adolescent peer pressure are all taking their toll. Educators are trying to determine the best way for teachers to deal with troubled students while preserving the safety of the classroom and the integrity of the teaching-learning process.

Many educators have found that the single most important factor in classroom management is the development of a positive relationship between the student and the teacher (Hall & Hall, 2003). For example, Marzano (2003) completed an analysis of 100 studies on classroom management and found that the quality of teacher-student relationships was the most important factor in all aspects of classroom management. Bender (2003) argued that a positive relationship is the basis of all effective discipline, and encouraged educators to consider the impact of any single disciplinary strategy on the long-term relationship they had with their students. Stipek (2006) emphasized that teachers should focus directly on their relationships with the students in the class that exhibit behavioral problems, but cautioned that teachers should not compromise on holding students accountable for their behavior.

Ferguson (2002) used a survey technique to inquire about disciplinary matters among a group of secondary students. The results indicated that students preferred to have positive relationships with their teachers and that African-American students, in particular, were highly responsive to teachers who showed that they cared about the student's learning and life. Clearly, there is a convergence among the researchers that a positive teacher-student relationship is the very basis of effective classroom management, and that in the absence of such a relationship, effective classroom management will be difficult.

If relationships are that important, then the more we know about them, the more likely we are to initiate and manage them effectively. With all the research focus in recent years on how the brain grows, develops, and learns, two questions now come to mind:

- Has the surge in neuroscience discovered more about the nature of human relationships?
- If so, can these discoveries suggest any classroom strategies that are likely to be successful?

Insights From Neuroscience

Human beings are social animals. Shortly after birth, infants begin to bond with their caregivers and mimic their actions (mirror neurons at work). They enjoy interacting with other toddlers and adults and often get cranky when left alone. A review of imaging studies on infants found evidence that social brain networks are developing rapidly during the first year (Johnson et al., 2005). As children grow, social relationships become an important environmental influence. The type of relationships that children and adolescents have with their parents, siblings, friends, and teachers form a knowledge base of experiences and emotions that will largely determine how those individuals respond in different social situations.

> *Human beings are social animals. Now neuroscience is exploring how our brain processes and assesses the behavior of others in a social situation and then determines our response.*

How people form relationships with each other has long been the study of social psychologists. For most of the 20th century, these studies collected data using self-reporting and measurements of behavior, such as response times along with recall and memory measures. Researchers avoided biological explanations of social behavior because they were thought to be incompatible with the broader concepts of social interaction and societal development.

Brain imaging technology, however, changed all that. Social psychologists realized that investigating how the brain processes information (i.e., cognition) could reveal how an individual appraises the meaning of an event and decides what emotional response to use in a social context. Social psychology became *social cognition*. Meanwhile, cognitive psychologists were using the new imaging technology and related techniques to explore the biological underpinnings of cognition— how the brain processes thought and how thought influences behavior. Cognitive psychology became *cognitive neuroscience.*

By the year 2000, some researchers recognized that merging social cognition with cognitive neuroscience would lead to a new field of study that

(1) would use cognitive neuroscience methods to study a wide array of social-emotional behavior,

(2) would use this combined methodology to shed more light on how the brain processes information, and

(3) did not identify with the types of research questions and content areas previously associated with related fields.

As a result, the new field of *social cognitive neuroscience* emerged (Ochsner, 2007).

What Is Social Cognitive Neuroscience?

Figure 5.1 illustrates how social cognitive neuroscience combines social psychology with cognitive neuroscience and aims to describe behavior at three levels using data from brain imaging and similar technology. The social level examines the experience and behavior of a person while interacting in various social contexts. The cognitive level looks at which brain regions are involved in information processing and how that processing gives rise to emotions and behavior that respond to a particular situation. The neural level explores the cerebral areas that are associated with social behaviors.

This is a new science, and researchers are attempting to understand the complex and dynamic relationship between the brain (and its related systems) and social interaction. As these fields combine, the resulting research is inevitably exciting and meaningful even though the underlying concepts are not easy to research. For instance, assessing personality traits and correlating them with task performance and biological data would seem relatively easy. These constructs, however, are rarely stable and they are dependent on so many other variables that designing experiments remains a challenge. Nonetheless, research in this area is advancing and already beginning to provide deeper insights into the neural mechanisms that influence our behavior in social contexts.

Some Research Findings

Medical professionals have long observed that the social behavior of some patients changed dramatically when certain brain areas were injured through a traumatic event, such as an accident or stroke. These observations led to the notion that social behavior may be processed in regions of the brain that were separate from the regions controlling non-social behavior. Consequently, one of the significant areas of research aims to answer this question: Are the cerebral processes and

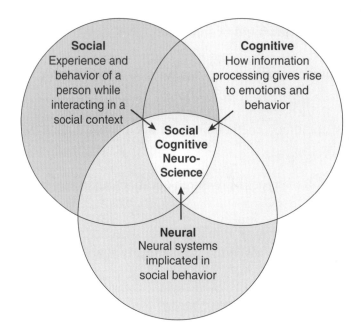

Figure 5.1   This diagram illustrates how three levels of investigation can be combined to form a new field of research known as social cognitive neuroscience.

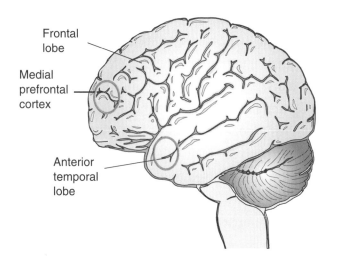

Figure 5.2   This diagram shows the location of two brain regions that are active when one processes social tasks. The medial prefrontal cortex is in the front center of the frontal lobe and the anterior temporal lobe is at the front of the temporal lobes located in each hemisphere.

neural systems that process social stimuli (e.g., forming relationships, comparing others to oneself, or interpreting the behavior of others) different from those that process non-social stimuli (e.g., dealing with hunger and sleep)? Apparently, the answer is yes. Recent studies indicate that specific brain regions are activated when subjects are faced with making social decisions and judgments as part of a performance task.

Numerous studies have found two brain regions that are substantially involved in social decisions, the *medial prefrontal cortex* and the *anterior temporal lobe* (see Figure 5.2). The medial prefrontal cortex is located just behind the center of the forehead at the very front of the frontal lobe. You may recall from Chapter 1 that the frontal lobe comprises the rational and executive control center of the brain, processing higher-order thinking and directing problem solving. In addition to these cognitive tasks, this region is also active when an individual is assessing how closely the mental state of another is like that of the individual in a social setting (Frith & Frith, 2006; Heatherton et al, 2006; Mitchell, Banaji, & Macrae, 2005).

The anterior temporal lobe is at the front end of the two temporal lobes, one in each brain hemisphere. Studies found this area to be particularly active when participants were judging which social concepts, such as one's needs and goals, described social behavior (Zahn et al., 2007). It may also be an area where social and emotional processing interact and where facial recognition occurs (Olson, Plotzker, & Ezzyat, 2007). These are important findings because they infer that the more similar another's mental state, social needs, and goals are to our own in a social situation, the more comfortable we will be with them. Thus, we are more likely to perceive that a positive social relationship exists between the two of us and that our behavioral responses will be similar.

Social Cognitive Development During Adolescence

In Chapter 1 we pointed out that the frontal lobe develops more slowly than the parts of the brain controlling vital processes and emotions. Full maturity of the frontal lobe, you may recall, occurs between the ages of 22 and 24 years. So it is no surprise that studies of social behavior also show differences in performance response with age. Because of its proportionally slower development period, the frontal lobe's ability to process and appraise social information will vary among children, adolescents, and adults. As any teacher or parent knows, the social skills of a primary school student can seem primitive when compared to those of a typical adolescent.

Studies verify that preadolescents are considerably slower than adolescents in determining the emotional intent of others. Adolescents, in turn, are slower than adults, but the difference is much less. This is likely due to the rapid increase in maturation that occurs in the frontal lobe during the middle and later adolescent years (Choudhury, Blakemore, & Charman, 2006; Giedd et al., 1999).

Although the area of social cognitive neuroscience is still new, studies over the last several years continue to reaffirm what most experienced teachers already knew: Social behavior is a critically important component of human development. What the science has done is confirm that this importance is signaled in the brain by the activity of specific regions that help individuals understand themselves as social beings, infer the intent of others, and decide the appropriate behavioral response for different social situations.

As we mentioned at the beginning of this chapter, one major component of social interaction in schools is the nature of the teacher-student relationship. Students today often spend more time with their teachers than with their parents, siblings, or peers. This fact alone accentuates the importance of how adequately the student and the teacher perceive, assess, and respond to each other's behavior. With that thought in mind, let's look at some strategies that have shown to be effective in helping teachers build meaningful and productive relationships with students.

DEVELOPING TEACHER-STUDENT RELATIONSHIPS

The Importance of Positive Relationships With and For Students

This section of the chapter focuses on establishing positive relationships with troubled students, including students with serious behavioral problems or students who merely seem aloof and unreachable. Prior to discussing specific interventions to build relationships, let's look at some general classroom management suggestions found in the research literature (Marzano, 2006; Stipek, 2006). Many teachers are using these strategies already. However, for others, perhaps the following synthesis can spur further consideration of various strategies that may not have been tried.

Building Positive Relationships With Troubled Students

- **Be proactive.** Positive relationships do not ordinarily evolve in most cases where students demonstrate consistent behavior problems. You really need to actively find ways to develop a productive relationship. Of course, this is challenging when the student in question has consistently demonstrated bad behavior in the class. Nevertheless, it is critical for you to develop a positive relationship with students in trouble, and the tactics recommended in this summary should assist.

- **Let students know you care.** Let students know that they are valued as individuals. Show that you care by making time to ask about a student's home life, weekend activities, or hobbies. Talking with students before or after class can go a long way in curbing future behavioral problems, so find the time for this important aspect of the relationship. A recent Gallup poll found that 78 percent of high school students polled said they work harder for teachers who have high expectations and who show that they care about their students' success (Gallup, 2004).

- **Show respect.** Always show respect for students, even in the event of misbehavior. If you feel angry about a misbehavior, you need to be doubly careful that your tone of voice does not indicate disrespect. Making this effort is critical. Also, whenever possible, point out positive behavior on the part of students with behavioral problems, and stress how such positive behavior benefits the entire class.

- **Set clear goals based on high expectations.** Students with behavioral problems need specific and clearly stated goals and must realize that you have high expectations for their work and behavior. Students often can and do behave better in their classrooms than in their home simply because their teachers set higher expectations for appropriate behavior than the students' parents.

- **Be assertive.** You are ultimately responsible for your classroom, and you should demonstrate appropriate assertiveness and appropriate levels of dominance. This does not mean rigid or unkind dominance, but rather a clear organizational structure that establishes your control of the ongoing classroom activities.

- **Use appropriate voice.** Experienced teachers have long realized that an assertive voice does not need to be an angry voice. Rather, in disciplinary situations, your voice should be firm and elevated slightly, but your demeanor should suggest a desire to calm down the situation and not inflame it. Calling a student's first name frequently results in calming the student.

- **Use appropriate body language.** Your body language can either defuse or aggravate a situation involving negative behavior. It is important to use erect posture and face the student without violating the student's physical space. In response to misbehavior, move toward the offending student while not appearing to rush. Also, avoid ritualized behaviors or body stances indicative of physical aggression (i.e., do not clench your fists at your sides or place fists on your hips).

- **Use clear class rules.** Some students with consistent behavior problems just do not realize that their behavior is unacceptable. For example, family members may interrupt each other when speaking, or respond loudly with a "that's a dumb idea" type of statement to each other. Very often, students bring such behaviors to class, not recognizing that it is inappropriate in a school setting. Thus, you should post clear rules in the class governing appropriate behavior and refer to them often. Developing these rules with the students allows them to take ownership of the rules. Typically, four to six class rules, stated positively as "dos" and not "don'ts," work best.

- **Use a variety of consequences for misbehaviors.** Although students need the structure that clear consequences bring, rigid adherence to any rule structure is not wise. Develop and use a range of responses to student misbehaviors, and implement the response that is appropriate to the level of the behavioral infraction. For example, walking toward the offending student may just be enough to refocus the student on the work. For a student loudly cursing at another student, however, ask that student for a meeting after class. Also, pointing out and rewarding positive behavior of others is always advisable.

- **Use hand and other signals.** Many teachers establish hand signals that assist in class management. For example, in some classes, when the teacher gets silent and raises her hand, the students are trained to look at the teacher, cease all talking, and raise their hands also. As the class gets more quiet even the offending student is likely to feel some peer pressure to get quiet. Other teachers use a hotel desk bell for the same purpose. When students hear the bell, they are to quietly look toward the teacher. Find a signal that works for you.

Reaching Unreachable Students With Dialogue Journals

For many students with behavioral problems, building a constructive relationship with anyone is a challenge because these students do not, or cannot, communicate well. Many of the factors that can result in behavioral problems in the classroom are exactly the same factors that may inhibit the building of effective relationships with either peers or adults in the classroom. For instance, if students are emotionally or physically abused at home, their sense of relationships will be skewed and their behavior in the classroom will likely be less than acceptable. Many students who demonstrate behavioral problems in the classroom today do not have any concept of how to build a successful relationship with an adult, or even how to respond when a teacher is attempting to develop a caring, positive relationship. Furthermore, these students may be distrustful of adults in general, and that factor alone can impede the development of relationships.

In many instances, the brain's emotional processing systems are frequently overriding cognitive reflection when these students deal with others, resulting in altercations or social withdrawal. Sometimes, they regret these confrontations but they lack a means to regulate their emotional responses. Taking the time to pause and reflect on thoughts that are to be written down can provide just the setting that allows the brain's rational processes to interact with the emotional regions, dampen their influence, and allow calmer communication to occur.

In situations where teachers find it difficult to get a student to open up to them, a dialogue journal might be the appropriate strategy (Peyton, 1997; Regan, 2003). A dialogue journal is a written continuing conversation that allows students with behavior problems and their teachers to communicate with each other in a non-pressured format. Students can write as much as they choose and they are assured of a teacher's response. The teacher uses the journal to ask questions of the student, compliment the student in some way, discuss a problem that might have occurred in the classroom, or all of these.

> *Dialogue journals allow teachers and students with behavioral problems to communicate in a non-threatening format by allowing the brain's rational areas to take control.*

The form of the journal involves letters that the teacher writes to the student and the student writes to the teacher. Some teachers have implemented this strategy in an effort to curb misbehavior while they teach writing, letter writing, spelling, or grammar skills. Other teachers use it to open a dialogue with a student who may be reluctant to communicate with the teacher in any other form.

Implementing a Dialogue Journal

Dialogue journals are easy to implement and typically involve implementation by the entire class rather than only one student. This strategy is particularly effective when a teacher is supported by a class paraprofessional, or co-teacher, who can assist in writing the letters for each student's journal. However, if it is not possible to use this strategy with the entire class, it may be used with a subgroup of students or with an individual student. Implementation takes approximately 15 minutes, and students should be required to write a letter in their journals a minimum of three times per week. Here are four steps to follow to implement this strategy.

- **Initiating the Journal Notebook.** Tell the students that a separate notebook will be used exclusively for the journal and that their journals will be kept in the classroom. Give the students time to personalize their journal in any way they wish, perhaps by drawing on it or pasting a photograph on the cover. Assure them that their dialogue journals will be seen only by the student and you. In the unlikely event, however, that a journal entry reflects a student's desire to do harm to self or others, you are obligated to share the journal with the appropriate authorities. If students ask about that possibility, you should answer their questions directly.

- **The Teacher's First Letter.** Begin by writing a letter to each student and placing it in the journal. Envelopes are not required, but the letter should reflect appropriate letter format and effective writing. The letters should be personal and directed individually to the students (which explains why this might be too time-consuming to do for an entire class of students without the support of a paraprofessional). You might start off by saying, "I'm glad we'll be doing this journal because I've wanted to get to know you better. I believe you said that one of your hobbies was . . ." In order to assist reluctant writers, your letter should include three to five specific questions that you would like the student to answer. Then, when the student reads the letter, you can point out the questions and help the student get started.

- **The Student's Response Letter.** The next day in class, the participating students are allowed 15 minutes of supervised time to write their response letters in their journals. Although your letters will be written on a page that is added to the journal, the students write directly on the journal page, in sequence. They respond on the page immediately behind your letter and you can staple your letter to the back of the student's response. In this way, the letters are paired for future reflection, and notebooks dropped on the floor do not result in a pile of mixed up letters. Avoid writing directly on the pages in the dialogue journal because students should feel ownership of that journal by being the only ones to write in it. All letters are dated and completed in appropriate letter format.

- **Developing the Relationship.** This strategy is likely to have a significant impact on a student's behavior after several letters have been exchanged. Over time, the content of your letters typically become more personal. You can question students about how their day has gone, how they perceived various social interactions, or their sense of what happened in a particular disciplinary situation.

A Case Study: A Dialogue Journal for Cynthia

Cynthia was a ninth-grade girl who seemed withdrawn and detached from the other students in her class. Mr. Fuller, her homeroom and English teacher, was concerned with her bizarre interjections into various conversations. She often interrupted other students with comments that were loud and wildly off topic. Mr. Fuller suspected that Cynthia made these comments both to get attention and to show her dislike for the other students who had seemingly rejected her. As a result, she was not accepted into the peer group and this, coupled with the fact that she was somewhat overweight, contributed to a very low self-esteem.

Mr. Fuller wanted to use an intervention that would allow him to gain insight into the cause of Cynthia's behavior, as well as allow him to work on her writing and communication skills. He wanted to build her up a bit before her classmates in order to assist her in developing a better sense of herself. He decided to do a dialogue journal.

To obtain information on the impact of his planned intervention, he discretely charted every inappropriate conversational comment Cynthia made during a one-week period in his English class. Although he may have missed a comment or two, he was confident that he counted almost all of Cynthia's inappropriate comments, especially because Cynthia was so loud. It was a simple matter to place a tally mark discretely by her name whenever she said something that was loud and did not fit the conversation. The baseline data indicated an average of seven such inappropriate comments each day, suggesting the need to provide some intervention.

After the other students began their seat work, Mr. Fuller took Cynthia aside to discuss the dialogue journal.

Mr. Fuller:	Cynthia, I'd like to try a new idea with the class, and I've selected you as my first student. If this idea works, I want to use it with everyone, but I want to do this with you first. It is called a dialogue journal. Would you help me with that?
Cynthia:	I don't know. What is it? What do I have to do?
Mr. Fuller:	Good question. A dialogue journal is simply a way for us to write letters to each other about a variety of topics. I'd like to get to know what your hobbies and interests are, so I'll probably ask about those first.
Cynthia:	So how is that going to happen? Will I get a letter from you?
Mr. Fuller:	Yes, you will. You'll get it right here at school. I'll write my letter and put it in this notebook here. This will be your notebook, and you'll be the only person in the class to have a dialogue journal notebook like this. Why don't you put your name on it.
Cynthia:	OK. (Cynthia writes her name on the cover of the notebook.)
Mr. Fuller:	After I write a letter to you, you will write one back to me and answer the questions that I've asked. You can tell me about your day or even ask me some questions if you like. Nobody will see this journal except you and me, and we'll keep it right here in the top drawer of my desk. OK? That way it won't get lost or anything, and we'll use it only in class.

Cynthia: OK. I'll give it a try. I guess this is one way we can get to know each other.

Mr. Fuller: Yes, we can, and I'll have a better understanding of how to teach you when I know what your interests are. That's why I want to do this eventually with the whole class, but you'll help me learn how to do it first, right?

Cynthia: OK. When do we start?

Mr. Fuller: I was hoping you would say that. I've already written my letter to you, so instead of doing the other assignment today, why don't you read that letter from me and then write one back to me. Make sure that your letter looks like mine and that you answer all of the questions I asked in my letter. Yours should not be a long letter, because you'll only have about 15 minutes, but do answer the questions and then ask me some if you like. When you finish, just put it in the journal, and then I'll read your response, OK?

Cynthia: OK.

Teachers who wish to implement a dialogue journal should consider using the script above as a guideline for their initial conversation with the target student. Note that Mr. Fuller showed a special interest in Cynthia in this discussion. He also asked her to assist him in something he was thinking about doing with the entire class, thus making the journal idea less threatening. Also, by approaching Cynthia in this fashion, he assisted in building her self-esteem.

The intervention data shown in Figure 5.3 demonstrate that Cynthia's inappropriate comments to others were reduced over a four-week period, suggesting that Mr. Fuller was correct that she was making those inappropriate comments to gain attention. Although such comments were not eliminated, the reduction was important because making fewer of these comments made Cynthia more acceptable to her peers. In this case, the personal journal had the additional effect of providing special attention to Cynthia in an appropriate fashion, and thus, she did not feel the need to make the improper statements as frequently.

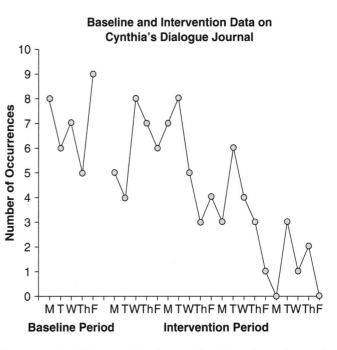

Figure 5.3 The graph shows the baseline data of Cynthia's inappropriate class comments and how they were significantly reduced over the four-week intervention period.

The dialogue journal is a simple and straightforward tactic that can assist in opening up students who are reluctant to communicate verbally with their teachers. It is easy to implement and costs only the price of a notebook and a bit of the teacher's time. The impact of this strategy can be impressive, as it was for Cynthia.

The Lunch Bunch: An Educator's Idea

Carla Gravits was a successful elementary teacher and, as the new assistant principal for Matt Elementary School in Forsythe County, Georgia, she saw a need for intervention with several students who had behavioral problems. As a first-year administrator, she managed the office disciplinary referrals and, in that role, students would frequently come to her office to "sit in time out" after misbehavior in class. Ms. Gravits wanted to let the students know that misbehavior would not be tolerated, but she wanted to do more than merely punish them. At times, students would engage her in a verbal power struggle in the office rather than merely sitting their time out. This caused her to question her own techniques, particularly with two troubled students whom we will call Tyrone and Damien. She picks up the story.

> *Having a few lunches with troubled students might be just the strategy for establishing a caring relationship that helps these students become more successful.*

At one point, when both Tyrone and Damien showed up in my office with another disciplinary note, I decided that rather than merely putting them in the time-out area I would invite them to just sit down and have lunch with me. I did it again the next week when they showed up, and it quickly became something I did with those two once or twice a week. I knew I had to develop a relationship with my students. I believed that if I established such a relationship, students would know that I really cared about their success in school and not just about their behavior problems. It worked. The behavior problems of these two boys became less frequent in just a few weeks, but that's not the end of this story.

Others who came to the office on a disciplinary referral also needed more attention, so I developed an informal Lunch Bunch program. Students struggling behaviorally are now invited to have lunch with me in my office once or twice a week. I take this time to talk with them and I try to relate to how they are feeling, concerns they have, and their difficulties in school. I often have three or four students in there at once, and I can talk with them together about appropriate and inappropriate behaviors. Sometimes, students actually coach each other about their behavior as we eat lunch together. At this point, the Lunch Bunch has become my favorite part of the school day. The only downfall I can see with the Lunch Bunch is that I have so many students who want to come eat lunch with me that it is often difficult to ensure that I see each one. Tyrone, Damien, and I now have a great relationship that has been beneficial to their school success. So now I love to see students coming toward my office with their lunch trays.

Like several suggestions made previously in this and other chapters, Ms. Gravits discovered a way to let these troubled students know that she cared for them, and that made all the difference. Disciplinary referrals for Tyrone and Damien decreased significantly, and the time they spent connecting with a caring adult contributed greatly to their success in school. This Lunch Bunch idea is something other schools should consider implementing for their troubled students.

Managing Serious Behavior Problems Through Adult Mentoring

Students with behavioral challenges may need more attention than even the most dedicated teacher can provide. This is not to say that teachers do not mentor, or that teachers do not wish to mentor, disruptive students. Rather, we are simply acknowledging the realities of today's classrooms where teachers have to meet the needs of 20 to 30 needy students. Certain students may require so much attention that teachers are just not able to meet their needs. To deal with this problem, programs using out-of-school volunteer mentors have been widely implemented in recent years in public schools. In some cases they are part of dropout prevention programs, while in others they are part of programs to curb serious behavior problems.

Adult mentoring is different from student-to-student mentoring or other types of mentoring programs. Specifically, adult mentoring involves a one-to-one relationship that is sustained over time between a non-faculty volunteer adult and a younger person, and where the relationship is formed to support the younger person through some aspect of development. Adult mentors can offer support for students in crisis and can often provide a sounding board when students reflect on their behavior.

> *Adult mentors can offer support for students in crisis and can provide a sounding board when students reflect on their behavior.*

A growing body of research attests to the effectiveness of well-conceived adult mentoring programs. Studies have found that mentoring can increase the chances of students staying in school, deter teen pregnancy, and decrease the probability of gang membership (Mecca, 2001). The students of adult mentors achieve a more positive attitude toward school, are more likely to trust teachers, possess higher self-confidence, maintain better attendance, and experience improved relationships with adults and peers (Curtis & Hansen-Schwoebel, 1999). Other studies found that students involved in mentoring had less drug and alcohol use, fewer incidents of hitting and violence toward others, less likelihood of becoming a teen parent, and improved relationships with their parents (Jekielek, Moore, Hair, & Scarupa, 2002).

Considerations on Adult Mentoring

Several factors need to be considered before a mentoring program can be implemented. We briefly describe some of those factors here but discuss them in greater detail later in this chapter.

Mentoring As a Group Effort. One of the first issues to consider is deciding who may implement an adult mentoring program. Typically, adult mentoring in public schools is implemented at the school level rather than by individual teachers. If individual teachers start an adult mentoring program, those teachers alone bear the burdens of implementation that we will describe here in addition to all their other responsibilities. Thus, in most cases, this strategy is done by the entire faculty or by a group of faculty within a school. For example, there are adult mentorship programs that focus exclusively on incoming freshmen in high school.

With that caution noted, adult mentoring for a single classroom may still be worth the challenges of implementation. For some students—typically those with very challenging behaviors—mentoring can make the class not only bearable for the teachers, but actually enjoyable. Mentoring can turn a student's misbehavior completely around and, for that reason, a teacher confronted with a particularly challenging student should consider providing an outside adult mentor. The guidelines described here focus on how an individual teacher might implement an outside adult mentor program.

Where to Find Mentors? Mentors are selected from the community, and finding those mentors may take some time. Educators have often approached community organizations, faith-based groups such as churches or synagogues, and civic clubs (e.g., Rotary, Lions, Pilot Clubs) to solicit mentors for their program. (Many states have established a mentoring support network, and you can find out if your state is a member by contacting the National Mentoring Partnership at www.mentoring.org.) However, when mentoring is supervised by a single teacher, that teacher typically invites a friend to mentor one or two students in the class, so finding multiple mentors is not an issue.

Should Gender and Race Be Involved in Matching Mentors to Students? A third consideration involves matching mentors to specific students. Mentorships generally work regardless of the similarities or differences between the mentors and their students. However, mentorships seem to work more effectively when the mentor and the student have some things in common. For instance, psychologists have recently emphasized the critical influence of a same-sex role model to assist children in becoming successful adults, and this same-sex factor should be considered in matching mentors with students whenever possible (Warshak, 1992). Some mentorship programs emphasize the importance of matching race in selecting mentors. Thus, one should consider pairing an African-American male with an African-American male student because the student may be more likely to bond with the mentor. This is the emphasis behind groups like *100 Black Men of Atlanta* and similar groups in other cities—African-American males spending some time each week mentoring African-American boys who are at risk for behavior problems.

Although educators often consider mentorship merely as instructional support, they can be much more than that, and they work regardless of the teaching that goes on in the mentorship. School-based mentorships can often move beyond the instructional interaction and into the interest areas or hobbies of the students and their mentors. What is really significant about the mentorship is not the content around which a mentorship is structured but the *relationship* that develops between the mentor and the student.

Finally, getting an adult mentoring program off the ground can be a challenge. As noted previously, mentoring programs can be large, highly visible programs for an entire school district involving school staff, parents, business representatives, community leaders, and perhaps students. Guidelines for such large programs are widely available. Here, however, we will focus on guidelines for individual teachers who might wish to implement a small mentoring program to assist one to two students in their own class.

Initiating a Mentoring Program

Like any other worthwhile program, planning is critical. The following is a list of initial considerations that we have gathered from a variety of sources (Clinton & Miles, 1999; Dappen & Isernhagen, 2005; Ryan, Whittaker, & Pinckney, 2002; Sonsthagen & Lee, 1996). The ideas are numbered because they closely represent the sequence in which the planning occurs.

1. **Establishing the Program's and Individual Student's Goals.** Well-articulated goals for the mentoring program center on building the competence of students in some way and include specific measurable objectives (e.g., reduction in office referrals for discipline). Clear goals reap a benefit on two levels.

   First, a mentoring effort that is driven by clear goals will run more smoothly because they keep administrative decision making in focus, thus avoiding misinterpretations or questions on the program's effectiveness.

   Second, clear and achievable goals for the program also translate into clear and achievable goals for the students. For example, the mentor and the student might work to improve certain academic skills or develop a mutually chosen hobby. Thus, the mentoring is given a structure—a common task at hand—that gives the relationship a foundation for growth. Such a common interest is frequently the stuff from which friendships are made, and a desirable interpersonal relationship is more likely to grow when it focuses on working toward a common goal than when it focuses on building a relationship. Some examples of program and individual goals are shown in Figure 5.4. Once such goals are established for the target student and the overall program, the teacher shares the entire plan with the principal.

2. **Delineating Activities and Procedures.** Most programs begin with the mentor offering instructional support, but the mentoring should be allowed to move beyond that stage.

Sample Goals for Adult Mentoring

Program Goals:

- By the end of the first week of school, I will describe this mentoring program to my principal.
- By the fourth week of school, four volunteer mentors will have been screened for the mentoring. Screening and training will involve two evenings concerning the purpose of the program, and each mentor will sign a document allowing school personnel to run a criminal record background check on them.
- By the sixth week of school, students with behavior problems will be targeted and paired with mentors.
- By the ninth week, eight out of 10 students will have mastered the first vocational skill area assigned (e.g., job application forms).
- By the end of the first year, incidents of aggressive or violent behavior involving students in the program will have decreased by 40 percent.

Individual Student Goals:

- By the ninth week, mentors will report having at least one in-depth conversation with their students about choosing alternatives to violence in specific situations.
- By the end of the first grading period, Tyrone and Damien will be sharing important personal information in their journals.
- By the sixth week, Anton will have collected a minimum of 15 pictures of trains for the student's scrapbook.
- By the end of week four, Tom's episodes of violent cursing in class will have decreased.

Figure 5.4   These are examples of program goals and individual student goals that can be part of an adult mentoring program. Clear and achievable goals are important for the success of this program.

Discussing other types of activities with mentors allows them to know the range of their options without exceeding their authority. Also, the planned activities need to be consistent with the goals of the program. If the primary goal is academic improvement, some form of content tutoring is appropriate. On the other hand, if a reduction of violence or aggressive behavior is the goal, then a common interest in a particular hobby may provide the nonthreatening framework that allows the mentor to engage the student in reflective conversations about choices and values. If the relationship develops, the weight of the mentor's influence will typically result in improved student behavior.

The daily school procedures for mentors will also need to be explained and shared with the mentors. These procedures typically involve school policies about signing in at the office and other matters. See Figure 5.5 for a sample list of guidelines for adult mentors.

Questions such as when, where, and how long to meet, how much flexibility there is in meeting times, assigned activities, family contact policy, and what is expected of students are addressed early on in the mentoring program or during the mentoring training period. This information is provided in written form, perhaps as a handout packet or handbook for the mentors. A calendar of classroom events is also included.

3. **Identifying Students for the Adult Mentoring Program.** In larger school-wide mentoring programs, participating students may be referred by other teachers, their parents, school

---

Guidelines for Adult Mentors

- Call the school before coming to find out if the student is present. If your student is absent, you may either miss that day or assist in the classroom during the mentoring period.
- Sign in at the school office when you arrive at school each day.
- Come into the class, pick up the student, and move into the mentoring area in the back of the class (or the library, or other designated mentoring area).
- If there is a time when you would like to give your student a special gift, the gift should be small, inexpensive, and serve as a reward for a job well done.
- All information such as test scores, behavior information, or family information regarding students is confidential. Discuss all concerns about confidentiality with the teacher.
- Monthly meetings are held for all mentors on the second Wednesday of the month at 4:30 p.m. in the classroom to discuss achievements, concerns, plans, etc.
- Training sessions for new mentors will take place during regular monthly meetings. If you have other adults you would like to invite to participate, please bring them along with you to the meeting.
- All mentoring sessions will be held on school campus during regular school hours. If you choose to undertake an off-campus trip or some activity after school hours, you must arrange that directly with the parents of the student. Such activities are not to be considered a part of the mentorship program here at school, and you alone will have the legal responsibility for the student during those activities.

Figure 5.5 This is a sample list of guidelines that should be shared with adult mentors. Having clear guidelines and procedures is essential for a safe and productive program.

guidance counselors, social workers, or the court system. In mentoring initiated by a single teacher, the students will typically be from that teacher's class. However, the student participants are almost always voluntary participants in the mentoring program, and teachers should bear that in mind. Prior to providing adult mentoring for a student, teachers should obtain permission from the student's parents to participate in a mentorship experience.

Teachers should carefully consider the type of student to be served by this program. The primary criterion in the selection process is whether mentoring is appropriate for a particular student. Successful mentoring programs are those that serve students whose academic or behavioral problems are not too severe and whose parents are likely to allow participation (Dappen & Isernhagen, 2005). Placing extremely violent students into adult mentoring programs is not recommended. These students are often difficult to manage and need to be supervised by a qualified teacher. Remember that the volunteer mentors are the heart of the program, and we want to retain them for future students. Pairing mentors to students with extreme behavior problems may result in losing those mentors from the program.

4. **Recruiting Mentors.** Finding only two or three suitable volunteers may be a significant challenge and must be done very carefully. For this reason, most mentoring programs arranged by teachers involve selecting two or three mentors from among the teacher's acquaintances. From the beginning, potential mentors must be aware of the time commitment involved and must also be informed about the hard realities of mentoring, so that only the truly committed ones will choose to continue with the program. As one suggestion, retired

educators are a great source for mentors, and they often wish to maintain some involvement in teaching after retirement.

Some states have laws regulating the screening of volunteer mentors. Persons with criminal records or a history of predatory behavior toward children cannot be in this program. Even if one selects mentors from among one's friends, a police screening is advisable (or may be mandatory) to assure that unsuitable applicants are not allowed to become mentors. Also, it is wise to limit the location of the meetings between the mentor and student to one's own class, perhaps in the rear of the room, or other public areas in the school.

5. **Training Mentors.** One or more training sessions are recommended for most mentoring programs. Certain basic issues are clarified during these sessions. Mentors need to understand how close the mentor relationship is expected to become, what parental involvement is anticipated, what costs are involved, and what happens if the relationship does not develop as expected. Trainers also provide mentors with suggestions on effective ways to work with parents.

6. **Providing Mentor Support.** Not only do mentors need training, they also need ongoing support from the teacher and from each other. Mentors should have periodic opportunities to compare notes with each other and to share ideas about approaches to try with various students. They need to be reassured that the teacher is reachable and available whenever problems arise. Also, the mentors should be recognized periodically for their efforts. Many programs hold a "thank you" dinner at the end of each year, inviting the students, their mentors, and parents to the event at which mentors may be recognized.

7. **Matching Mentors and Students.** Teachers should give careful consideration to matching mentors and students. As we discussed earlier, mentoring relationships that do not result in a connection between the mentor and the student, for whatever reason, do not lead to improved behavior, and may result in withdrawal by either the student or the mentor. Students who participate in mentoring, unfortunately, may have become all too familiar with being let down by adults, and they do not need yet another disappointment in their lives.

The task of matching mentors and students involves two primary issues: the degree of choice afforded to the participants and the degree of similarity between mentors and students in terms of race/ethnic background, gender, hobbies, and interests. There are no clear research data about whether giving mentors an opportunity to choose their student makes a difference in terms of outcomes, though most large adult mentoring programs include this feature. Various larger mentoring programs use questionnaires or profiles completed by both mentors and students to help identify areas of common interest, though this goes beyond the scope of what most individual teachers can do. Still, some careful consideration of these matching factors is likely to result in more effective mentoring to reduce behavior problems.

The literature suggests that teachers ought to avoid extreme social or socioeconomic differences between mentor and student (Bernard, 1992). Cross-race or even cross-gender pairs may not always be the ideal, but these mentors can still bond with, and be beneficial to, students with behavior problems, especially if the socioeconomic spread is not too great. Actually, some socioeconomic difference is desirable as a means of expanding the horizons of the students involved in the mentoring program. Even though a mentor from outside the student's daily world may not fully comprehend the realities of that world, the adult can still be an effective mentor (Dappen & Isernhagen, 2005). It is the caring attitude of the adult that is critical to the mentorship's success. In some situations, cross-race mentoring itself can bring the added benefit of building appreciation for cultural diversity—certainly a desirable outcome in today's world.

For oppositional or aggressive students, additional care is needed in matching mentors and students. With the goal in mind of establishing a bond between the troubled students and their mentors, consideration should be given to the disciplinary style and disciplinary flexibility that particular mentors are likely to demonstrate. In these instances, the mentors should be strong, firm disciplinarians who are not threatened by behavioral outbursts, but who can contain them while maintaining their own composure. In doing so, the mentor models for the student how to control one's own behavior. As a more intimate mentoring relationship is established, mentors can help their students reflect on their behavior and consider other behavioral options for situations in which their rage builds up.

8. **Assessing the Effectiveness of Mentoring.** The effectiveness of mentoring for small programs should be based on the degree to which the initial goals of the mentorship were met. Were the behavior problems of the student reduced after mentoring began? Does the mentor sense that a productive bond has been established with the student? Teachers should keep some type of baseline and intervention data to determine the effectiveness of the mentorship based on the stated goals. The data should be shared with the mentor on a periodic basis as one way to provide reinforcement for that person's efforts.

9. **Evaluating and Revising the Program.** For teachers who implement mentoring with more than one mentor and student, some evaluation of the overall effectiveness of the program should be conducted. A mentor evaluation questionnaire that solicits the mentors' view of their impact is useful, as is combined data on the behavioral problems displayed by the students during the baseline and mentoring periods.

Depending on the age of the participating students, teachers should also consider using a student questionnaire that solicits their assessment of how the mentorship experience went. A report summarizing these data for the entire program will assist in evaluating and, if necessary, revising the program at the end of the school year. Information on the effectiveness of one teacher's mentoring program might motivate other teachers in the school to consider such a program in their classes, thus leading to broader implementation of mentoring at that school.

A Case Study: A Mentoring Example

Ms. Barkeley was a fifth-grade teacher who found that, by the end of the third week of school, she was becoming frustrated by continuing disciplinary problems in her class. Although she had the usual collection of students with attention problems and oppositional behaviors, one particular student, James, seemed sullen and withdrawn much of the time, and this concerned her greatly. She knew that James lived with his elderly grandmother and that no other students lived near him. Thus, he was often alone during the afternoon hours after school.

James seemed to have few friends at school and rather than joining the other boys playing basketball or other sports during the morning recess, James would often stand near the school watching the other students. However, James's problems went far beyond withdrawal. Ms. Barkeley also noted that James would frequently explode into violence, either calling other students names or hitting them if they passed by his desk. Unlike the usual demonstrations of hitting at that age, James seemed intent on seriously hurting someone. In most cases, those hitting episodes were not provoked by the other students.

Based on these observations, Ms. Barkeley decided to obtain some baseline data on his behavioral eruptions. James demonstrated either physical or verbal aggression about four times each day. Ms. Barkeley considered different types of potential interventions. Because James seemed so unconnected to her and to his peers, she decided to provide a same-sex adult mentor in an effort to reach James and reconnect him to his school and classmates.

To initiate her adult mentoring intervention, Ms. Barkeley reviewed the considerations noted earlier in this chapter and then discussed James's behavioral issues with the principal. During that discussion, she presented the baseline data on James's instances of hitting and verbal aggression. Ms. Barkeley shared with the principal her thoughts on James's need for an adult role model and mentor, and indicated that she had a candidate in mind—a retired male teacher named Howard Pursey whom she had known for years and who still attended her gym. While exercising at the gym, Ms. Barkeley often discussed her class management issues with Howard, and she had been impressed with his sensitivity to the needs of unruly students. With the principal's approval, Ms. Barkeley telephoned Mr. Pursey, told him about her idea of having him mentor James twice a week for 45 minutes in her class, and asked if he would be interested.

Note that many of the issues raised previously on implementing a mentoring program are immediately addressed when one uses a retired teacher for that role. In instances such as this, Ms. Barkeley and her principal could be assured that Mr. Pursey would not require a great deal of preparation concerning legal policies of the school or on what types of management procedures were appropriate. To be prudent, they decided that Mr. Pursey had to undergo a police screening even though he had been a retired teacher for only a year. They were confident that Mr. Pursey could manage any temper behaviors or violence that James demonstrated in a manner consistent with the school's disciplinary policy. Once the basics of the mentoring plan were in place, Ms. Barkeley contacted James's grandmother to explain the mentoring program and her belief that this might be of benefit to James. The grandmother readily agreed to allow James to receive these mentoring services twice each week at school.

Most of the mentoring was set for James's 10:00 a.m. recess time because he had little connection with the other students during recess and showed no interest in joining their play. Thus, every Tuesday and Thursday, Mr. Pursey arrived in Ms. Barkeley's class just before recess and picked up James. Because the mentoring was occurring during recess, no academic work was included. Rather, Mr. Pursey began the mentoring by taking James down to the cafeteria where he had arranged to have ice cream available for them.

While eating the ice cream, Mr. Pursey casually inquired about James's family, how long he lived with his grandmother, how he liked school, and what subjects he liked best. As any veteran teacher might suspect, James was at first reluctant to converse with Mr. Pursey and usually responded in one-word answers. During week two of the mentoring period, Mr. Pursey, on a whim, brought along some pictures of old trains, because trains were his hobby. James showed interest when Mr. Pursey explained that his father had worked as a railroad engineer for all of his life, and he asked James if he would like to see a genuine old steam engine that was on display in a local history museum.

James seemed to come to life at that suggestion and asked when they could go. After obtaining permission from the grandmother, Mr. Pursey took James to the museum on one of their mentor days, and thus began James's interest in old trains. From that day on, the two collected pictures of trains and pasted them into a scrapbook. They searched for pictures on the Internet and found stories of old train wrecks in the local newspapers' archives. James seemed proud that he was building a scrapbook of train wreck photographs and, after a time, Ms. Barkeley found an opportunity to have James share his pictures with the class during a social studies lesson.

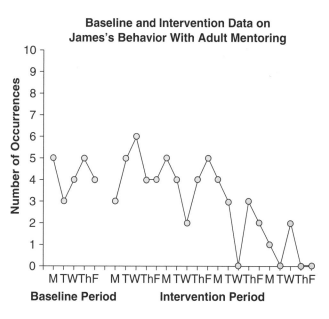

Figure 5.6 The graph shows the baseline and intervention data on James's changes in behavior before and after the adult mentoring intervention.

The data on James's behavioral problems indicate that the mentoring worked well (see Figure 5.6). Like most mentoring programs, immediate results are rare and should not be expected because mentors typically work with students only once or twice per week. In this case, however, the results were becoming obvious by the third week of mentoring, barely one week after Mr. Pursey discovered James's interest in trains. The data shown in Figure 5.6 demonstrate a gradual decrease in behavior problems from the third week on, and by the end of this intervention, James's aggressive problems had been reduced significantly.

Of course, not every mentoring program will be as easily established or evolve as quickly as this example. In most cases, students should not be expected to give up their recess time, and teachers must make tough choices about what lesson content to forgo in order to provide time for the mentoring experience. With those concerns noted, James's and many other true examples confirm that mentoring holds the potential to reach the "unreachable" student. Teachers confronted with the time dilemma should ask themselves what is best for the student. Should a student remain in all of the content classes, misbehaving continually, or could that student's needs be better served by providing some time for adult mentoring? The Big Brothers Big Sisters Organization has useful information on starting and maintaining mentoring programs. See the **Resources** section for more information about this site.

SUMMARY

We are social animals. Forming relationships with others was wired into our ancestral brains because it represented another pathway to survival. The significance of relationships becomes more important to individuals as they grow from child to adolescent to adult. Some students misbehave mainly because they have not established any trusting relationships with their parents, peers, or adults. Teachers who take the time to establish meaningful and trusting relationships with troubled students often find that behavior problems decrease significantly. Pairing troubled students with volunteer adult mentors has also proved to be an effective strategy for building a student's self-concept and leading to more acceptable social behavior.

Using Peer Relationships to Modify Behavior

EXAMINING PEER RELATIONSHIPS

Social neuroscience has made one thing very clear: Forming social relationships is such a powerful innate influence that the brain has developed mechanisms to help us establish and assess the value of such relationships. Chief among these mechanisms appears to be the mirror neuron system that we discussed in Chapter 3. You will recall that this system allows us to infer what is going on in the mind of another. More recent studies suggest that the mirror neuron system does not act alone when an individual is trying to infer the mental state of another in a social situation. Other areas of the brain are also activated, and their activation depends on how one's brain is appraising the actions of another.

In a study using fMRI technology, researchers noted that mainly the mirror system (areas 1 and 2 in Figure 6.1) was activated even when the individual was watching inanimate objects move. But when animate objects were in motion, other brain areas representing the social network (areas 3 through 7 in Figure 6.1) showed immediate activation (Wheatley, Milleville, & Martin, 2007). The social network includes areas associated with biological motion (area 3), biological form (area 6), cognitive processing (areas 4 and 5), and emotional processing (area 7). Not surprisingly, similar fMRI studies show that the social network is much more likely to be activated when a subject is playing a game with a real person than with a computer (McCabe, Houser, Ryan, Smith, & Trouard, 2001).

As the frontal lobe, mirror neurons, and social network mature during adolescence, they help the brain attune itself to the mental state of the person with whom we are interacting. As a result, we adjust our own feelings and actions so that they are synchronized with those of the other person.

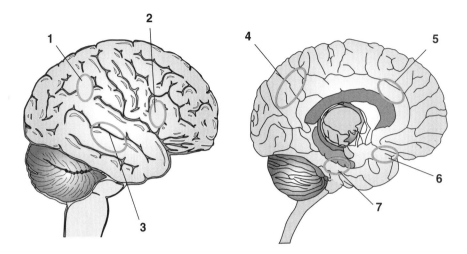

Figure 6.1   The mirror neuron system is represented by areas 1 and 2 on the surface of the brain. Other regions, considered part of the social network, were activated by biological motion (area 3), including the internal areas for biological form (area 6), cognitive processing (areas 4 and 5), and emotional processing (area 7).

Source: Adapted from Wheatley, Milleville, & Martin, 2007.

When we see someone with a happy, sad, or angry expression, mirror neurons activate circuits in our own brain for happiness, sadness, or anger (Iacoboni et al., 2005; Iacoboni, 2007).

These discoveries further explain why personal relationships can be such a useful vehicle for modifying behavior. We discussed at length in Chapter 5 that teacher-student and adult mentoring relationships can be very effective strategies for addressing undesirable behavior in students. Because students spend a lot of time with their peers, another question comes to mind: Can peer relationships also be effective in curbing undesirable behavior in students? Before we answer this question, let's do a quick review of the effects of peer influence on the developing adolescent brain.

Dealing With Peer Influence: A Two-Edged Sword

We explained in Chapter 1 that during adolescence the frontal lobes of the brain undergo rapid development, enabling them to communicate more effectively with other brain regions for higher-level decision making. This control over emotional impulses and perceptions originating in other parts of the brain gradually produces the judgment, self-control, and analytical ability characteristic of older adolescents and adults—and important for resisting undesirable peer influences.

Peer influence is a two-edged sword. On the one hand, peer pressure can lead students with weak self-control to perform risky and undesirable behaviors, such as unsafe driving, smoking, drugs, and alcohol. On the other hand, it can serve to moderate undesirable behaviors, such as boorishness or aggression, because they are incompatible with a peer group's norms. Recent research studies continue to confirm this dichotomous nature of peer influence (Allen, Porter, & McFarland, 2005; Collins & Laursen, 2004; Diego, Field, & Sanders, 2003).

> *Peer influence can either lead students to perform undesirable behaviors or it can moderate undesirable behaviors because they are incompatible with the group's norms.*

Research on Responding to Peer Influence

Young Adolescents. It would seem that if young adolescents are able to resist undue peer pressure, then there is a greater likelihood that they would continue such resistance as they get older. In a study to determine who was better able to resist peer influence in early adolescence, Grosbras and her colleagues used functional magnetic resonance imaging (fMRI) with 35 10-year-olds (Grosbras et al., 2007). The researchers found striking differences in the brain activity between students with high and low resistence to peer influence. Individuals with high resistance showed a highly coordinated pattern of brain activity in the neural systems underlying perception (mirror neurons) and decision making (prefrontal cortex executive center). These subjects also scored high on tests of self-control. The scans of the two groups were so consistent in their differences that they actually allowed the researchers to predict a subject's resistance to peer influence. Another study of more than 350 10- to12-year-olds found that those with high self-control were much less likely to respond to peer pressure to start smoking than those with low self-control (Perrine & Aloise-Young, 2004).

The findings in these and similar studies are important because they show that, even at 10 years of age, the frontal lobes of some students are sufficiently mature to attain the right balance between acknowledging the influences of peers and maintaining one's independence. They also demonstrate the importance of self-regulation. Adolescents' sense of self and how they relate to others will fall either under executive control or impulse control. Those adolescents who have trouble controlling their impulses will most likely respond inappropriately to peer influence.

Older Adolescents. In a unique study, researchers had adolescents participate in an experimental conversational forum over networked computers (Cohen & Prinstein, 2006). Instead of real people on the other end of the computer, however, the 16- and 17-year-old students responded to computer-generated entities manipulated to appear like either highly popular/liked classmates or unpopular/unliked classmates. The researchers found that adolescents publicly conformed to the behavior of high-status peers when others viewed their responses. They also privately internalized the aggressive and risky attitudes of highly popular/liked peers, endorsing these attitudes even when their responses were no longer visible to others.

The results showed that the effects of peer influence were remarkably strong, predicting the adolescents' aggressive and risky responses even more than their overall levels of past aggressive behavior. It seemed that the adolescents' social anxiety (i.e., their fears about others not liking them) was one factor affecting their vulnerability to peer influence. Those adolescents high in social anxiety were especially likely to be influenced by peers, even those who were not highly popular/liked.

Here we have a study whose implications for understanding and remedying adolescent aggression and risky behavior are profound. For example, many interventions try to change adolescents' aggression and risky behavior using rational arguments, persuasive information, and appeals to fear that emphasize the negative consequences of such behavior. But these results indicate a more effective route involves changing not adolescents' own attitudes but their perceptions of the attitudes of their peers. In other words, successful interventions lead these adolescents to think: "This behavior does not fit with my group or with the group to which I want to belong."

The Desire to Be Liked

Students' responses to peer influence seem largely based on their desire to be liked and accepted by their peer group. Any behavior that advances their likability in their group is apt to be repeated; any behavior that lowers it, will not. This is why a youngster's initial selection of a peer group is so critical. That group's norms will establish the guidelines as to which behaviors are acceptable, and which are not, in order to remain in the group.

Numerous studies have been done to uncover the traits that students use to determine who is popular or unpopular in a group. One typical study examined the likability preferences of more than 400 boys and girls in grades four through eight. Not surprisingly, students who were viewed by their peers as sociable and attractive were considered popular. Those who were viewed as antisocial, unattractive, deviant, and incompetent were considered unpopular (LaFontana & Cillessen, 2002).

Another study examined early adolescents' stereotypical descriptions of two types of youth who were seen as popular by their peers. Participants included nearly 300 13- to 14-year-olds. Early adolescents distinguished two types of popular peers: a "populistic" type (popular but not necessarily well liked) and a "prosocial-popular" type (popular, well liked, and accepted). These two types differed in terms of academic and interpersonal behaviors. Populistic adolescents were seen as overly aggressive, stuck up, vulgar bullies who were academically disengaged. But they were also seen as leaders, influential, and arrogant more than were the prosocial-popular adolescents. Adolescents in the prosocial-popular group were seen as cooperative, helpful, and academically engaged. Both types of popular youth were seen as attractive and fashionable (deBruyn & Cillessen, 2006).

One interesting finding in this study is that adolescents make a clear and important distinction between popular and likable. Obviously, there are students who would prefer to be either or both. Again, there are no other major surprises here, indicating that the traits adolescents use to determine likability or popularity have not really changed much over the years, nor has the desire to be liked and popular.

Adolescents make a clear and important distinction between popular and likable.

Adolescents certainly have opportunities to find peer groups that will support and encourage undesirable behaviors, as the research on deviant peer influences confirms (Gifford-Smith, Dodge, Dishion, & McCord, 2005). Yet other peer groups can influence an adolescent to moderate misbehaviors. Let's now look at some strategies that can make that happen.

PEER-MEDIATED BEHAVIOR MANAGEMENT STRATEGIES

As children enter puberty, peer group influence increases dramatically. For that reason, a variety of peer influence strategies have been used by teachers for instructional purposes, such as cooperative learning, peer tutoring, and peer modeling. But peer-centered strategies have also been developed to assist in managing classroom behavior problems. These strategies generally allow teachers to tap into the power of the peer group to facilitate more appropriate behavior in the classroom.

Peer-Mediated Anger Management

For students with anger management problems, one successful strategy is the use of peers as teachers of anger management strategies (Presley & Hughes, 2000). In this strategy, peers assist in helping students with behavior problems to learn anger management skills. One example of an anger management tactic is the adapted version of the *Triple-A Strategy,* which was initially developed by Walker and his colleagues (1988). This adapted version is shown in Figure 6.2.

Presley and Hughes (2000) demonstrated the impact of this approach. They identified four target students with behavioral disorders who demonstrated anger management problems in their peer interactions in school. Two of these students were in grade nine, one in grade 10, and one in grade 12. The researchers then selected three peer trainers from a one-credit class for high school seniors called "Peer Buddies." Three senior girls were chosen as trainers and were trained in the *Triple-A Strategy* during two instructional sessions. Then the peer trainers taught the strategy to the

---

The Triple-A Strategy

Assess

1. Student does not speak aloud for at least three seconds in order to assess the situation.
2. Student asks and answers aloud, "What is going on?"
3. Student asks and answers aloud, "Why did he/she do or say that?"
4. Student asks and answers aloud, "Did he/she do this on purpose or is it something that just happened?"
5. Student asks and answers aloud, "How does she/he feel about the situation?"
6. Student asks and answers aloud, "Is he/she upset or just kidding?"

Amend

7. Student chooses an appropriate alternative response to anger (e.g., not responding verbally or non-verbally, initiating another conversation, or walking away).
8. Student tells the other person how the situation made him/her feel (e.g., "I am upset that you would not just ask me for paper or to see my homework. I'm surprised you took my notebook without asking me.").
9. Student asks the other person to tell him or her how this makes him/her feel.

Act

10. Student responds to the situation using ASSESS and AMEND steps.
11. Student evaluates his/her initial response to the situation and makes changes, if necessary.

Figure 6.2   This list shows the steps involved in the Triple-A Strategy.

target students using a variety of methods, including directly reviewing the *Triple-A Strategy*, role playing, and providing feedback on the role play performance of the target student. During the role play, a target student would be expected to participate with a peer trainer, and another peer trainer would serve as the "coach" by providing feedback to the target student.

The results indicated that peer-mediated anger management using the *Triple-A Strategy* was effective in increasing the number of times the target students used the strategy's steps. For each student, there was a significant increase in the number of steps from the *Triple-A Strategy* that the student completed during the role-play activities. Also, during the training and follow-up phases, the number of anger management events reported by teachers dropped for three of the four students in the target group, thus demonstrating the effectiveness of this strategy in a real classroom setting.

Factors to Consider in Peer Mediation

Here are three factors to consider before selecting this strategy.

- **Availability of trainers.** In the study just described, the peer mediators were earning course credit for this coaching work, but that might not be the case in other secondary schools. If you wish to use this tactic, and such a class is not offered in your particular school, you could select peer trainers from senior honors courses, psychology courses, or studies skills classes.

- **Age difference between trainers and target students.** Note the age difference between the trainers and the target students in the previous example. All but one of the target students were in the first two years of high school, and they were being coached by seniors. This age difference plays a role in the overall effectiveness of the strategy because underclassmen usually look up to seniors.

- **Emphasis on anger management strategies.** Providing a structured curriculum for anger management such as the *Triple-A Strategy* helps to focus the peer mediation efforts. Peer mediation is more effective when the effort is focused specifically on an appropriate strategy rather than viewed as a friendship or general coaching situation. Although some bonding is likely to occur between the target students and their peer coaches, the emphasis is on the mastery of anger management tactics themselves and not on the relationship-building aspect of this training.

A Case Study: Reducing Gail's Anger Through Peer Mediation

Although the research on anger management has focused mainly on older students, it seems that enraged students are showing up in all grade levels in the schools today. Like most interventions, the sooner they are started, the better. Here is an example of using peer mediation in an elementary classroom. Ms. Tierney, a fifth-grade teacher, noted that one of her students, Gail, would often arrive ready to fight with someone. Gail would lose control of herself on those days and her body and general demeanor indicated as much. She would literally get red in the face, clench her fists by her side, and turn to confront any student who angered her. In most cases, a serious bout of cursing ensued, though no physical violence ever resulted.

Nonetheless, this anger and rage were disruptive in the classroom, so Ms. Tierney counted the episodes where Gail lost control over the period of three days. On one of the days she was fine and appeared to be totally in control. On the other two days, however, Ms. Tierney noted at least four instances where Gail lost control. Initially, Ms. Tierney had sent Gail to the office to cool down, but she felt she should be offering Gail something more than the cooling down option. She decided to implement a peer-mediated intervention based on the *Triple-A Strategy.*

This strategy is based on role playing various situations that might make students angry. Ms. Tierney first needed one or more students to serve as trainers or coaches. There was one student who related fairly well to Gail, so Ms. Tierney decided to use that student as one coach in the role-play situations. She asked that student to pick another student as the other coach. Ms. Tierney had decided that others in the class might benefit from the *Triple-A Strategy* and thus wanted a couple of trained coaches to use later with other students beside Gail.

Ms. Tierney talked with the two prospective coaches and asked if they would do some role play with her during the morning break. She promised each of them an ice cream for each day they did it, and they readily agreed. Then she spoke privately with Gail just prior to the end of the morning break. Here is her conversation.

Ms. Tierney: Gail, I wanted to invite you to spend the next several morning breaks with me and two other girls playing out some short plays about what to do when someone gets angry.

Gail: Why is that?

Ms. Tierney: Good question. I've noticed that a number of students in the class sometimes get angry and are ready to fight, and I think I'd like to use this idea with a number of my students.

Gail: I sometimes get mad.

Ms. Tierney: Yes, you do, just like many others, so if you can help me figure out how this works, it will help you and a lot of other students in the class.

Gail: What do I need to do?

Ms. Tierney: We'll begin tomorrow during the morning break. We'll spend about 10 minutes each day doing some of these role plays and then I can figure out if I should do this with others in the class. Deborah and Sandi will be doing this with us. I know they like you and you all get along well together.

Gail: What do we do then?

Ms. Tierney: I'll give two of you a short sentence that presents a situation where someone might get angry, and then we'll talk about a *Triple-A Strategy* for how to control your anger.

Gail: I get angry a lot.

Ms. Tierney: I have noticed that, and for the first week you'll be the "angry" person in the role-plays, but in the next week, one of the others will be. Can we start tomorrow?

Gail: I guess so.

After that brief introduction, Ms. Tierney laminated a description of the *Triple-A Strategy* steps found in Figure 6.1. She then wrote the following three scenarios representing situations in which Gail had become angry.

1. *When you come into class, you see several girls look in your direction and begin to laugh. You think they might be laughing at you.*

2. *One of the guys in class was joking with a friend and shoved him backward. He bumped into you and made you drop your books, and then everybody in the hallway laughed when you were picking them up.*

3. *You got a low grade on an assignment in class, and it really bugged you because you had studied and expected a better grade. You got angry when you heard other students talking about their grades which were higher than yours. They asked what your grade was, and it made you feel dumb.*

Using one scenario each day, the three girls worked together with Gail playing the role of the angry person for the first week. Deborah was the other "actor" while Sandi was the "coach." Deborah acted out the scenario with Gail, and Gail showed how she would respond. Then they considered the steps on the chart and repeated the scenario, while talking about how Gail could respond using the Triple-A Strategy.

Gail at first was reluctant to voice her statements aloud because she thought that might seem dumb. However, because this is required by the strategy, she agreed to do so when Ms. Tierney pointed out that, "It's better than going to the office again!" After the role play was done twice, the teacher and the girls discussed all of the steps and then returned to their morning break. The entire intervention took only about 10 minutes each day.

The data in Figure 6.3 show a significant decrease in Gail's angry outbursts. Note that Ms. Tierney had only three days of baseline data at the start instead of the recommended five days. However, even with that limitation, it was clear that Gail's angry outbursts decreased within the first week of this intervention and were all but eliminated within two weeks.

Results from the second week are particularly interesting. Frequently, the disruptive behavior decreases when the target student is the main "actor," but note that it also decreases when that student serves as a "coach," as Gail did here. This is because students will understand the strategy better after having portrayed both the actor and the coach, in effect getting two different perspectives on the strategy. Another important result occurred after the intervention was completed. Because Gail liked the social aspects of this strategy, Gail asked Ms. Tierney if she could practice this with "two of my other friends." Thus, the strategy was shared with others beyond Gail and the other coaches.

Not every intervention works out as well as this one, but the power of peer influence is hard to overestimate. Peer-mediated

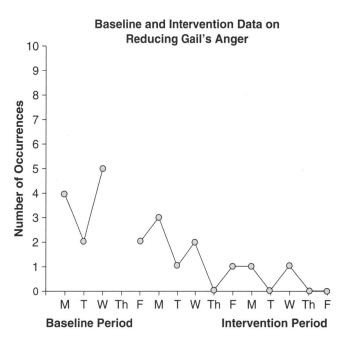

Figure 6.3 The graph shows the frequency of Gail's anger outbursts during the baseline days and during the two weeks of intervention using the Triple-A Strategy.

interventions such as this tend to reinforce appropriate behavior for most pre-teens and teenagers much more than teacher applied interventions precisely because students during those years are so acutely attuned to the opinions of their peers. Results like those shown for Gail are not uncommon, and teachers from grades four and up should seriously consider using peer-mediated anger management strategies.

Peer Confrontation To Curb Misbehavior

Another strategy that draws on the influence of peers is the peer confrontation or peer pressure strategy (Sandler, Arnold, Gable, & Strain, 1987). This strategy, like the previous one, hinges on involving the peers of a target student in a discussion of the misbehavior that occurred, reasons for that misbehavior, and alternatives for that behavior (Salend, Whittaker, & Reeder, 1992; Tanaka & Reid, 1997).

Peer confrontation is a strategy that is appropriate for students from grade four through high school. This strategy is not recommended for students prior to grade four because neither the influence of the peer group nor a student's social judgment is sufficiently developed during those early years. As students reach the middle grades, peers become increasingly important as a referent for acceptable behavior. Teachers should take full advantage of that fact in the management of their class.

> *Peer confrontation can successfully control misbehavior and is an appropriate strategy for students from grade four through high school.*

The peer confrontation strategy is effective because it is designed to moderate inappropriate behavior by

1. Removing the audience for inappropriate behaviors

2. Eliciting a discussion of appropriate behavior through the use of peer discussion, and

3. Helping students develop an understanding of their own behavior.

A Case Study: Decreasing Cursing Using Peer Confrontation

When a student consistently interrupts the class or demonstrates a problematic behavior, the teacher should collect baseline data on how often that misbehavior occurs. A simple frequency count usually suffices for this. For example, Ms. Bullock was the teacher in a fourth-grade classroom in which Tyrell enjoyed widespread audience attention for cursing in class. Every time Tyrell cursed, the class snickered until Ms. Bullock reestablished control. As a result of Tyrell's cursing, Ms. Bullock had sent him to the principal and called his parents in for a conference about the problem, but neither action decreased the problem behavior. Ms. Bullock decided to use the power of peer influence and to eliminate Tyrell's audience for his misbehavior by implementing a peer confrontation procedure.

Figure 6.4 shows the baseline frequency count of how many times Tyrell cursed in class in one week. Information for this chart was collected during the morning instructional period between the first bell and recess when most of this behavior seemed to occur. To collect the information, Ms. Bullock marked on a notepad for one week each time Tyrell cursed during the morning period. In that way, the data were collected without disturbing the class instruction.

The peer confrontation technique should be used when a student demonstrates the misbehavior eight to 25 times during a single day. In Tyrell's case, a count of the frequency of the misbehavior during a five-day period provided enough data to demonstrate a very disruptive problem.

The peer confrontation procedure itself involves four steps that resemble a problem-solving process, and is intended to identify the problem, discuss the problem, describe alternatives to misbehavior, and solicit the student's cooperation in agreeing to use one or more of those alternatives.

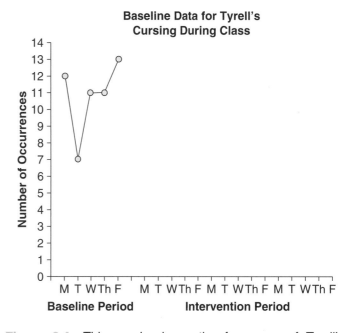

Figure 6.4 This graph shows the frequency of Tyrell's cursing during the week when baseline data were collected.

Step 1: Identify the Problem. On Monday of the second week, when Tyrell cursed at someone, Ms. Bullock began the intervention, using questions that were intended both to defuse the situation and to elicit the assistance of the class in a discussion of the misbehavior. Ms Bullock's questions were also intended to remove Tyrell's audience—namely, the class members laughing at the misbehavior. The following dialogue provides an example of what Ms. Bullock said when Tyrell cursed. In a voice loud enough to get every student's attention, Ms. Bullock began the strategy by saying: *"Wait a minute, everyone. We just saw an inappropriate behavior that disrupted our work. What problem behavior just stopped our work?"*

Note that the focus of this question is on the misbehavior and not on who did it. The statement is phrased to make the inappropriate behavior seem to be an offense against the class and not an offense against Ms. Bullock. Also, when Ms. Bullock asked these questions, she purposefully did not look at Tyrell. Rather, Ms. Bullock was engaging the entire class in a discussion of inappropriate behavior.

The desired response is for another student in the class to accurately describe the behavior problem that disrupted the class without mentioning or criticizing the offending student by name. Ms. Bullock's statements should focus not only on the behavior problem, but on the disruption to the class. However, she needs to be prepared if other students' responses do not focus on the behavior. In this instance, one student said, *"Tyrell is being a jerk!"*

Clearly, this is not where Ms. Bullock wanted the discussion to go, so she redirected it by stopping students from calling others names (i.e., using a firm look toward the student who called Tyrell a name) and said, *"We don't call others names in this class. I just want to know what happened that stopped our work."* After this statement, Ms. Bullock stepped back to disengage from the student who did the name-calling and waited to get a response that focused on the offending behavior. At that point, another student raised her hand and said, *"Somebody just cursed in class."* Ms. Bullock responded by saying, *"Yes, Jessica, someone did curse in class and that disturbed our work!"*

Let's analyze what has happened so far. Tyrell disrupted the class, but Ms. Bullock has not engaged him. She has not even looked in his direction. When another class member called Tyrell a name, Ms. Bullock defended Tyrell. At this point, Tyrell is surprised that he has not been punished, and he has even heard Ms. Bullock defend him. That alone will empower Ms. Bullock in this situation because she has effectively removed Tyrell's audience for the misbehavior. The class is looking at Ms. Bullock now rather than snickering at Tyrell.

Step 2: Analyze the Behavior. After a student gave an answer that identified the behavior problem, Ms. Bullock held a brief discussion of why students might misbehave in that way. She started with the following questions: *"Can anyone guess why someone might do that? Why would anyone do that?"*

Ms. Bullock is attempting to get the class to participate by stating possible reasons for the misbehavior. Still somewhat puzzled, Tyrell listens as his peers analyze his behavior. This is a powerful deterrent and further empowers Ms. Bullock because students at this age, who are heavily influenced by their peers, do not like having those same peers coolly and critically analyze their misbehavior. Also, the various reasons for the misbehavior that are mentioned by other students can lead to a positive discussion of behavioral options. For example, students may suggest that Tyrell cursed because he wanted attention or could not do the required work.

As Ms. Bullock elicited responses from other students about why this misbehavior occurred, she complimented each student who provided a reasonable response. In effect, Ms. Bullock had the class critically analyzing a misbehavior rather than snickering, and she had thus removed Tyrell's audience. Also, notice that Ms. Bullock has still not engaged Tyrell directly, thereby avoiding an unpleasant power struggle with him.

Step 3: Identify Alternative Behaviors. Next, Ms. Bullock led the discussion in the direction of alternative behaviors that are considered more appropriate. She encouraged the class to continue their problem solving by suggesting other behavioral options for when a student wants attention or cannot do the work. She facilitated that discussion with the following statements: *"OK, I understand why someone might curse in class. He might need help or might just be tired of the work. Now, can we suggest other things someone might do if he needs help? We are not here to criticize anyone, but we do want to help all of you to control your tempers and stop cursing. Can someone suggest what a student may want to do when he feels he is getting angry?"* Ideally, responses from the class will involve more constructive options to frustration. Answers from the class included: *"He could put his head down on his desk for a minute,"* or *"He should raise his hand and ask for help."*

Note that even if this procedure fails as an intervention for Tyrell, the rest of the students have engaged in a two- to three-minute problem-solving discussion about appropriate and inappropriate behaviors. This discussion would benefit almost any classroom.

Step 4: Elicit Student Participation. The final step involves eliciting the cooperation of the offending student. Ms. Bullock's goal is to discuss the problem behavior and the behavioral options with Tyrell and to get him to agree to try the solution(s) that the class mentioned. For some mild behaviors, where the student is not overly angry or otherwise emotionally involved, Ms. Bullock might turn to Tyrell and say something like: *"Tyrell, the class believes you might need some help with the work, or might just need a brief break. We would like to ask that next time, rather than cursing and disrupting our work, you merely raise your hand and ask for either some help or a one-minute break. Could you do that for the class?"*

This careful phrasing makes clear that the misbehavior is an offense against the class, and that the class is making this request of Tyrell. The research shows that this will work for most students who are not involved in strong feelings of anger or embarrassment. Thus, the teacher should engage in this step immediately after the first three steps are completed.

However, for some more aggressive behaviors (e.g., fighting, angry verbal attacks, or overt name calling), disruptive students might be too emotionally charged after this procedure to agree to participate. In those instances, one option would be to wait until some time has passed before moving to Step 4. For example, after Ms. Bullock completed Steps 1 through 3 above, she might have said something like: *"OK, I think we've discussed that behavior problem enough for now. Let's return to our work."* She should then call Tyrell aside at the end of the class period and complete the fourth step with him by discussing the offense against the class, the alternative behaviors the class mentioned, and soliciting Tyrell's cooperation.

As the behavioral intervention plan data in Figure 6.5 indicate, this intervention was successful with Tyrell. His inappropriate behavior dropped significantly upon implementation of this strategy. Teachers in grades four and higher should consider using this intervention to harness the power of the peer group to support appropriate behavior in the class.

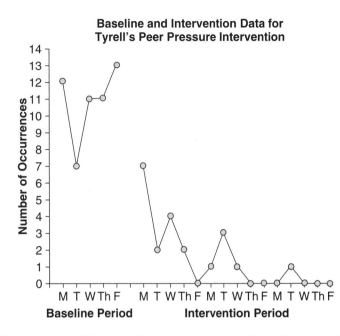

Baseline and Intervention Data for Tyrell's Peer Pressure Intervention

Figure 6.5 This graph shows the baseline data for the frequency of Tyrell's misbehavior and the data for the three weeks during the peer pressure intervention.

When to Try Peer Confrontation

Almost every elementary and middle school teacher has seen students use misbehavior to show off for other students. Remember that at this stage of brain development, networks are being established to help the individual assess the importance of social interaction and acceptance. Young adolescents who misbehave are often rewarded by peer-group admiration, and this can lead to increased behavior problems. Consider the peer confrontation strategy when you have students who are using defiance or humor to gain attention or to play off the attention of other students. By doing so, you get rid of the audience for misbehavior by getting that audience to work *for* you rather than *against* you.

Unlike some of the other strategies in this book, the peer confrontation strategy is useful for situations in which students are angry or heavily emotionally involved in other ways. Even when students are about to or have come to blows, a peer confrontation strategy can be used after the students are separated and calmed. For students who consistently bully others, overtly act out, are constantly seeking attention, or use fists to get their own way, this strategy works.

When to Avoid Peer Confrontation

Peer confrontation, however, is not appropriate for some students. It should be avoided if less intrusive strategies will work or if a particular student appears devastated by even the smallest degree of class attention or embarrassment. Many teachers have had the experience of teaching intensely shy students, or students who would feel particularly sensitive to any open discussion of their behavior. Although some embarrassment is often the natural by-product of this strategy, it is intended primarily to remove the audience that supports the misbehavior, to help students analyze their own behavior, and to find ways to get their needs met without misbehavior. Embarrassment is not intended to be the primary outcome, and if a student is particularly easy to embarrass, this is not an appropriate strategy.

Peer confrontation depends on mild social pressure from peers for its success. Consequently, it might not be effective in situations where a student is primarily socialized to students other than those in the class, or for students who do not care about the opinions of others. Although some students pretend not to care (and this strategy is appropriate in those situations), there are students who are so disconnected from their peers that peer pressure is not likely to be effective. Peer confrontation would most likely not work in those cases.

The Mystery Motivator/Mystery Character Intervention to Decrease Inappropriate Behavior

The Mystery Motivator/Mystery Character intervention involves using the power of peers along with some "mystery" to curb inappropriate behavior (Jones, Boon, Fore, & Bender, in press; Murphy, Theodore, Aloiso, Alric-Edwards, & Hughes, 2007; Musser, Bray, Kehle, & Jenson, 2001). Mystery motivators involve providing a "mystery prize" for completing a specified behavior, and the prize can be for the entire class or a subgroup within the class. The mystery character (Jones used the term "hero") is a student whose identity is kept secret until the end of the lesson and who can earn rewards for the entire class.

Jones and her colleagues (in press) implemented these procedures to curb inappropriate verbal remarks in a sixth-grade specialized reading class that included only seven males. Those students joked too much with each other about being in a special class, calling each other names, and talking about each other as "being stupid!" Although most of this was only the robust banter common among young males, on several occasions, these disrespectful statements resulted in serious verbal altercations in the classroom.

Ms. Jones wished to curb the number of verbally disrespectful statements these students made to each other. She defined these statements as any that showed disrespect to others or to her. This included statements like, "Shut up!" or "I can't believe you missed that," or "You're an idiot!" Even if these statements were made between friends in a joking fashion, they were still counted as disrespectful statements during this intervention.

Ms. Jones placed a tally sheet with each student's name on her desk, and without mentioning this to the students, she placed a mark beside the name of any student who made a disrespectful statement. With this simple method, she could track not only the total number of disrespectful statements but also the number of such statements made by individual students. Furthermore, she could continue her teaching while collecting the baseline data.

After several days, she informed the class of the "mystery motivator" and "mystery character" intervention, as follows.

Ms. Jones: I want to find a way in our class to stop calling each other disrespectful things because I want us all to enjoy this class and to help each other out when we need it. Will you guys help me with that?

Class: Sure. What do we do?

Ms. Jones: I'd like to give everybody in this class a mystery motivator reward every day from this list of rewards (e.g., 10 minutes of educational game or computer time, or five minutes time off before the next period, etc.). However, you only earn the mystery motivator reward if one of you—called the mystery character for that day—says no more than one disrespectful thing in the entire class. That way, you will all need to stop saying disrespectful things to each other, in case you are mystery character that day.

Student: How will we know who you're watching?

Ms. Jones: That's part of the mystery. You won't know who the mystery character is, and I'll be watching everyone every day.

Student: You mean we won't know who's the character? Is that right? How will we know who wins?

Ms. Jones: That's right, but whoever that guy is, he can win a reward for the whole class.

Student: How will we know what the reward is?

Ms. Jones: That's the other part of the mystery. The mystery motivator reward for any given day is a mystery too, unless the character wins it. Then we'll open the envelope for that day to see who the character is and see if his behavior earned anything for the class.

After this explanation, Ms. Jones began the intervention. As she taught the lesson, she tallied the disrespectful remarks made by anyone. The class quickly noted when she made a tally mark and would often encourage each other to "shut up!" Of course, Ms. Jones then pointed out that the statement to "shut up" is disrespectful and suggested that the class merely call someone's name softly as a reminder not to say disrespectful things.

Near the end of the period, Ms. Jones announced it was time to open the envelope to see who the mystery character was and whether he had won the mystery reward for the class that day. Ms. Jones looked first at the name of the mystery character and then at her data for that student to see if the mystery character had used no more than one disrespectful remark. If so, she announced to the class the mystery character's name, and the class applauded. Then Ms. Jones looked back at the information in the envelope and read out the mystery motivator that the character had won for the class.

If, on the other hand, the mystery character had made more than one disrespectful remark, Ms. Jones told the class they had not won, and she continued the lesson for an additional 10 minutes without revealing the name of the mystery character for that day. That way, no student was singled out when he failed to win the mystery motivator reward.

In Figure 6.6, the data showed a significant decline in disrespectful comments made by the class as a whole. Over a period of only two weeks, the disrespectful comments were almost eliminated by this intervention, and the data collected for each student likewise showed a significant decline. This strategy can be used in larger classes, but general education teachers should not attempt to collect data on every student in such classes. Rather than a "mystery character," general education teachers should collect data only on the one or two target students in the class (see the discussion that follows of other group contingency interventions). Still, this mystery motivator/mystery character is a powerful peer influence strategy because the target students can earn rewards for the entire group.

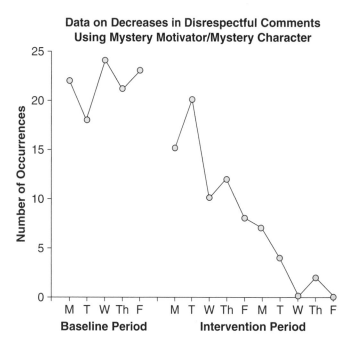

Figure 6.6 The graph shows baseline data on the frequency of disrespectful comments and the decrease that occurred during the two-week period of the mystery motivator/mystery character intervention.

Group Contingency Interventions

Many other strategies also involve the option for rewarding groups of students contingent upon their behavior. These are typically referred to as *group contingency strategies*. Imagine a general education teacher dividing the class into three roughly equal groups based on their behavior. That teacher could then record the misbehaviors of the students in each group and reward the best behaved group. That is one example of a group contingency because the reward is contingent upon the behavior of each member of the group. In this type of strategy, peer influence is important because students usually coach each other toward more appropriate behavior in order to get the reward (Jones, Boon, Fore, & Bender, in press; Salend, Whittaker, & Reeder, 1992). Even students with aggressive, disruptive, or inattentive behaviors frequently respond well to group contingency strategies (Jenson & Reavis, 1999).

Students generally can find ways to improve their behavior when provided an opportunity to

> *Group contingency interventions often result in developing a positive group identity that can serve as a relationship builder for students with otherwise disappointing social relationships.*

earn positive reinforcement for their classmates. Even ingrained or habitual behavior can be addressed using this intervention because the peers are likely to verbally remind the offending student to behave appropriately. Drastic changes in behavior are not only possible, but likely, whenever the power and influence of the peer group is brought to bear.

Perhaps as importantly, using this strategy often results in the development of a positive group identity that can be a powerful relationship builder for many students with otherwise disappointing social relationships. Students with learning disabilities, emotional problems, attention disorders, or oppositional defiant behaviors often have difficulty making and fostering interpersonal relationships. Using a group contingency strategy can build more successful interpersonal relationships for many of these students.

Different Group Contingency Options

Jenson and Reavis (1999) identified several specific types of group contingencies. In the *individual-all group contingency* situation, the behavior of one individual determines the reward for the entire group, as was the case in the example of the mystery character we just described. In the *group-all group contingency*, the specific target behaviors of every member of the group are recorded, and the reward is based on the total group's behavior. The teacher must make a choice as to which type of contingency to use. In the individual-all group contingency, the behavior of one person has a dramatic impact on everyone, and the peer pressure is likely to be stronger for that person to improve behavior. The advantage of the group-all group contingency strategy is that the entire group will be monitoring and seeking improvement in the behavior of every member of the group, and the strategy is likely to result in improved classroom behavior overall.

Considerations for Implementing Group Contingencies

There are several issues to consider prior to using this strategy.

- **Age of the peer group.** This strategy is dependent on the influence of the peer group. Even though teachers in lower grades may try this strategy—it can often work well in the lower grades—the strategy is more effective for students in the fourth grade and higher. This is because the power of peer influence is profound in the upper elementary and higher grades and, therefore, this strategy will work for older students with a wide range of behavioral problems.
- **Risk of losing control.** Implementation of group contingencies involves the risk of the teacher losing control of the strategy. If, for example, an aggressive or violent student is asked to "please work more quietly" by a classmate, the aggressive student may explode, and this angry outburst could flair into verbal or physical aggression toward the other student. Teachers may wish to avoid this strategy where certain violent students are involved.

- **Setting up the group.** Although different models of group contingency interventions exist, there are several implementation tasks for teachers that are common to all of these interventions. Initially, teachers must make certain to establish comparable groups, specifying a target behavior for each student or group member. Next, the teacher must state the ground rules for making the polite requests for appropriate behavior between group members. In addition, teachers must establish an easily understood contingency along with an appropriate reward system. Here is an example.

A Case Study Using Group Contingencies

Ms. Morris sought to curb certain mild misbehaviors in her fifth-grade class and decided to implement a group contingency intervention in which subgroups in the class compete against each other for rewards. In particular, Ms. Morris was concerned with the frequent disruptive off-task behaviors of three specific individuals in her class of 21 students.

Ms. Morris decided to break the class into three groups of seven students each, and each one of the three target students was placed in a different group. Ms. Morris also took care in placing other students because some had demonstrated various inappropriate behaviors in the class. She did her best to make certain that the groups were balanced. She then rearranged her class seating chart so that groups of students working together could subtly and politely remind each other of appropriate behavior.

After the groups were established, Ms. Morris carefully selected a specific behavior for each target student, making certain that the behavior for each student was clearly defined and easily observable. She met with the target students individually to ask if they wanted to be "characters" by earning rewards for their group. Then she discussed each target behavior with the student and made certain that each student understood that the target behavior may be different for other students.

Next, Ms. Morris prepared her class by writing some sample polite requests on the board. These included forms for particular requests students might make to each other, as follows:

> *"Burrell, please remember to do your work quickly."*

> *"Luis, please remember that this is work time, and our group wants to win the prize for today of extra recess time."*

> *"Charles, could you please work more quietly so that I can finish my work on time?"*

Finally, with the permission of the target students named above, she then explained the contingency to the class, as follows:

Ms. Morris: Class, I've invited Charles, Burrell, and Luis to become our class "characters." They have agreed to try to earn 10 minutes of extra computer time for good behavior, and they will share that time with some of you each day. I want everyone to participate. Are you interested in extra computer or educational game time?

Class:	Sure! Yeah!
Ms. Morris:	Then I'm forming some new groups in the class. When I call your name, I'll tell you which group you are in, and we'll arrange the desks so that these three groups are sitting together. (Ms. Morris goes through the roll, forms three groups, and has the students arrange their desks so that groups sit together.)
Student:	What do we do now?
Ms. Morris:	As you can see every group in the class includes one of our class characters. I've explained to the characters that I will be counting the number of times they disrupt the class and that the character who disrupts the class least wins the reward for his whole group on that day. We'll do the computer or educational game time just after lunch, before we go to our special classes and afternoon activities.
Student:	What if Burell misbehaves and our group loses?
Ms. Morris:	Good question. No one likes to lose, and that's why everyone in the group should help the character by reminding him to get back in his seat and be quiet. Each group member should use a respectful statement like one of those I've written on the board. Let's practice some of these. Thomas, you're in Burrell's group. Imagine he is making noises, and you want to remind him to behave. Use one of these statements on the board and politely make that request.
Thomas:	I guess I would use the one: "Burrell, please remember to do your work quickly and quietly."
Ms. Morris:	That's exactly right, Thomas. Use a quiet voice and make the requests politely while you look toward Burrell. You're trying to remind him that he can be the character for your group, and you politely remind him of that. I also noticed that you added "quietly" at the end, and that's great, as long as it is polite and respectful.

Notice that Ms. Morris emphasized supportive ground rules regarding the comments that students might make to the character students in their group when reminding them of appropriate behaviors. Because of the inappropriate conversation models often promoted by movies, television, recordings, and other mass media, it is not uncommon to find students today who do not know how to make a polite request. Thus, the skill of politely requesting something can be taught directly to the students when implementing this strategy, just as Ms. Morris did.

In some cases, teachers might wish to ask the students to ignore any angry remarks made by the character in response to a polite request for better behavior. While Ms. Morris did not do that in this example, such anger can sometimes occur. If it does, the teacher should immediately step in and deal directly with the angry student.

In establishing the specific contingency, teachers should clarify what specific behavior is expected. Teachers may also wish to extend some reinforcement for more than one group each day. For example, the teacher could explain that, *"The group with the best behavior earns 10 minutes of extra computer education time this afternoon if we are able to work effectively today with no one interrupting our concentration. The next best behaved group may earn up to five minutes of extra time. The third group doesn't earn any extra time."*

The group contingency options are limited only by the teacher's imagination and time. All types of rewards may be offered and all types of groups involved. Alternatively, the teacher may merely focus on one student to earn rewards for the entire class. Still, research has shown various group contingencies to be highly effective, and general education teachers should be prepared to implement some version of this strategy when dealing with misbehaving students.

SUMMARY

Peer influence is a strong encourager or mitigator of adolescent behavior. Social networks and mirror neurons in the brain help us to understand ourselves, appraise the intentions of others, and foster the desire to be accepted as part of a social group. Teachers can use the power of peer influence to moderate undesirable behaviors while supporting desirable behaviors. Strategies such as peer mediation, peer confrontation, mystery motivator/mystery character, and other group contingencies serve as effective techniques whereby peers can control misbehaviors and reinforce positive behaviors.

Chapter 7

Managing Oppositional Behavior

WHAT IS OPPOSITIONAL BEHAVIOR?

All children get cranky, angry, spiteful, and defiant at times. Adolescents are moody and argumentative. It is part of growing up and the natural result of interacting with other peers and adults. Typical youngsters are always pushing boundaries as they try to get their needs met, and it is normal for them to display oppositional behaviors at certain stages of their development. When their behavior is unacceptable, parents and teachers usually step in with corrective action and the misbehavior subsides. On the other hand, some oppositional behaviors may persist and be clearly disruptive to the family, home, or school environment.

The primary behavioral difficulties of individuals with oppositional behavior is their persistent pattern of disobedience and hostility toward parents, teachers, or other adults, and their refusal to follow commands or requests by adults.

Causes of Oppositional Behavior

Various factors probably contribute to oppositional behavior. There are currently two primary theories offered to explain how children develop oppositional behavior patterns. The first is a developmental theory and researchers believe it suggests that the problems begin when children are toddlers. Children and adolescents who develop oppositional behavior may have genetic deficits that made it difficult to develop autonomous social skills. From this perspective, the bad attitudes characteristic of oppositional behavior are viewed as a continuation of the normal developmental issues that were not adequately resolved during the toddler years.

The second view involves learning theory. It suggests that the negative characteristics of this behavior are learned attitudes reflecting the effects of negative reinforcement techniques used by parents and authority figures. The use of negative reinforcements by parents increases the rate and intensity of oppositional behaviors because it achieves the desired attention, time, concern, and interaction with parents or authority figures. As the discussion on the causes continues, there is general agreement that the following four factors play a significant role in the development of the oppositional behavior (see Figure 7.1):

- **The Child's Inherent Temperament.** Temperament is a function of the interaction of numerous genetic, biological, and neurological factors. Brain imaging studies indicate that youngsters who demonstrate severe oppositional behavior display lower activity in the frontal lobe than typical youngsters, and this finding may explain their limited ability to develop appropriate social skills.

- **Parenting.** How did the family respond to the child's temperament at the first displays of oppositional behavior? Did they ignore it, tolerate it, get into power struggles, get angry, or use excessive punishment? Were there marital problems or evidence of child abuse?

  The interactions of a persistently irritable child with parents who are harsh, punitive, and inconsistent often lead to a coercive, negative cycle of behavior in the family. In this pattern, the child's defiant behavior tends to intensify the parents' harsh reactions. The parents respond to misbehavior with threats of punishment that are inconsistently applied. When the parent does punish the child, the child learns merely to respond to threats. When the parent fails to punish the child, the child learns that compliance is not necessary. Studies indicate that these patterns are established early, in the child's preschool years. If left untreated, the pattern development accelerates and worsens by the time the child enters school.

  Another aspect of parenting relates to the use of alcohol. A study of 226 families with children aged from 18 to 48 months old found that children in families with nonalcoholic parents had significantly lower levels of aggression and oppositional behavior throughout the age span than children with one or more alcoholic parents (Edwards, Eiden, Colder, & Leonard, 2006).

- **Biological Factors.** There is research evidence that biological factors may contribute to persistent oppositional behavior. Researchers have recently found that defects in several genes can lead to conduct problems and antisocial behavior, particularly in males (Beaver et al., 2007; Hudziak et al., 2005). Studies indicate that problems in parts of the neuroendocrine system, such as the hypothalamus and the pituitary and adrenal glands, can lead to increased behavior problems in children (van Goozen & Fairchild, 2006). Other research findings seem to indicate that disturbances in the system that regulates the neurotransmitter serotonin may have an impact on aggressive and oppositional behavior in children and adolescents (Snoek et al., 2002). Further investigations into the neurobiological factors associated with disruptive behavior may lead to the development of new forms of interventions.

Possible Causes of Oppositional Behavior

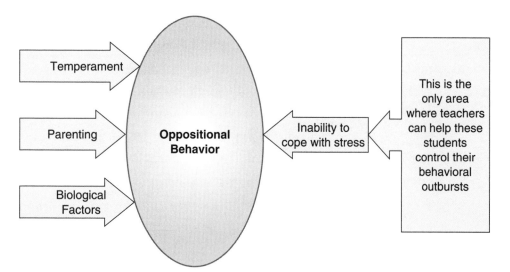

Figure 7.1   Four of the most commonly accepted explanations for oppositional behavior are the student's temperament, the nature of the student's parenting, biological factors, and the student's inability to cope with environmental stressors. Of these, teachers can address only the type and extent of stressors in the student's class and school environment and help the student deal with them.

- **Inability to Cope With Stressors in the Environment.** Causes of stress (stressors) are always present in our environment. Typically, as we grow and develop, we learn to deal with stress by recognizing its symptoms, assessing it, and deciding what to do to alleviate it. Some individuals may have been exposed to persistent stressors as toddlers and, for whatever reasons (including possible genetic contributions), did not develop the skills necessary to cope with them. Because these individuals have difficulty coping with stress, stressors in the environment lead to frustration and serve as "triggers" for oppositional behavior.

Of the four major potential causes of oppositional behavior, teachers can address only one: helping students to cope with stressors in the class and school environment. As we shall see later in this chapter, the strategies we suggest for teachers to consider in dealing with students with oppositional behavior are based primarily on reducing causes of stress in the classroom and assisting these students with coping techniques.

STUDENTS WITH OPPOSITIONAL BEHAVIOR IN THE CLASSROOM

Many teachers have experienced momentary opposition from students in the class, and even the best students sometimes refuse to complete work or comply with classroom rules. However, as we noted earlier, some students demonstrate a consistent pattern of noncompliance over a period of months or years. They typically refuse to comply with rules, blame or argue with others, lose their temper, curse, demonstrate low self-esteem, and consistently annoy others (Salend & Sylvestre, 2005). Students who consistently demonstrate these behaviors will be a challenge to teachers, and many teachers feel frustrated when first confronting them (Abrams, 2005).

In some ways, such frustration is justified. Research studies indicate that few behavioral interventions have produced significant, sustained, positive results in students with oppositional behavior (Carey & Bourbon, 2006; Walker, Colvin, & Ramsey, 1995). Furthermore, few of the typical behavioral interventions used in schools (e.g., suspension, expulsion, and in-school suspension) seem to work for these students over the long term (Blankenship & Bender, 2007; Carey & Bourbon, 2006). Although these interventions may remove a child from the general education class, many educators would prefer more effective, proactive strategies that allow a teacher to successfully manage these disruptive behaviors in the classroom.

Teacher Knowledge of Oppositional Behavior

Despite the challenge of managing students with oppositional behavior, there are things teachers can do. One is for teachers to examine their own knowledge and beliefs about such students. Studies show that educators sometimes inflate their ratings of students with oppositional behavior to include hyperactivity and inattentiveness as well. Consequently, they are more likely to believe that these students have attention-deficit hyperactivity disorder (Jackson & King, 2004).

Not all oppositional behaviors are the same, and certain types of behaviors manifest at different ages. For example, temper tantrums are more common in young children. Some children may display tantrums when they do not get their way in the classroom or simply because they get frustrated while attempting to do an academic assignment (Hall, Williams, & Hall, 2000; Salend & Sylvestre, 2005). Others may display an angry, vengeful, or aggressive response to the slightest provocation, and for others no provocation seems necessary at all. In older students, verbal aggression is more common.

Regardless of the causes of the oppositional behavior, teachers can only deal with the stressors to which a child is exposed in the classroom. Consequently, in planning ways to manage these students, teachers should give careful attention to the types of stressful events that might set that child off. Such stressful, unplanned, or unstructured events in the classroom are called *triggers* because they often set off an oppositional episode. If those triggers can be avoided, the student will be much easier to manage in the class (Hall, Williams, & Hall, 2000). Later in this chapter we will discuss how to avoid triggers.

School administrators and teachers should be encouraged to do some serious self-reflection when dealing with children who display oppositional behavior. Abrams (2005) encourages teachers to become more "therapeutic" in their outlook. For example, Abrams encourages teachers to examine their own behavior patterns, their management of the stress of teaching, their efforts to control the behavior of the students in their class, and their level of flexibility in their class management procedures. Although all of these may be tested to the limit by some students

> *Flexibility is perhaps the single most important factor when dealing with students with oppositional behavior.*

with oppositional behavior, flexibility is perhaps the single most important factor. Furthermore, educators should not assume that all students who display oppositional behavior have a permanent developmental disorder that can be addressed only in special education settings.

Teacher Frustration and Countercontrol

The concept of countercontrol deals with a simple question: Who is controlling whose behavior? Although students with various behavioral problems can be challenging and frustrating to teach, most veteran teachers say that children and adolescents with oppositional behavior are among the most difficult students to manage in the classroom. Their behavior is often beyond the tolerance level of most teachers, and when confronted with students with oppositional behavior in the classroom, many teachers feel they lack control over their own class (Abrams, 2005). Students with oppositional behavior may seem quite

> *Countercontrol is a tactic that students with oppositional behavior use to manipulate the behavior of the teacher—and it frequently works!*

powerful and influential, and their influence does not usually create an environment conducive to learning. Carey and Bourbon (2004) have suggested the concept of *countercontrol* to explain this sense of disempowerment that some teachers experience when teaching students with ODD.

Countercontrol is a concept that was first discussed in the 1950s by psychologist B. F. Skinner (1953), but this idea has been given little attention in the educational literature until recently. Skinner suggested that as some individuals (in this instance, teachers) attempt to control the behavior of others (i.e., students with oppositional behavior), the persons being controlled may sense a powerlessness and frustration, and that could result in their attempts to countercontrol their controllers. Carey and Bourbon (2004) believe that this countercontrol phenomenon may explain the mutual frustration felt by students with oppositional behavior and their teachers in the classroom. Because Skinner provided no precise definition of countercontrol, Carey and Bourbon (2004) defined countercontrol as the actions taken by a controllee (student) to manipulate the behavior of the controller (teacher). Consider the following scenario:

Ms. Bothell had been working with Kenesha for only two weeks in her eighth-grade science class, and already she was feeling frustrated by Kenesha's consistent defiance. When Ms. Bothell gave an assignment, Kenesha said something like, "That's dumb! I'm not going to do that over the weekend!" Other defiant acts included slamming her books down on her desk when she came into the room and cursing at others whenever she felt slighted. Whenever Ms. Bothell spoke to her in an attempt to discipline her, Kenesha cursed her loudly in the classroom.

Ms. Bothell collected baseline data on Kenesha's outbursts and then tried several interventions. First, she met with Kenesha daily for two weeks in an effort to discuss each behavioral outburst and to explain the unfavorable impact her behavior had on the class. After two weeks, it was clear that this approach was not working, so she tried to ignore the problem for the next three weeks. However, Kenesha's behavior became even more blatant and outrageous. Ms. Bothell then sent Kenesha to the principal's office whenever an outburst occurred.

This is an excellent example of countercontrol. Kenesha responded to Ms. Bothell's attempts at behavioral manipulation by becoming more out of control and, thus, began to control Ms. Bothell. The end result was that Kenesha could avoid class assignments any time she wished by staging a behavioral outburst that resulted in her being sent to the principal's office for punishment. In countercontrol, the teacher often feels more frustrated than the student because the student is really exerting more control in that situation than the teacher.

Carey (2002), in one research study, asked teachers and students about control issues in the classroom and got some useful insights into countercontrol situations. Teachers at all levels of experience said they were involved in countercontrol situations at various times in their career. Carey found that the teachers' sense of just how controlling they were was unrelated to the students' perception of control attempts by their teachers. Rather, the variable that seemed to matter most was the students' perception of how controlling teachers were *attempting* to be. In situations where teachers were perceived as highly controlling, more students reported that they attempted to countercontrol the teacher's behavior. Furthermore, students reported more countercontrol when they were *told* to do something than when they were *asked* or were provided with choices. You may recall from previous chapters that students with overt behavior problems respond more appropriately when provided with choices about their assignments or about other factors in the class.

Perhaps the best test of countercontrol is the teacher's sense of the classroom dynamics. When a teacher feels constant frustration or high levels of stress with a particular student, the teacher may want to examine the relationship with the student in question, and reflectively ask, "Have I been attempting to control that student's behavior beyond the bounds necessary for the requirements of the classroom?" By seriously reflecting on which rules truly make a difference and which rules do not, teachers are likely to become more flexible in their classroom expectations. Flexibility on less important rules can mean the difference between effectively managing a student with oppositional behavior or becoming increasingly frustrated by failed attempts to manage the same student as the year progresses. One tactic the teacher can use for such self-reflection is called the "So What" test.

The "So What" Test

Although structured classrooms, governed by clear rules and expectations, are important in the management of challenging students, not every rule infraction warrants an intervention or confrontation with the student with oppositional behavior. Townsend (2000) recommended that teachers apply the "So What" test whenever a student commits some infraction or acts defiantly in the class. Before deciding whether to engage the student and address the misbehavior, the teacher reflectively asks, "So what if the student did that, and didn't get punished?" This momentary pause allows the teacher to quickly examine the rule and the infraction and determine if it is important enough to cease instruction and start a discussion with the student.

Using this "So What" test can lead to the differential enforcement of class rules. Ideally, all rules should be applied equally to all students in the class, but in reality, this is rarely the case. Because many infractions go unnoticed by teachers, or because some students are good at hiding their infractions, rules are often not consistently applied and enforced in the classroom, even when teachers make every effort to do so. Townsend (2000) suggested that teachers be flexible and vary their rules and expectations for students with oppositional behavior by

> *The "So What" test is one of the best means of determining what action to take when a student misbehaves.*

enforcing only those rules that clearly matter, while enforcing all classroom rules for other students in the class. Such flexibility can free the teacher to accept behaviors that, in other students, would be unacceptable, but for the students with oppositional behavior, may represent an actual improvement in behavior.

Many teachers will have concerns with the rule flexibility recommended here. There are those teachers who firmly believe in the old adage, "Give them an inch and they'll take a mile." Others may believe that "If I let one student get away with that, everyone else will test me!" Fortunately for educators, neither of these statements is actually true. A teacher ignoring one student's overt misbehavior does not immediately result in every other student in the class emulating that behavior. Misbehavior is not an instantly contagious disease that threatens to take over one's classroom. For most overtly inappropriate behaviors, the exact opposite occurs—students are likely to observe the misbehavior and then ignore it, especially if they see the teacher doing so.

Furthermore, when teachers tell their students to ignore overtly disruptive behaviors, they remove the audience that sometimes reinforces the misbehavior. Therefore, we suggest that teachers should consider the rigid application of rules with some students and a more lenient application with others. If students challenge such rule application (as some will), teachers might respond: "It is not my job to treat you all the same. It is my job to do the best teaching I can for every one of you, and sometimes I'll have to treat you differently to do that."

Defiant Students: Explosions Waiting to Happen

Power Plays With Students

Students who are angry or frustrated will sometimes initiate power plays with their teachers. Power plays may be defined as situations in which students wish to demonstrate their power and influence in the class through open defiance and misbehavior (Albert, 1996). Sometimes students appear to be explosively angry and actually want to interact with their teachers in a negative way. Most veteran teachers have had the experience of seeing students walk into class, slam their books down on the desk for no apparent reason, or loudly curse at a classmate who merely brushes past them. On many occasions, these students are providing teachers observable warning signs prior to a violent behavioral outburst. Sometimes their warnings are more subtle and include things like tense facial expressions or a stressful body posture (Lopata, Nida, & Marable, 2006).

Alert teachers can often predict a student's mood through observation and intervene to prevent violent or disruptive behavior. Walker (1998), for example, noted that in three of every four physical attacks on teachers, the student provided some pre-attack warning signs.

Avoiding power plays with students is a wise course of action for one simple reason: When teachers allow themselves to be trapped in power struggles with students, the students always win. Students who initiate power plays will invest themselves entirely in the power play situation. Teachers, on the other hand, cannot do so. As adults, they should avoid such destructive behavior because they need to remember their responsibilities to the other students in the class. Of course, teachers can ultimately eject students from their classroom, but even in this situation, one must inquire as to who won that power struggle? Didn't the student avoid the class work? Thus, instead of engaging in power struggles, teachers should master a set of quick responses that can help defuse the angry, potentially violent student who is actively seeking a power play with the teacher. Here are a some ideas worth considering.

> *Students with oppositional behavior tend to create power struggles. Avoid them. When teachers allow themselves to be trapped in power struggles with students, the students always win.*

Defusing Techniques

There are several techniques that you can use to avoid power struggles with students and to calm down an explosive or potentially violent student. Although few techniques are 100 percent effective, the following have been shown to work (Albert, 1996).

- **Use repetitive instructions.** When a student shouts angrily about not wanting to do an assignment, you should repeat the instructions in a calm voice. If the student shouts again, repeat the instructions again, in a softer voice, taking care to say the same things that were said the first time the instructions were given. Students find it difficult to argue with someone who is repeating the same instructions. When using this technique, do not respond to any objections the student may raise. Just repeat the same instructions, using a quieter voice each time. After three or four repetitions, turn and walk away. You have not responded to the student's effort to initiate a power play, and even if that student does not immediately begin the work, others in the class will, and the student is left arguing with nobody.

- **Call the student's name.** Hearing one's first name called softly, in a nonthreatening manner, has a calming effect on most individuals. Trained negotiators use this technique in hostage situations in their attempts to calm the hostage takers. You can apply the same technique to calm students who may be escalating toward a behavioral outburst. Use a softer voice than the student is using and calmly call the student's first name each time the student demonstrates a verbal outburst.

- **Use humor.** Allow yourself to joke about noncompliance. When a student refuses to do any work, you could make a statement such as, "Well, that's one way to go, I guess" as you walk away from the student. One caution here: Humor at the expense of the student is never recommended because such humor is really sarcasm and is likely to only inflame the situation. However, in this example, the humor actually targets the teacher's presumed control of the classroom and is not focused explicitly on the offending student.

- **Ask about the student's anger.** When a student initiates a power play, inquire in a calm voice about the anger, hoping that the student will discuss the cause of the upset. If the time and situation allow, say something like, "I can see that the assignment upsets you. Is it something we can talk calmly about? We can return to that assignment later." Having a three-minute discussion now about the underlying cause of the student's anger is preferable to having an escalating power struggle that will take much longer to resolve and likely result in overt misbehavior.

- **Share power with students.** When students challenge you about an assignment and mention something else they would like to do, consider their desires. If possible, share power by negotiating with them about their desired activity and the required task. Allowing these students just a few minutes on their desired task may be enough to get their compliance afterward to do the assigned task. This sharing of power can be very effective provided the students' desired tasks do not require large amounts of instructional time.

- **Postpone the discussion of behavior problems.** When a student who has misbehaved is highly emotional or very angry, postpone the discussion of the misbehavior to a later time. Let the student know that a discussion will take place, but that it need not take place immediately. Sometimes, showing that you were sympathetic to the student's emotional distress can defuse an ongoing behavioral problem.

- **Understand and respect personal space.** Personal space in most Western societies is shaped like an oval in front of each person. The oval extends farther in the front than to one's sides and rear. Understand personal space and realize that students who are emotionally upset will frequently attack when their personal space is invaded. You should avoid invading the personal space of students unless they become an imminent danger to themselves or others. Respect their personal space and use other defusing techniques to alleviate the students' tension and stress.

- **Use voice tone matching techniques.** We have described in previous chapters how our brains are hard-wired to attune our behavior to those with whom we are interacting (Remember the mirror neuron system?). This behavior matching occurs in a variety of ways, including voice quality, tone, volume, facial expression, emotional intensity, and body stance. Understanding this tendency to match the behavior of others can empower you in several ways. Resist, however, the natural tendency to match the students' violent or emotional intensity because this only inflames the situation. Instead, subtly encourage students towards calmer behavior by using their natural inclination to match your voice tone, facial expression, and lower emotional intensity. When confronted by aggressive or potentially violent students, use a softer voice tone, keep your facial expression concerned but not judgmental, and call the student by name. This serves to calm the student, even during an emotionally intense situation.

A Case Study: Defusing a Potentially Violent Situation

Mr. Tibo entered his sixth-grade science classroom after lunch one day to find Jason and Rupert confronting each other with clenched fists. Jason was an average student who rarely got into trouble, but Rupert was a student with oppositional behavior who frequently got into fights on school grounds. Mr. Tibo sensed the emotional tension in the room and was certain that the students would have been physically fighting had he not entered the class. He had to defuse that potentially violent situation immediately and he chose a few of the defusing techniques described earlier. Here's the ensuing scenario:

Mr. Tibo: (Using a calm voice and without physically approaching the combatants, he said) Rupert, I can see you are upset, and we'll need to talk about this. Please come outside with me for a moment.

Rupert: It's not my fault. He hit me!

Mr. Tibo: Rupert, I can see you are upset, and we'll need to talk about this. Please come outside with me for a moment. (This was said with a softer voice)

Rupert: Damn it! Why does everybody pick on me? He hit me first!

Mr. Tibo: (Softer still). Rupert, I can see you are upset, and we'll need to talk about this. Please come outside with me for a moment. (Mr. Tibo walked out of the room without turning his back on the two boys, and he was glad to see that Rupert followed.)

Mr. Tibo: (Now alone with Rupert in the hallway.) Rupert, thank you for coming along. I want to make sure that I hear your concerns because I can see you are very angry. Maybe we should talk about this a bit after you and I calm down.

Mr. Tibo was able to prevent a violent fight by using several defusing techniques. He softly called Rupert's name, which had a calming effect. He repeated the same instructions and avoided discussing who was initially at fault. Although teachers should explore who is at fault in these instances, the time to do that is after the situation is over and not while the threat of violence is still a real possibility. Finally, Mr. Tibo expressed concern for Rupert's feelings and asked about his anger. When teachers have these techniques at their fingertips, they can use those that are most comfortable for them and most appropriate for the situation.

We should note that these defusing techniques are not behavioral improvement interventions in the strictest sense, because they are intended to immediately alleviate stress and avoid a potentially violent situation in the classroom rather than reduce behaviors over time. Thus, in addition to these techniques, teachers should seek to be more proactive in managing students with oppositional behavior by considering ways to avoid triggers that lead to misbehavior.

> *Teachers can learn simple techniques for defusing tense situations involving students with oppositional behavior.*

Avoiding Triggers For Misbehavior in the Classroom

Another way to avoid behavioral outbursts in the classroom is for teachers to become aware of emotional triggers. Unlike the previous techniques, avoiding triggers for behavioral outbursts is a proactive technique that can empower teachers to more effectively manage a variety of challenging students, including those with oppositional behavior.

It is no secret that the breaks between classroom activities, or the transitions to out-of-class activities, often provide opportunities for disruptive behavior. Any of those transition times could be a trigger for oppositional behaviors. Sharply-worded directives from the teacher or other students, unexpected changes in class routine, or even tasks that tax a student's intellectual ability, can all serve as triggers (Hall, Williams, & Hall, 2000; McIntosh, Herman, Sanford, McGraw, & Florence, 2004). Here is a classroom example.

Travon was a fourth-grade student who frequently burst into loud, aggressive name calling when he felt frustrated. Mr. Timmons, the general education teacher, knew about Travon's outbursts and was careful to use both proximity and prewarnings with Travon concerning upcoming transitions. When it was time to move from reading to mathematics, for example, Mr. Timmons collected any necessary items he needed for the first part of the mathematics lesson and then casually moved nearer to Travon's desk. Travon got some reassurance from that proximity and was less likely to have a behavioral outburst. Also, just before telling the class to put away their reading books and get out the math workbooks, Mr. Timmons prewarned Travon by leaning next to Travon and whispering, "It's almost time for math. Would you like to be the first one to get your math book out today?" On most days, once Travon had his mathematics book on his desk, Mr. Timmons could then give instructions to the other students, and Travon was fine. In short, the prewarning technique coupled with proximity worked on most days.

However, one day, just as Mr. Timmons was moving toward Travon to provide the prewarning, the class loudspeaker came alive with the voice of the principal announcing an assembly during the last period of the day. Before the announcement was over, Travon was up and shouting toward the speaker, "You can't do that! I'll miss my PE!" Then he began cursing loudly, aiming most of his creative language at the principal.

In this example, Mr. Timmons was using the appropriate techniques for students with oppositional behavior and had found the right combination of ideas that usually worked with Travon. However, even in the best of circumstances, things go wrong, such as the ill-timed announcement that caused Travon's behavioral outburst. Such events notwithstanding, teachers should seek tactics that assist in avoiding triggers in order to more successfully manage students in the classroom.

Strategies for Avoiding Triggers

Here is a list of strategies and tactics from a variety of sources that you can use for avoiding triggers (Hall, Williams, & Hall, 2000; McIntosh, Herman, Sanford, McGraw, & Florence, 2004; Salend & Sylvestre, 2004; Zuna & McDougall, 2004).

- **Use physical proximity**. Because many students with oppositional behavior do not feel secure in the classroom, your physical presence can often make an outburst less likely to occur. When transitions are planned, or when unexpected events occur, you should physically move toward the students without threatening them by invading their personal space.
- **Give a prewarning.** Because so many students have difficulties with transitions between subjects or activities in the classroom, consider prewarning students with oppositional behavior of such transitions. In that way, these students can get prepared first and not feel frustration if it takes them a few seconds longer to get through the transition.
- **Offer students choices.** Students with oppositional behavior need a sense of control over their environment. Offering choices can empower them and may prevent defiance. For instance, assignment sheets could be used that cover the same topic in various ways (e.g., an outline to complete or a graphic organizer on the same content). Students could be given a choice of which assignment they wish to do, and having some choice reduces the incidence of defiant behaviors.

- **Partner students together.** Use a buddy system that partners typical students with those who have behavior problems. In many cases, the partner of a student with oppositional behavior can assist in curbing misbehavior for various in-class and out-of-class activities.

- **Teach specific behaviors for transitions.** Although most young students can quickly grasp the concept of "forming a line" in the hallway, some defiant students are perplexed by that simple request. This results not from a lack of cognitive understanding of what "forming a line" means, but from fear, frustration, or social isolation. Students with oppositional behavior may be saying to themselves, "Who should I stand next to? Nobody likes me!" Thus, as other students form a line, students with oppositional behavior remain standing in the middle of the hallway trying to determine their position in line. Teaching specific behaviors, such as "lining up along the wall" could assist such students, especially if you point out that it really makes little difference whom one stands next to.

- **Give clear, short, and simple instructions.** Students with oppositional behavior who sense frustration are likely to respond with an emotional outburst. One way to prevent that is to use clear, short, directive comments. For example, avoid saying, "Is everyone finished? Put away your papers now, get out your history text, and turn to page 138." In this example, students who are not finished may be embarrassed and feel frustration. Further, the instructions included four different things to which the student must attend. Consider, instead, short, politely-phrased directives (teachers should always model politeness), and include pauses or breaks between the directives: "Please put your papers in your desk and get out your history book." Pause for about 10 seconds, then say, "Turn to page 138."

- **Emphasize class routines.** You can emphasize class routines by writing the class schedule on the board and discussing it with the students. Use caution when making changes in routine. Teachers may vary routines for a wide variety of reasons, and although this is sometimes advisable, care should be taken when the class includes students with oppositional behavior. For example, you could tell the class, "Today, get your history texts and we'll do our lesson on the playground because it's so nice outside." Changes in routine of this nature do enrich the class, but they also run the risk of becoming a trigger, since students with oppositional behavior gain security from the structure of the class routine.

Teaching Students To Relax

Another proactive strategy that teachers should consider for students with oppositional behavior is teaching them relaxation techniques (Lopata, Nida, & Marable, 2006). We know that students with oppositional behavior are easily stressed. You may recall from Chapter 3 that when someone is under stress, cortisol enters the bloodstream causing physiological changes in the body. One of these changes is the tightening of the body's muscles, a survival reflex to prepare for fight or flight. As muscles tighten and squeeze blood vessels, blood pressure increases, cognitive processes slow down, and emotional responses ramp up, thereby increasing the likelihood of a strong emotional outburst. Relaxing those muscles can retard and reverse this process and reduce the chances of an emotional blowup in the classroom. Surprisingly, medical studies have not yet revealed the *exact* physiological mechanisms by which relaxation calms the body, but numerous studies show that this technique works (Arntz, 2003; Conrad & Roth, 2007; Gorenstein et al., 2007).

Learning and using relaxation strategies can be a challenge at a time when every minute of the school day is devoted to instruction on statewide educational standards in reading, mathematics, and other subjects. Yet many teachers who have found the time to teach relaxation techniques to students with oppositional behaviors have reported success. These strategies can empower students to take greater control over their own behavior, and that is a worthwhile goal even in this day of highly-emphasized, standards-based learning.

> Simple relaxation techniques can lower the emotional arousal of students with oppositional behavior and calm tense confrontations.

Although some students thrive on defiant behaviors and seem to seek out ways to show defiance, other students are defiant as a result of the manner in which they were raised. If the social structure of the family was such that aggressive power plays were dominant in family life, then most of the children from that home will use such domineering tactics in their own relationships with peers and teachers. These types of relationships at school are, of course, dysfunctional and children in these situations soon realize that. Consequently, some students with oppositional behavior honestly desire to learn alternatives to their defiant behavior so that they can be accepted by their peers. For those students, teaching them a relaxation strategy provides such an alternative (We should also point out that many of the other strategies previously covered in this book—verbal self-control, dialogue journals, and self-monitoring—can be used for students with oppositional behavior as well). Here is an example of a relaxation strategy that is very appropriate for students from kindergarten up through grade three.

The Turtle Technique (Grades K to 3)

The turtle technique is an instructional procedure that involves teaching young children to relax whenever they feel frustrated or angry. For students with oppositional behavior, feelings of frustration are common, and knowing an alternative to overt misbehavior can assist these students in behaving more appropriately. This technique has been around for some time and the early research demonstrated that behavioral problems among young children can be reduced using this procedure (Fleming, Ritchie, & Fleming, 1983; Robin, Schneider, & Dolnick, 1976).

Generally, the technique should be taught to the entire class and then used when necessary for individual children. Like all preventative techniques, this technique needs to be specifically taught *before* the misbehavior occurs.

A Case Study: Teaching Students to "Do a Turtle"

Mr. Goff had two students in his second-grade class whom he believed would particularly benefit from this technique. Henrico was a violent youngster who was living with a foster family. He used threats and intimidation to bully and manipulate other students in the class. Prior to his foster care placement, he had witnessed many violent incidents in his first family, including seeing physical violence between his father and mother. Clearly, Henrico needed to learn more appropriate behaviors for getting along with others.

By contrast, Alfred was not violent, but he was defiant. It seemed that everything Mr. Goff said was a point of argument. Alfred was one of seven children living with his mother, and Mr. Goff believed that such defiance was the only way Alfred gained attention at home. Mr. Goff decided to teach the turtle technique to the entire class so that he could subsequently use it with individual class members, particularly with these two young boys. His goal was to teach the students to pretend to become turtles by withdrawing into their protective shells, whenever he or the students felt it was necessary. Mr. Goff used the following dialogue for training the students in the turtle technique.

Mr. Goff: Let me tell you all a story that will help everyone behave better in our class. This is about a turtle. How many of you have seen a turtle before?

Student: I have. I saw one on the road.

Student: My dad brought me one last year!

Mr. Goff: Well, that's good. Then you may know that the turtle is a wise animal. It knows that whenever it feels unsafe, or angry, or when someone says something nasty to it that hurts its feelings, it can find an escape. Where do turtles escape to when someone hurts their feelings or they are feeling angry or frightened?

Student: They go into their shell!

Mr. Goff: That's right. They go into their shell, where they are safe. What happens when the turtle is in its shell?

Student: They sleep. They keep their eyes closed.

Student: They stay in there for a while.

Mr. Goff: That's right. They rest and stay safe, because nobody can bother them. They ignore the world outside their shell. Do you think they like it in their shell?

Student: Yes! They are safe and they stay in there.

Mr. Goff: The shell for the turtle is safe and warm, and the other animals know not to bother the turtle when it is in its shell. Also, the turtle knows not to talk with any of the other animals for a minute or so, until its anger or its fear goes away. How many of you wish you had a shell like that? Wouldn't it be nice to just escape when we are feeling angry or when someone hurts our feelings? Do you think that we could pretend we have a shell like the turtle?

Student: If I had a shell, I'd go in every day!

Student: I'd like to have a shell like that!

Mr. Goff: What would that look like? How could we pretend we have a protective shell when we feel angry or hurt?

Student: We could put our heads down like this (she puts her head on her arms on the desk).

Mr. Goff: That's a great idea, Kathryn. Let's everyone pretend to be a turtle right now for just a few seconds, just like Kathryn. Everyone, do a turtle! (Children put their heads on their desks.)

Mr. Goff: This is really great. Now everyone look back at me, please. We'll do a turtle whenever someone needs to calm down a bit, and if you folks are feeling angry, or someone hurts your feelings, you can become a turtle any time you like. The rest of the class will remember not to bother you when you are a turtle, and I'll make sure that you have a minute or so in your safe, warm shell. How does that sound? Does everyone want to do that when they feel angry?

Student: Yeah! Let's all do that.

Mr. Goff: Let's all try it one more time. This time, I'll make some noise over here, and I want you to just ignore it and keep your heads down. Do you think you can do that? Just stay in your safe, comfortable place just like the turtle. Everyone, do a turtle! (Class becomes a turtle, and Mr. Goff makes some noise.)

Mr. Goff: Everyone did that great! Now look back at me, please. I'd like to pretend that I see one student getting angry or upset. When I do, I'll ask only that student to do a turtle. Of course, the rest of you should just ignore that student and go on with your work. Let's try that now. Kathryn, do a turtle! (Kathryn puts her head down.)

Mr. Goff: That's great Kathryn! You put your head down and you didn't say anything to anybody. Let's try someone else. Jason, do a turtle! (Jason puts his head down.)

Mr. Goff: Good job. Now someone else. Alfred, do a turtle! (Alfred puts his head down. Mr. Goff continues with several other students, making sure to also include Henrico.)

During this training and practice session, note that Mr. Goff emphasized that when he asks an individual student or the entire class to "Do a turtle," that person, or the class, should immediately stop talking and put their head down. He could have also emphasized that turtles don't talk back to others, don't peek out of their shell, and stay in their shell until the teacher talks with them.

The baseline and intervention data showed that this technique was effective for both Henrico and Alfred. Mr. Goff had kept baseline data for five days on both Alfred and Henrico, as shown in Figure 7.2. After the class was trained in this intervention, Mr. Goff used the turtle for various students in the class, and continued to count and chart the misbehavior of Henrico and Alfred. The behavior of each of these students improved considerably, and Alfred's defiant behaviors were almost eliminated.

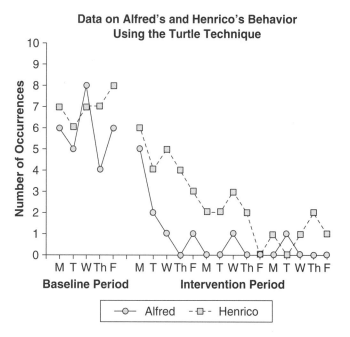

Figure 7.2   The graph shows the frequency of Alfred's and Henrico's misbehaviors during the one week baseline period and the three weeks of intervention using the "do the turtle" technique.

Using the Turtle Technique

You can use the turtle technique in the following ways:

- As shown in Mr. Goff's scenario, instruct specific students to "Do a turtle" when those students begin to lose control or display inappropriate behavior. This often prevents disruptive behaviors thereby improving the climate for the entire class.
- Individual students should be allowed and encouraged to "Do a turtle" when they feel the need to do so because they are angry or their feelings have been hurt. This teaches students with oppositional behavior that they do have some control over their feelings and over the environment.
- You can tell the entire class to "Do a turtle" when conflict arises that may get out of control, as when students are arguing loudly or when they are fighting. It also removes the audience for the misbehavior.
- In certain situations, you may wish to teach this technique to only one or two students who need help controlling their emotions. This technique is particularly effective for students with oppositional behavior because both the student and you can observe the signs of an impending emotional outburst. In those cases, explain to the class that when Henrico has his head down, the class should ignore him and not talk to him or about him.

Relaxation Strategies for Older Students

Various relaxation strategies have been shown to be effective for students with emotional problems at all grade levels (Kellner & Turtin, 1995; Lopata, 2003; Lopata, Nida, & Marable, 2006).

Adapting the turtle. For older students in grades four to 12, you may wish to use the same general technique as "Do a turtle" described earlier without referring to the turtle. Rather, use the term "time out" for hurt feelings, anger, or frustration. Teachers have used this idea in middle and high school classes, and it is effective for many students with oppositional and other behavioral issues. Mr. Goff's dialogue can be adapted for the age group and used to teach relaxation and the "time out" strategy in much the same way as the turtle technique.

Progressive relaxation. Another option involves teaching other relaxation strategies to the students, as recommended by Lopata and his colleagues (Lopata, 2003; Lopata, Nida, & Marable, 2006). These researchers point out that much aggressive behavior is preceded by various physical indicators of emotional arousal. Indicators include increased breathing and heart rate, changes in skin temperature, clenched fists, or sweaty face and palms. When teachers observe these indications of emotional arousal in older students, they should consider using a relaxation strategy that involves progressive tightening and loosening of the muscles, referred to as *progressive relaxation.*

In using this technique, ask the students to lie down flat on their back with arms out to their sides. Then ask them to look straight up at one spot on the ceiling, or to close their eyes, if they prefer. Next, ask them to tighten the muscles in their forearms by making a tight fist and to sustain that tension for a few seconds. After about five seconds, the student is told to relax. Next, the students should tighten the upper arms for several seconds, and then relax. You then progress through the major muscle groups in the body, including calf muscles, thighs, stomach muscles, chest muscles, and then all muscles at the same time. In each case they are asked to tighten these for several seconds and then release. This exercise takes only about two minutes to complete, but it reduces tension and stress that the students may be feeling and can thus prevent major behavior problems. Numerous research studies confirm that this strategy gives students control over their aggressive and oppositional behaviors (Kellner & Turtin, 1995; Lopata, 2003; Lopata, Nida, & Marable, 2006).

Other Strategies

More so than with other students, teachers working with students with oppositional behavior are well advised to implement a variety of class management tactics. Here are some additional strategies and accommodations to consider when working with these students. The list covers all grade levels, although some of the strategies need to be adapted for the age of the particular student (MACMH, 2007; MGH, 2006):

- Post the daily schedule of activities in the classroom so students know what to expect.
- Praise students whenever they respond positively. This includes collaborative efforts such as successfully sharing a computer with others.
- Make sure academic work is at their appropriate achievement level. When the work is too difficult, students become frustrated. When it is too easy, they become bored. Both reactions lead to behavioral problems in the classroom.
- Identify the student's good efforts even if the results are ultimately unsuccessful. Describe what the student did right and clearly indicate what needs to be corrected.

- Avoid infantile materials to teach basic skills. Materials should be positive and relevant to students' lives.

- Systematically teach social skills, including anger management, conflict resolution strategies, and how to be assertive in an appropriate manner. Discuss strategies that the students may use to calm themselves when they feel their anger escalating, such as the turtle technique or relaxation strategies. Do this when students are calm.

- Select instructional material that encourages student interaction. Students with oppositional behavior need to learn to talk to their peers and to adults in an appropriate manner. However, all cooperative learning activities must be carefully structured and monitored.

- Maximize the performance of low-performing students through the use of individualized instruction, cues, prompting, the breaking down of academic tasks, debriefing, coaching, and providing positive incentives.

- Structure activities so the student with oppositional behavior is not always left out or is the last one picked.

- Establish a place in the classroom (confidential and quiet) where the negotiation of conflicts can occur.

- Ask parents what strategies work at home.

WHAT ABOUT OPPOSITIONAL DEFIANT DISORDER (ODD)?

When children and teenagers have a persistent pattern of unruly behavior toward their parents and other authority figures, they may have oppositional defiant disorder (ODD). It occurs clinically in only about two to five percent of the population, although parents alone tend to report a higher percentage. Recognizing the difference between a youngster who is strong-willed and one with ODD is not easy. The key seems to be the *persistence* of the behavior.

Before puberty, the condition is more common in boys. After puberty, however, the occurrence is nearly equal in boys and girls. Because the disorder is associated with defiance, disobedience, and hostility directed toward authority figures, the following symptoms may regularly and consistently appear in someone with ODD:

- Being easily annoyed
- Refusing to comply with adult requests
- Having frequent temper tantrums
- Being resentful and vindictive
- Blaming others for mistakes
- Showing aggression toward peers
- Arguing with adults
- Using obscene language
- Deliberately annoying other people

ODD is a spectral disorder, ranging from mild to severe, so each of the these symptoms may be present in lesser or greater degrees depending on the individual. ODD often occurs along with other behavioral or mental health problems such as attention-deficit hyperactivity disorder (ADHD), anxiety, or depression. Because many of the symptoms of these disorders overlap, it may be difficult to distinguish ODD from those of other behavioral or mental health problems without professional observation and testing.

> *ODD is a spectral disorder, ranging from mild to severe, so each of the symptoms may be present in lesser or greater degrees depending on the individual.*

Development of ODD

The behaviors associated with ODD change with the child's age. By the time they are of school age, children with patterns of oppositional behavior tend to express their defiance with teachers and other adults, and they exhibit aggression toward their peers. As these students with ODD progress in school, they experience increasing peer rejection due to their poor social skills and aggression. These students may be more likely to misinterpret their peers' behavior as hostile, and they lack the skills to resolve social conflicts. In problem situations, students with ODD are more likely to resort to aggressive physical actions rather than verbal responses. They often do not recognize their role in peer conflicts and thus blame their peers (e.g., "He made me hit him."), and they usually fail to take responsibility for their own actions.

Treatment of ODD

ODD is a persistent disorder in that about 75 percent of children diagnosed with ODD continue to show the symptoms well into adolescence. Medication is not usually prescribed unless the ODD coexists with attention-deficit hyperactivity disorder (ADHD) or other disorders. Treatment usually includes group, individual, and/or family therapy, and education. Of these, individual therapy is the most common. Individual psychotherapy has been shown to be effective for some children, but no long-term studies have been done to date to determine its overall success rate. Therapy can provide an orderly daily schedule, support, consistent rules, discipline, and limits. It can also help train children to get along with others and modify their behaviors.

Parent management training (PMT) focuses on teaching the parents specific and more effective techniques for handling the child's opposition and defiance. Research has shown that parent management training is more effective than family therapy. One variation of PMT, known as Parent-Child Interaction Therapy (PCIT), appears to be helpful over the long term (Herschell, Calzada, Eyberg, & McNeil, 2002). A group of Australian researchers recently reported that families who were given a course of PCIT maintained their gains two years after the program ended (Nixon, Sweeney, Erickson, & Touyz, 2004).

A modified skills component of a treatment known as Dielectical Behavior Therapy (DBT) implemented in a group therapy format has shown to be effective with adolescents who display oppositional behavior. This approach helps group members learn to use specific skills that are broken down into four modules: core mindfulness skills, emotion regulation skills, interpersonal effectiveness skills, and distress tolerance skills. In one study of 32 adolescents, this treatment not only decreased negative behaviors but also increased positive behaviors (Nelson-Gray et al., 2006).

SUMMARY

Teachers should realize that students with oppositional behavior are likely to challenge their ability to effectively manage the classroom. Therefore, small successes are critically important for these students, and the teacher's flexibility is the key. Because some of the available disciplinary techniques may not work as well with students with oppositional behavior, teachers should consider what flexibility they can allow in their classroom rules and procedures. Certainly seeking ways to avoid triggers is critically important, and some of the various other strategies described in this chapter may also be effective. Only a small percentage of students have Oppositional Defiant Disorder (ODD) and many of the strategies in this chapter can be effective with them as well.

Developing Positive Self-Esteem

THE NATURE OF SELF-ESTEEM

Among the most effective teachers are those who realize that they are about the business of helping children and adolescents develop into young adults. To accomplish this, educators teach students curriculum content and skills and attempt to modify their behaviors so that they will move forward more successfully in life. Through the complex social interactions that occur in schools and classrooms, educators hope that their students will feel confident to meet the challenges that will face them after they leave school. Just how confident these students feel will depend largely on what they *know* about themselves, called *self-concept,* and how they *feel* about themselves, called *self-esteem.*

Self-Concept and Self-Esteem. There is research evidence indicating that we become aware of ourselves by the end of the second year after birth (Prudhomme, 2005). As we grow, we accumulate information about ourselves, such as, "I have curly hair, I am tall, I go to school, and I am a male." This growing body of knowledge forms our self-concept. We also begin to develop feelings about this information and these feelings form the basis of our self-esteem. Given the same set of facts, an individual who feels, "I hate having curly hair, I hate being tall, I hate going to school, and I hate being a male," will have a very different level of self-esteem than one who feels, "I like having curly hair, I like being tall, I like going to school, and I like being a male." Teachers and parents generally can not do much about

> *Self-concept and self-esteem are not the same. Self-concept is what we know about ourselves. Self-esteem is how we feel about ourselves.*

changing the facts that contribute to a student's self-concept, but they can often influence how the student feels about those facts. In other words, teachers can have a significant impact on changing a student's self-esteem.

The Power of Self-Esteem

If individuals see themselves as good people worthy of praise and respect, then they have high self-esteem. On the other hand, those who see themselves as flawed and not worthy of praise or respect have low self-esteem. How people act and the decisions they make are often motivated by their self-esteem. For example, students with positive self-esteem are more likely to have the confidence to pursue different challenges, whether it is studying to do well on a test, trying out for a sports team, or answering a question in class. These students are not overly afraid of failure. They recognize that failure is a natural part of life and whether they fail or succeed at something has little to do with their overall worth and ability as a person. Students with low self-esteem, however, are less likely to try their best at anything. They are so certain they will fail that they approach tasks and challenges with so much worry or fear that they are unable to concentrate. Some students consistently compensate for this anxiety by misbehaving (Ybrandt, 2007).

In this book, we have explained some of the major reasons why otherwise typical students are disruptive in schools. Students with frequent behavioral problems often have negative feelings about learning, their school, and sometimes about themselves. Because of their past misbehaviors, these students may have experienced rejection from their peers (and perhaps some teachers, too) and believe that they cannot succeed in school. Their misbehaviors have given them plenty of opportunities to look bad, and their school experiences have offered them few opportunities to look good. Consequently, they may very well have low self-esteem and low expectations for their own academic success. As we mentioned earlier, self-esteem is a major factor driving people's actions.

Cautions About Self-Esteem

Although research studies continue to show that raising self-esteem in students with behavior problems can be effective, some cautions are in order. Many people assume that high self-esteem leads directly to positive outcomes and that low self-esteem often results in undesirable behaviors. But this is not always the case. A nine-year longitudinal study of disruptive and non-disruptive boys, for example, showed an almost equal number of low and high self-esteem students in each group. It should be noted that no sustained interventions were undertaken with the disruptive boys during the course of the study (Tremblay, Saucier, & Tremblay, 2004).

The research on how self-esteem correlates with positive outcomes continues to be mixed. Contrary to popular belief, bullies do not typically suffer from low self-esteem, nor do those prone to drug and alcohol abuse. Also, raising self-esteem does not *automatically* translate into improved behavior or academic achievement. Sometimes, attempts to boost self-esteem in disruptive students may backfire if the focus is *primarily* on making them feel good about themselves. High self-esteem does not appear to prevent children from drinking, taking drugs, smoking, or engaging in early sex. However, motivation, achievement, and behavior *do* improve when self-esteem interventions center on instilling a sense of personal responsibility for acceptable social interactions and academic performance (Baumeister, Campbell, Krueger, & Vohs, 2005).

> *Raising self-esteem does not automatically translate into improved behavior or academic achievement. However, motivation, achievement, and behavior do improve when self-esteem interventions center on instilling personal responsibility for social behavior and academic performance.*

In this chapter, we focus on building and developing a student's self-esteem. We do so in the belief that a number of students who misbehave do so because a good portion of their interactions in school have focused on their misbehavior and not on their strengths or interests. With that in mind, let us examine first the research on how positive feelings about oneself can lead to more acceptable behavior and raise self-esteem. Then we will look at some strategies that support helping students develop a better sense of self. In doing so, however, we do *not* want to give the impression that raising self-esteem is the cure-all for solving all the behavioral and social problems that beset schools. Rather, what we offer are suggestions that are just *one* part of a multi-step approach to helping teachers be successful in dealing with troubled students.

Research on Self-Esteem

Hundreds of studies around the world over the past few decades have looked at the impact of self-esteem on human behavior. As we mentioned earlier, the results are mixed, but some common findings do emerge.

Factors Influencing Self-Esteem

Studies continue to show that age, gender, parenting, and socioeconomic status are major factors affecting one's self-esteem.

- **Age:** Self-esteem tends to grow steadily up until middle school. The transition of moving from the familiar and sheltered environment of elementary school to an unfamiliar setting with new social and intellectual demands has an impact on self-esteem. Self-esteem will either continue to grow after this period or begin to decline.

- **Gender:** Girls tend to be more susceptible to having low self-esteem than boys. This may be the result of increased social pressures that emphasize appearance rather than intelligence or athletic ability (Ge, Conger, & Elder, 1995).
- **Parenting.** Perhaps the most important influence on young people's levels of self-esteem are their parents—partly as a result of genetic inheritance and partly through the degree of love, concern, acceptance, and interest that they show to their children. Physical and sexual abuse are especially damaging to children's self-esteem (Emler, 2001).
- **Socioeconomic status:** Researchers have found that children from higher-income families usually have a better sense of self-esteem in the mid- to late-adolescence years than children from lower-income families (Twenge & Campbell, 2002). This may be due to the biases that parents reveal to their children about low socioeconomic people by their words or deeds.

Other Research Findings

A meta-analysis of many studies about self-esteem, including longitudinal studies, reveal the following (Emler, 2001).

- Low self-esteem is not a significant risk factor for delinquency, violence towards others (including child and partner abuse), drug use, alcohol abuse, educational under-attainment, or racism.
- Low self-esteem is a risk factor for suicide, suicide attempts, depression, teenage pregnancy, and victimization by bullies. However, in each study it was only one among several related risk factors.
- Although the causal connections remain unclear, low childhood self-esteem appears to be strongly associated with adolescent eating disorders, especially in females (Dunkley & Grilo, 2007; Granillo, Jones-Rodriguez, & Carvajal, 2005; Hill & Pallin, 1998).
- Young people with very high self-esteem are more likely than others to hold racist attitudes, reject social pressures from adults and peers, and engage in physically risky pursuits, such as drunk-driving or driving too fast.
- Students' self-esteem can be raised by parenting programs and planned interventions in school, but scientific understanding of why particular interventions are effective is limited.

It is worth noting that, although we encounter many students with low self-esteem, there are some students who have extremely high self-esteem who can also become behavioral problems. High self-esteem is far from being an unconditional benefit. Our language contains many unflattering words to describe people with high self-esteem, such as *arrogant, smug, conceited*, and *boastful.* To some degree, very high self-esteem can be as much a problem in need of treatment as exceptionally low self-esteem. However, most researchers agree that the number of students with low self-esteem far outnumber those with very high self-esteem.

Biology and Self-Esteem

Brain Imaging. In several of the previous chapters we discussed research studies that showed parts of the brain that were activated during emotional processing and decision making. Exactly what parts of the brain are involved in self-esteem remain a mystery. Several imaging studies have found that different parts of the brain were activated when subjects were doing internal reflection about themselves than when they were engaged in external problem solving (Goldberg, Harel, & Malach, 2006; Hannula, Simons, & Cohen, 2005). As shown in Figure 8.1,

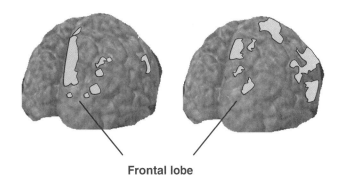

Frontal lobe

Figure 8.1 These representative images show the major areas of brain activation during self-reflection (left image) and during problem solving involving sensory processing (right image). Note how the degree of frontal lobe activity during self-reflection decreases noticeably when the brain's attention is diverted to processing sensory information.

Source: Adapted from Goldberg et al., 2006.

when the subjects shifted from introspection to solving the external problems, the brain areas involved in the internal reflection switched off as other brain regions were being recruited for problem solving. The implication here is that getting students involved with meaningful academic and other school activities may significantly reduce the amount of time their brain devotes to worrying about their self-esteem.

Pleasure and Anxiety Chemicals. Medical researchers have known for a long time that our emotional moods alter our body chemistry. Without going into the complex biochemistry of the body's natural mood-altering chemicals, we can reduce the process to looking at those chemicals likely to be present in greater amounts while experiencing pleasure or anxiety (see Figure 8.2).

Individuals who are enjoying an experience and who have positive views of themselves are likely to have an increase in the amount of *endorphins* in their body. Endorphins are the body's natural pain relievers, but they also produce a feeling of euphoria, have a mild

> *Getting students involved with meaningful academic and other school activities may significantly reduce the amount of time their brain devotes to worrying about their self-esteem.*

sedating effect, and reduce stress. They also enhance cognitive processing. While in this state, people are likely to be productive, pleasant, and attentive to learning.

Conversely, individuals who constantly reflect on their low self-esteem are often under stress. When that occurs, endorphin levels are low, but the amount of another natural chemical, called *cortisol,* increases. We discussed cortisol in previous chapters, and you may recall that it is the body's stress hormone. When cortisol is present in large amounts, individuals have a difficult time focusing on nonessential cognitive tasks, such as schoolwork, because they are preoccupied with the causes of the stress.

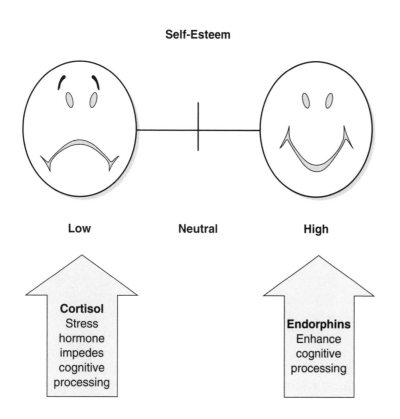

Self-Esteem

Low   Neutral   High

Cortisol
Stress
hormone
impedes
cognitive
processing

Endorphins
Enhance
cognitive
processing

Figure 8.2   Individuals with low self-esteem often are under stress and have higher than normal amounts of cortisol, a hormone that impedes nonessential cognitive processing. Those with high self-esteem often experience increases in endorphins that enhance cognitive processing as well as provide a feeling of euphoria.

Guidelines for Building Self-Esteem

Strategies designed to build self-esteem need to take the research findings into account if we expect positive student outcomes. Consequently, we should consider the following ideas, some of which have been mentioned in earlier chapters:

- **Offer genuine praise only.** Praise for a student must be genuine. Insincere praise can do more harm than good because it builds resentment and disrespect. Worse, exaggerated praise may cause students to believe that they can accomplish feats that are actually outside their capabilities, thereby guaranteeing failure.

- **Use students' names when addressing them.** When students hear their name, it reminds them that you know who they are as individuals, and this tactic can strengthen the student-teacher relationship.

- **Avoid assumptions.** Avoid making assumptions about a student's behavior, and separate the behavior from the person. Remember that most misbehavior is not directed against you *personally*.

- **Point out positives.** Mention positive aspects of a student's work and behavior. We will discuss more about this important approach later in this chapter.

- **Consider giving students a classroom responsibility.** Sometimes just giving a student with behavioral problems a regular classroom responsibility (e.g., taking attendance, passing out materials, setting up technology) is enough to dampen or eliminate misbehaviors.

- **Make failure positive.** Look for ways to help students turn a failure into a positive experience. This is one aspect of working with misbehaving students that is frequently overlooked. For example, if a student project or presentation did not go as planned, you could say: "You worked carefully, patiently, and had just this one step out of order. Once you fix that, you will be able to figure out the rest."

- **Include students in some decisions.** By allowing students to participate in making decisions about some aspects of class work (e.g., what kind of report to do or the selection of a guest speaker) gives them a sense of ownership and the realization that you have trust in their decisions.
- **Know the student.** We have mentioned in previous chapters about the value of getting to know more about your students, especially those with behavior problems. Ask about their other activities in school and about their life outside of school (without prying). We will discuss later in this chapter how this information can be a crucial part of an intervention strategy.
- **Use cooperative learning groups/peer-assisted learning.** Because poor self-esteem often includes low academic self-concept, studies show that including these students as part of cooperative learning groups increases their feelings of academic competence, thereby decreasing undesirable behaviors (Hänze & Berger, 2007). Peer-assisted learning also improves social behaviors and builds self-esteem and self-concept (Ginsburg-Block, Rohrbeck, & Fantuzzo, 2006).

What follows next are several practical techniques that have been shown to help teachers design interventions for troubled students with low self-esteem. They will not work with all students who have behavioral problems, nor will they work with the same student all the time. However, these interventions have been successful on many occasions and are definitely worth considering.

BUILDING A NEW PERSPECTIVE ON THE TROUBLED STUDENT: THE STRENGTH-BASED ASSESSMENT

What Is Strength-Based Assessment?

Teachers who choose to help students build a more positive self-esteem need to have some insights into the home life, personality, after-school activities, and hobbies of these students. Recently, the concept of strength-based assessment has been recommended as a means of gaining those insights. Strength-based assessment involves a coordinated attempt to identify strengths within a student's environment in an effort to find a way to reach troubled students. Michael Epstein of the University of Nebraska originated this concept and became an early proponent (Epstein, 1998, 1999; Rudolph & Epstein, 2000).

Epstein recognized a weakness in the assessment procedures for students with significant behavior problems. Traditional behavior management assessments and planning options were rooted in identifying behavioral deficits rather than strengths. Instead, Epstein shifted from the traditional behavior management process for students with behavior problems to identifying strengths in the student's home or environment that could be the basis for more effective interventions (Epstein, 1999).

In the typical assessment and remediation plan for most students with behavior problems, one could find an assessment of intelligence, and perhaps an assessment of academic achievement. One could also anticipate that these data would contain an abundance of negative findings. Epstein, in contrast, recommended that teachers and educators seek to identify the strengths that benefit a student with severe behavioral problems. According to Epstein (2000), such a strength-based assessment may involve a chat with a student and a discussion with the parents on the student's overall contextual environment. Figure 8.3 presents a series of questions that could be included in such a strength-based assessment interview with the student.

These questions may be easily adapted for use in an interview with parents about their child's behavior. Note that these questions do not involve documenting behavioral concerns so much as seeking positive attributes in the life of the child. The interview itself should be open, and every effort should be made to foster a comfortable atmosphere for the student. In this context, surprising findings of potential strengths may be unearthed which go beyond the litany of deficits that result from traditional assessment practices. Here is an example.

A Case Study: Strength-Based Assessment on Noshawn

Noshawn was a fifth-grade student with significant behavioral problems. His teacher, Ms. Fore, counted the number of times that Noshawn presented a disciplinary problem in the class. These instances included each time Ms. Fore had to discipline Noshawn, as well as each time Noshawn did not have his homework completed. After a three-day baseline period, Ms. Fore sought some assistance in managing Noshawn's behavior problems. Within a week, the local school psychologist completed a psychological report of Noshawn and recommended that Ms. Fore consider conducting a strength-based assessment in addition to the usual academic assessments. Ms. Fore used the student interview in Figure 8.3 and a telephone interview with Noshawn's mother, asking essentially

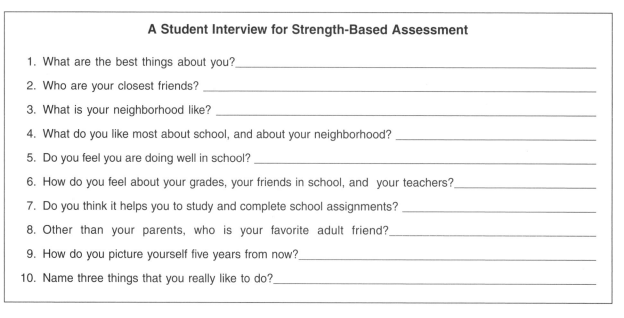

A Student Interview for Strength-Based Assessment

1. What are the best things about you?_____

2. Who are your closest friends? _____

3. What is your neighborhood like? _____

4. What do you like most about school, and about your neighborhood? _____

5. Do you feel you are doing well in school? _____

6. How do you feel about your grades, your friends in school, and your teachers?_____

7. Do you think it helps you to study and complete school assignments? _____

8. Other than your parents, who is your favorite adult friend?_____

9. How do you picture yourself five years from now?_____

10. Name three things that you really like to do?_____

Figure 8.3   This is an example of a strength-based assessment used with a student who has behavioral problems. See the Appendix for a black-line master version.

the same questions. Here are the insights from both the traditional assessment and the strength-based assessment for Noshawn.

Conclusions from a Traditional Assessment on Noshawn

- Has lower than average IQ (IQ = 87)
- Sent to in-school suspension five times in three months
- Had two fights with other students
- Has poor academic skills in reading and all reading-dependent subject areas
- Has turned in homework only rarely
- Occasionally manifests aggression and other bullying behavior

Conclusions from a Strength-Based Assessment for Noshawn

- Plays basketball with a minister in the community several afternoons each week
- Functions on grade level in mathematics
- Is sportsmanlike on the basketball court under adult supervision
- Mother is actively involved and comes to all IEP meetings; will support interventions at home, and check homework if requested.

Note how the strength-based assessment offers possible connections with Noshawn, whereas the traditional assessment is merely a catalogue of problems offering no potential solutions. Teachers and parents are often frustrated when they are presented with such a catalogue of negative findings. When reviewing these findings, some veteran teachers may feel as if they could have written the evaluation based merely on their preliminary observations—such is the consistency of this negative litany of deficits. Youngsters with serious behavior problems are often similar in their areas of deficit, and behavioral deficits often lead to or coexist with academic deficits. Thus, the traditional assessment rarely presents any revealing findings that suggest positive intervention possibilities (Epstein, 2000).

In contrast, the conclusions from the strength-based assessment provide some options for reaching Noshawn. A strength-based assessment poses a variety of questions not typically asked in traditional assessments, and many of those questions focus on relationships that are meaningful for the student. Epstein (1998, 2000) maintains that, unlike traditional assessment, strength-based assessment frequently offers something positive for parents and teachers to discuss about the student. This factor alone can enhance the relationship between the parents and the teacher, as well as between the teacher and the student.

In the case of Noshawn, the strength-based assessment indicated several possible strengths in Noshawn's environment, including an involved, caring mother and a local minister who was spending considerable time with Noshawn and other youth in the community. Ms. Fore decided to build an intervention strategy that used these strengths. She requested the mother's permission to invite the minister to a meeting. In that meeting the mother, the minister, Noshawn, and Ms. Fore discussed together Noshawn's behavior and that little homework was being completed. The minister agreed that, each weekday right after the basketball game, he and Noshawn would look over the homework assignment together. The mother also agreed to do the same.

As her contribution, Ms. Fore asked Noshawn to start a homework agenda that Ms. Fore and the mother would review and sign each day. To address the behavior problems in class, the minister said that he would be happy to get a call from Ms. Fore and that he would then discuss the behavior problem with Noshawn.

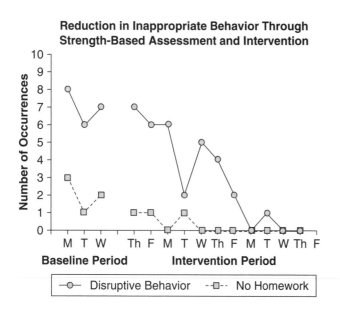

Figure 8.4 The graph compares Noshawn's inappropriate behaviors from the three-day baseline period through the two-week intervention period using strength-based assessment.

This simple and straightforward intervention was effective. Figure 8.4 shows the baseline and intervention data for Noshawn. The behavior problems in class were reduced over time and the problem of homework completion was solved virtually overnight. It is clear that a strength-based assessment in this case provided Ms. Fore with the insight she needed to reach Noshawn. Because this concept of strength-based assessment is relatively new, we recommend that teachers review this research and use this tool in the classroom for students with disciplinary problems.

MOTIVATION AND ATTRIBUTION RETRAINING

Motivation Research and Attribution Theory

Many teachers bemoan the lack of motivation displayed by some students with behavior problems. Yet it is not easy finding research-based interventions that directly address student motivation. In part, this is a result of the disassociation between teachers' terminology and researchers' terminology. When researchers investigate motivational issues, they typically use the concept of "attribution theory."

For most of us, motivation is related to the notion that what we do has a direct impact on our world and, thus, involves the control that we believe we have over our own environment. If we believe that behaviors such as hard work, demanding study, and appropriate social conduct lead to success, then we are motivated to do that work and study. For this reason, the majority of students in school today are motivated to study hard and behave appropriately.

Unfortunately, many students with behavioral problems and low self-esteem believe that they cannot exercise much influence or control over their world at all, and thus, they are not motivated to improve their behavior (Salend & Sylvestre, 2005). These students attribute control over their fate to factors outside themselves over which they exercise little influence. For example, if students believe that they are inherently "weird," or "uncontrollable," they are very likely to act that way, and misbehavior is often the result. Likewise, if students perceive that they have little control over their classroom environment, they will emotionally withdraw from that environment, even though they are forced to physically remain in the classroom. This situation results in their lack of attention to what is going on in class and becomes frustrating for the teacher.

At other times, students seek some control in negative ways, as in the countercontrol examples we discussed in Chapter 7. Recall that some students feel most influential in their environments exactly when they misbehave because that is when the teacher's focus is totally on them. The most influential factor in this scenario is the students' perception of who or what controls their environment. Thus, the attributions students make about their environment play a critical role in influencing their behavior.

Many students with behavior problems believe that they cannot exercise much influence over their world and, thus, are not motivated to improve their behavior. When teachers help students change this attitude, both behavior and academic achievement improve.

A body of research over the last several decades has investigated students' attributions of the factors they believe control their world. This research focuses on the factors to which students attribute their success or failure in various situations such as classroom tasks, social events at school, or getting along at home (Bryan, 1986; Masood, Turner, & Baxter, 2007; Salend & Sylvestre, 2005). We all attribute events to various causes, and for most of us, these attributions influence our subsequent actions and behaviors. We seek to behave in a way consistent with our beliefs. For example, Masood, Turner, and Baxter (2007) studied parents' attributions for the cause of their children's disabilities. They found that parents who believed their child's disability was related to something that the parents had done developed more negative relationships with those children. Clearly, the negative attribution by the parents lead to a negative result—an impaired parent-child relationship.

Most of the attribution research in recent years has concentrated on academic tasks and not on inappropriate behavior. The research has shown that training in appropriate attributions can lead to increased effort on academic work (Salend & Sylvestre, 2005). However, Bryan (1986) used attribution training to modify classroom behaviors of a group of students with learning disabilities, showing not only that attributions can have an impact on behavior, but also that changing the students' attributions can modify their behavior. Because students with behavior problems often attribute their problems to factors other than their own behavior, teachers should consider interventions that change the students' attributions.

To accomplish this, teachers first need to know their students' attributions. By using the strength-based assessment interview (see Figure 8.3) that we previously discussed, the students' answers to questions 4, 5, 6, and 7 may indicate that the students attribute problems in their relationships in school to factors other than their own behavior and efforts. Also, some casual questions from the teacher might reveal the degree to which students make attributions to outside forces rather than to their own efforts. For example, when asked why they frequently get disciplinary referrals to the office, students with behavioral problems might say that "The teacher hates me" rather than "I lose my temper and misbehave in class." Likewise, if students struggling academically are asked what caused a failing grade, they may say that "The work was too hard" or "We didn't cover it in class" rather than "I should have studied more." These students are prime candidates for attribution retraining.

Educators are discovering that when they specifically intervene to modify the attributions of students with behavior problems, their behavior improves (Salend & Salvestre, 2005). Although this technique is similar to the examples of self-talk to curb behavior that were presented in Chapter 3, the focus in the following example is specifically on changing the students' attributions, resulting in a positive impact on their behavior.

A Case Study of Attribution Retraining

In her 18 years of teaching ninth-grade science, Ms. Draton had never experienced a ninth-grader like Joshua. Joshua was of average intelligence, though he would often say things about himself like, "I'm just dumb!" Still, Ms. Draton knew that Joshua could easily succeed in the lessons with some effort—an effort which he apparently was not willing to make. Joshua's older sister had been in Ms. Draton's class only two years earlier, and she was a class star who subsequently became one of the academic leaders in the school. Ms. Draton believed that Joshua may have compared himself with his sister and, believing that he was less academically able, developed a negative attitude toward himself and his abilities. In a previous parent meeting, Joshua's mother (the father did not live at home) had even made that comparison between Joshua's lack of school success and the success of his older sister. Ms. Draton feared that such comparisons may have been made in the home in an effort to motivate Joshua, but, in reality, they had the opposite effect of lowering his self-esteem.

Moreover, Joshua's poor grades were overshadowed by his inappropriate behaviors in class. For example, he entered the class and often placed his head on his desk for most of the period, apparently asleep. Ms. Draton called on him in class to get his participation, but it never seemed to work. He just laid his head down again as soon as the teacher continued with the lesson. However, he was never really asleep. If anyone mentioned his name in class, even jokingly, he immediately lifted his head to curse at them, leading to repeated referrals to the principal's office. Ms. Draton decided that something else had to be done to directly address the root of the problem—Joshua's beliefs about his lack of ability in school. Because she knew of the attribution research, she began a behavioral improvement plan based on changing Joshua's beliefs about himself and improving his inappropriate behaviors.

To start, Ms. Draton collected data on two target behaviors: the number of negative comments Joshua made about himself and his schoolwork and the number of times he put his head down in class. Next she began the intervention with a private conversation with Joshua, as follows.

Ms. Draton:	Joshua, I want you to do better in science than you are doing. I'm not sure if you know this, but science is one area in which boys almost always do well.
Joshua:	I bet my sister got straight As! She's smarter than me in everything.
Ms. Draton:	I don't remember how well your sister did, but I do want you to know that you can do very well in science with some more effort.
Joshua:	I'm not that smart. I don't do school work that good.
Ms. Draton:	I disagree, and that type of statement is exactly what I want to talk to you about.
Joshua:	What do you mean?
Ms. Draton:	First of all, I really don't care how smart others might be. What I want to know is, do you think you're smart?
Joshua:	Yeah, about some things, I guess. Not school.
Ms. Draton:	There you go again, making another negative statement about yourself in school. Do you think that is wise?
Joshua:	What do you mean?
Ms. Draton:	Do you think that what people say about themselves is important? Is it possible that sometimes we begin to believe what we say about ourselves somehow?
Joshua:	I guess. I'm not sure.
Ms. Draton:	Well, I think what we say to ourselves can be important because if we say something enough, we begin to believe it. Joshua, if I looked in the mirror every morning and said to myself, "You are an ugly 39-year-old school teacher and you shouldn't try to put on makeup and make yourself attractive," do you think I would eventually believe it?
Joshua:	You're not ugly.
Ms. Draton:	Thank you for that, but the question is, do you think that I'd begin to believe what I said to myself if I said it often enough?

Joshua:	Yeah, I guess.
Ms. Draton:	Then it is important to consider what we say about ourselves, isn't it? We need to say more positive things about ourselves, don't we?
Joshua:	What do you mean?
Ms. Draton:	Well, I should get up in the morning, look in the mirror, and say something like, "You look pretty good for a 39-year-old teacher, so get that face on and go to school and enjoy your students today!" If I said that to myself, do you think I'd enjoy my day more than if I said the things I said before?
Joshua:	Yeah. You'd do better at school.
Ms. Draton:	That's right, I would, and I'd enjoy school more. Now let's talk about you in science class. What do you need to say to yourself about science?
Joshua:	I guess I could try to be as smart as my sister was in science. So, I could do better, huh?
Ms. Draton:	You certainly could, but I want you to make a much stronger, more bold statement than that. You are a very strong young man, so I want a very strong statement. I want you to say, "I can do well in science, and I'll study hard so I can succeed!" Repeat that with me. (Together they say: "I can do well in science, and I'll study hard so I can succeed!")
Ms. Draton:	Let's say it again. (They repeat the phrase together and then she asks Joshua to repeat the phrase alone.)
Ms. Draton:	This will be your "bold statement," since it is a bold, positive statement about yourself. Repeat it one more time please, so you can remember it.
Joshua:	"I can do well in science, and I'll study hard so I can succeed!"
Ms. Draton:	That's great. Now, Joshua, I notice many times that you lay your head on your desk. You can't do really well in science with your head on the desk, can you?
Joshua:	I'm still listening when my head is down!
Ms. Draton:	I believe you are listening when your head is down, but you will still not do as well laying your head down as when you watch me and watch what I'm showing the class on the board, will you?
Joshua:	I guess not.
Ms. Draton:	So, every time you lay your head down, I'm going to walk over to your desk and say your name gently to help you remember to pay attention. When you hear that, it will remind you to lift your head up, pay attention, and say that bold statement quietly to yourself. Can you do that?
Joshua:	I don't have to say it out loud, do I?

Ms. Draton: No, you don't. I just want you to say it silently to yourself. It will be our secret statement. OK?

Joshua: I guess so.

Ms. Draton: Good, I think saying that bold statement can help you remember to study more, and I believe your grades will go up.

Joshua: I hope so.

Ms. Draton: Trust me, Joshua. They will go up, and you can do very well in this science class using that bold statement.

Note that in this discussion Ms. Draton focused Joshua on his attending behavior as well as his attributions on his poor work in science class. She was addressing not only the irritating behavior problem (i.e., a student who pretends to sleep in class), but also the underlying cause (his negative attributions based on the belief that he could never do as well as his sister in any school subject).

Ms. Draton continued to count the number of times he placed his head on his desk, as well as the number of negative, self-deprecating statements Joshua made about himself in relation to his schoolwork. As shown in Figure 8.5, Joshua's behaviors changed within three weeks of beginning this intervention. During the baseline period, he was putting his head down at least eight times during science class, but that decreased to almost none during the intervention (solid line on graph). The number of negative statements Joshua made about himself also decreased over time (dashed line on graph).

Along with this intervention, Ms. Draton made every effort to find times to praise Joshua in front of the class (without embarrassing him, because ninth-grade students are highly sensitive to the perceptions of their peer group). In one instance, Joshua assisted another

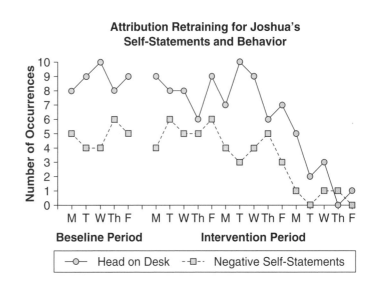

Figure 8.5 The graph shows the decrease in frequency of Joshua placing his head on the desk and his negative self-statements from the one-week baseline period through the three-week intervention period.

student with a lab project during the intervention period, and afterward, Ms. Draton called on him to do part of that lab demonstration for the entire class. Activities of this nature are the focus of the next strategy in this chapter. Such activities, coupled with the attribution intervention, assisted Joshua in curbing his non-attending behavior and improving his attributions. As a result, his motivation for learning science and his behavior in class both improved.

The "Shine My Light" Strategy

All students need attention from time to time, and teachers must often provide that attention for either positive accomplishments or negative behaviors. In the previous case study, you may have noticed how Ms. Draton found a way to focus the class's attention on Joshua's accomplishment. This tactic provides just the attention that some students require, and the "shine my light" strategy involves providing exactly that type of opportunity for positive attention. This strategy offers a student with low self-esteem and behavior problems a chance to be proud of some accomplishment or hobby.

> The "Shine My Light" strategy offers students with behavior problems a chance to be proud of some accomplishment or hobby.

As discussed numerous times in this book, some students will find ways to gain attention through inappropriate behavior. One thing teachers and parents can do to fill the attention needs of students with behavior problems is to create ways for the students to receive attention for their positive accomplishments. In other words, we should seek ways for students to "shine their light!" Favorable attention from classmates and the teacher also assists in developing a positive self-esteem over the long term and thus tends to reduce behavioral problems overall.

Students with learning disabilities, behavioral problems, and attention-deficit hyperactivity disorder are particularly prone to lower than normal self-esteem. When considering these and other factors that place students at risk for poor behavior (e.g., troubled home life, poverty, etc.), the development of a strong, positive self-esteem is the single biggest factor in fostering resiliency in these students. Consequently, whenever parents and teachers assist an at-risk student in fostering a hobby, activity, or talent that can reap positive attention, they enhance the student's self-esteem as well as decrease behavior problems.

Beginning a "Shine My Light" Strategy in the Classroom

Before you begin this strategy, consider a few simple guidelines.

- **Help the student select an area of interest.** Obviously, you cannot get a student to practice at the local recreation league or the go-cart race track because these are after-school activities. However, you can encourage students to explore other areas of interest. For instance, if a student shows an interest in painting, you could assist in arranging special visits by the art teacher. Project assignments in class could offer artwork as one option for demonstrating understanding of the subject matter. You may be able to use a student's interest and ability in art to make that student a tutor for others on various art projects in a variety of subject areas.

Mentors can likewise foster a student's hobby or interest. You may recall from the adult mentoring example described in Chapter 5 that the mentor fostered an interest in trains and train wrecks that lead to a class presentation by James.

- **Consider what options the school and community offer.** For a student with an interest in music, band may be a course that you recommend. An interest in karate, basketball, gymnastics, swimming, cooking, or automotive engines may be encouraged by carefully selecting related reading material for classroom work. Helping students find reading materials in their hobby or areas of interest may also result in increased and improved reading skills for troubled students.

- **Talk with other teachers about a student's interests.** In early childhood, a number of hobbies turn out to be short-term interests, particularly prior to puberty. However, somewhere around the fifth grade, many individuals develop the interests and hobbies that stay with them for a lifetime. Watch closely and talk with the student's previous teachers about any interest or hobbies they may have noticed. Encourage the development of hobbies covertly, not overtly. For students with behavior problems, overt pressure from parents or teachers to develop a hobby can be counterproductive, so subtle encouragement is the key. For example, you could mention to students that the community has a soccer league or a scout troop for their age group. Almost any hobby will do if it provides the students with something that they can be proud of, and occasionally demonstrate, for others.

- **Take the time to show interest in the student's hobby.** For a student who is taking karate lessons, try to find the time some afternoon to drop by the karate school, perhaps with the parents, to observe the student's practice. This bit of extra attention can go a long way in working with students with low self-esteem and certainly will endear you to the parents.

- **Be aware of the costs involved.** Any expense associated with the hobby or interest area should be considered. Identify, if possible, a hobby that can be done inexpensively and with other students (e.g., shooting hoops in the yard, tennis, stamp collecting, etc.). For students with behavioral issues, finding an inexpensive hobby or interest that fosters appropriate social interaction can provide a timely opportunity to practice social skills.

- **Encourage public performance of skills.** Identify hobbies that offer regular opportunities to show one's skill (e.g., dance recitals, science or social studies projects in school, musical performances, talent shows, etc.). The public performance of skills is the aspect that enhances self-concept, and if students are willing, such public performances should be encouraged. Also, you should realize that students at certain ages may not be willing to show off their strategy, but even for some of these students, the shine my light strategy can still be a benefit in terms of building self-esteem.

A "Shine My Light" Planning Activity

In order to develop a list of options for particular students, you may find the planning sheet in Figure 8.6 helpful. Note that the first part of the sheet involves collecting some information and observations on the students' behavior as well as their hobbies and interests. Also, in contemplating the use of this strategy, you and the parent should consider the subtle hints that may reveal a student's interests. How does the student spend free time? Even video game preferences may provide subtle clues. For instance, does the student prefer video games that challenge the mind with mysterious activities, offer sports and games, or allow one to fly spaceships?

A Teacher's and Parent's Planning Guide for the "Shine My Light" Strategy

I. The Student's Behavior and Interests

Identify a student who has demonstrated problem behaviors in the classroom. Consider first, the types of behavior that have been demonstrated.

1. What behaviors suggest the student needs attention? Describe it here. _____

2. Has this student demonstrated this problem behavior before? If so, when?_____

3. What was the student's primary motivation for this behavior? Did this result in laughter from the rest of the class? _____

4. Does the misbehavior itself suggest a particular task or a particular type of attention the student would like? _____

5. Does the student's interest show in his or her academic work in the class (e.g., a child who always writes stories about bicycles)? _____

6. What do others (e.g., parents, peers, and other teachers) say about the student's interests?_____

7. What does the student identify as hobbies or areas of interest? _____

II. Exploration of Options

List below any possible hobbies/interest areas identified above.

_____   _____   _____

_____   _____   _____

1. Which of these options are the least expensive? _____

2. Are all of the options available, given the expense associated with almost any hobby?_____

3. Which options take advantage of community resources (recreation leagues, ball fields, etc.)?_____

4. Which options, if any, parallel the interests of other siblings? _____

5. Is some formal or informal training available to the student for any of these options (e.g., band training at school)? _____

6. Can family or other students in the class provide informal training in this area at no cost?_____

7. Do these options offer regular opportunities for this student to demonstrate the newly acquired skill? _____

8. Based on this, which is the best option to explore? _____

Figure 8.6   This is a sample planning guide that teachers and parents can use to help students select a hobby or area of interest as part of the "Shine My Light" strategy. See the Appendix for a black-line master of this guide.

Clues to a student's interests may be anywhere. Some students misbehave in school by always being out of their seat. But why? The student may be attempting to do preferred tasks. Does the student stop work and go to the computers in the back of the room for computer work or games? Does the student head for a DVD or other technology in the room, or to the reading corner to find a particular type of book? Does the student complete assignments in science or choose to play in the science corner instead of doing other assigned tasks? These types of misbehaviors can suggest particular areas in which a student is interested.

The next part of the planning guide involves noting ways to explore the identified areas of interest as well as any potential barriers to such exploration. Considerations here include the expense associated with the hobby and what resources are available within the school and community. Resources that allow the student to explore a hobby or interest area are important, and the planning guide will help you and the student explore options more completely prior to selecting something. Youths often need only a small amount of encouragement to assist them in exploring fields of interest to them. You may wish to use the planning sheet with them periodically (perhaps once every six months) until a lasting hobby is found—one the student will do without prompting from the parent or teacher. Finally, you may also wish to share this form with the parent for planning purposes.

Recommend the "Shine My Light" Strategy to Parents

The "shine my light" strategy can potentially be much broader than just a classroom intervention. Because teachers are occasionally in a position to make suggestions to parents on child-rearing issues, this is a great tactic to recommend to parents. Children's behavioral problems often have an impact on everyone in the family. For children with overt and consistent behavior problems, it is all too easy for the entire family to focus the majority of their child-rearing effort on the disability or behavior problem. This approach may give the child a sense of defeatism—the belief that, "I can't do this or that because of my disability." Such a narrow focus may deprive other siblings of the attention and parental time that they also require. Moreover, parents whose sole focus is on their child's behavioral problem often miss the joy that these children can provide for the family.

In talking to PTAs and other parent groups, we frequently recommend that parents of children with disabilities, behavioral problems, or other developmental delay issues identify a hobby or a talent to foster with the child. Even an inexpensive hobby (e.g., karate lessons, sports, dancing, playing a musical instrument) can be a point of great pride for children and adolescents, and such activities can provide an identity of which they can be justifiably proud. Specifically, karate seems to be worshiped by today's youth, based on the many movies where the hero uses this technique during the climactic duel at the end. Classes which allow children and adolescents to develop this discipline give them a point of pride and a focus for their identity that can drastically modify inappropriate behaviors. If cost is an obstacle, various self-defense classes are often taught for free in youth programs at the YMCA and other community organizations. Again, any hobby that gives a youngster bragging rights to some special knowledge or skill may work to enhance self-esteem and provide positive attention for those youths who need it.

Caring parents as well as involved teachers will look for just this type of opportunity to give students a hobby in which they will grow. One recent Hollywood movie, *October Sky*, focused on a caring teacher who encouraged a student's interest in rockets as an escape from an uninspiring life in a West Virginia coal mining town. The student began with small rockets fired from a local field and ended with a career in the exploration of outer space. Hobbies can create an identity or even a profession for a troubled youth. They also allow individuals who may otherwise seek attention in less than positive ways to shine their light in a more acceptable way.

SUMMARY

How we feel about ourselves (self-esteem) has a great influence on our behavior. Students with low self-esteem feel that they cannot accomplish much in school and can respond to this sense of inadequacy by frequently misbehaving. They often attribute their failures to outside forces over which they believe they have little or no control. By finding ways to change these notions through building a more positive self-esteem and attribute retraining, teachers can greatly help these students be more successful both in and out of school. In many cases, these interventions may be the key that unlocks the potential of otherwise troubled youth.

Chapter 9

Putting It All Together

In the previous chapters, we have discussed what recent research in neuroscience says about how the brain influences behavior. We have also suggested ways in which this research may be used to determine the kinds of approaches that would best help educators manage disruptive behavior and help troubled students become more successful in school. Our suggestions have included strategies for controlling impulses and inappropriate social behavior, self-verbalization, dealing with unruly boys, developing productive adult and peer relationships, coping with students with oppositional behaviors, and improving students' self-esteem.

In this final chapter, we discuss how all these topics and strategies are tied together under one overarching concept: The *educational climate* in which students with behavior problems spend their days. Educational climate is the umbrella that encompasses both *school climate* and *classroom climate*. We will focus here mainly on classroom climate.

What is Classroom Climate?

Classroom climate deals directly with the happiness and overall comfort level of students in the classroom context. It has been discussed widely in the educational literature for the last decade or so, and most experts agree that students perform much better when their learning environment is comfortable, when they are happy, and when they are relatively free from stress. Specifically, classroom climate deals with the emotional impact of a particular learning environment on the individuals in that environment. The following questions should be considered:

- Are students and teachers happy to be together in the classroom?
- Do they all seem to enjoy themselves most of the time?

- Are academics and social learning being stressed in a positive, enjoyable way?
- Does everyone feel valued in the class?
- Do all students feel that they can contribute meaningfully to the class?

As these questions indicate, classroom climate bears a strong relationship to how all students experience their overall school endeavors. Some researchers have suggested that classroom climate is a particularly important variable with minority students (Garcia & Ortiz, 2006; McKinley, 2006), but a positive classroom climate will result in improved behavior for most students (Freiberg, 1998; Goleman, 2006; Hansen & Childs, 1998; Sterling, 1998).

The term *school climate* refers to the relationships among students and all their teachers, the various relationships among teachers, and those among teachers and administrators. Schools are open social systems that are in constant flux. The beliefs, values, and attitudes of the students, teachers, parents, administrators, and others determine how they interact with and influence each other. School climate also involves establishing predictable expectations for social behavior, emphasizing academic success, fostering mutual trust and respect, and ensuring personal safety.

Goleman (2006) suggests that school climate is the sum of all positive and negative interactions among all participants in the school, and that the overall tone of those interactions is largely influenced by the unspoken habits and norms that guide the behavior of those individuals. So school climate involves how various participants "feel" and "sense" their environment and what they perceive to be their "worth" to others in that environment. When all of these perceptions are positive, a person can feel happy in that situation. The school climate, therefore, has a major impact on classroom climate.

The Biology of Happiness

Some readers may be wondering whether we have lost our way because we are discussing here the concept of happiness. This is, after all, a book about how the brain influences behavior, and one thing that is emerging from social cognitive neuroscience is the significant role that a feeling of happiness plays in determining the way we view and interact with our world. If we are serious about learning how the brain works and about using that information to improve teaching and learning, then we need to understand the biology and behavioral impact of happiness.

What Brain Scans Show

Happiness and sadness are processed differently. Although psychologists have long recognized the positive effects that being happy can have on an individual's performance and behavior, it is only in recent years that the technology of neuroscience has allowed researchers to see how happiness is expressed in the brain. In 1995, one of the first major studies using PET scans discovered that emotional opposites, like happiness and sadness, resulted in different patterns of brain activity. Happiness produced highly activated areas in the left frontal lobe but only low activation in the amygdala. Sadness, on the other hand, was centered more in the limbic area with high amygdala activity (George et al., 1995). These areas are outlined in Figure 9.1.

In a similar but expanded study, Damasio and his colleagues used PET scans on 39 subjects and found that happiness, sadness, fear, and anger each stimulated different combinations of brain areas. Their results confirmed that happiness stimulated the left prefrontal lobe region while sadness produced high activity in the front region of the limbic area (Damasio et al., 2000). The

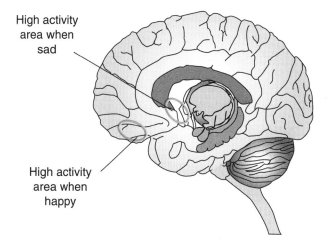

Figure 9.1   Happiness and sadness activate different brain regions. The more highly activated areas are shown here. Happiness activates a region in the left prefrontal lobe, while sadness activates a region at the front of the limbic area.

Source: Adapted from Damasio et al., 2000.

researchers suggested that the main reason these four emotions feel different when we experience them is because they involve different brain regions that trigger different combinations of neurochemical reactions. Subsequent studies using PET, fMRIs, and electroencephalograms confirm these findings (Johnstone, van Reekum, Oakes, & Davidson, 2006; Kringelbach, 2005).

You now have the explanation as to why we have included this discussion in the book. You will recall from Chapter 1 that the frontal lobe plays a crucial role in attention and in the processing of new information. If happiness activates this brain area, then the likelihood that students will give attention and process information in the lesson significantly increases. Conversely, the likelihood of disruptive behavior occurring under these conditions significantly decreases.

Happiness and trust. Another interesting aspect of these studies is the connection that the brain makes between happiness and trust. An fMRI study looked at how the brain is activated when dealing with trustworthiness, happiness, sadness, and anger. Not surprisingly, the researchers found that trustworthiness was positively correlated with happiness and negatively correlated with anger and sadness (Winston, Strange, O'Doherty, & Dolan, 2002). Translated to a school setting, these findings mean that students are much more likely to trust a teacher who is happy—and who, by extension, provides an environment where the students are happy—than a teacher who is not.

The Brain's Happiness Chemicals

Researchers have studied the neurochemistry of sadness and depression far longer and more intensely than that of happiness. Although a large portion of research on emotions has focused on the negative, it is only recently that researchers have begun to examine the chemical mechanisms at work when we are in a positive frame of mind. Studies are now looking at the chemicals that circulate in the prefrontal cortex, the area that shows high activation during happiness.

There is research evidence that some people are predisposed to being happy more often than others. Exactly what is the physical difference, though, between a left prefrontal cortex that is predisposed to happiness and one that is not? It most likely has to do with neurotransmitters, the chemicals that carry signals from one neuron to the next. Figure 9.2 shows that as an electrical nerve impulse traveling along a neuron reaches the end of the fiber (called an *axon*), it causes sacs (called *vesicles*) to release neurotransmitters. These chemicals travel across the tiny synapse between neurons and bind to receptor sites in adjacent neurons that are specifically designed to receive only those molecules. This activity stimulates the receiving neuron to continue the electrical signal. After the neurotransmitters bind to the receptors, they return to the original neuron through the transporter areas and reenter the vesicles for later use.

Although the prefrontal cortex is awash in many neurotransmitters, including dopamine, serotonin, glutamate, GABA, and more, researchers believe that dopamine is especially important when it comes to feelings of joy and happiness. Although other neurochemicals called opiates (such as endorphins) are also involved in these complex pleasure and desire cycles, dopamine facilitates the transfer of signals associated with positive emotions between the left prefrontal area and the emotional centers in the limbic area of the brain. People with a sensitive version of neural receptors that accept dopamine tend to have better moods, and researchers are actively studying the relationship between dopamine levels and feelings of euphoria and depression. Dopamine pathways may be especially important in aspects of happiness associated with moving toward some sort of goal, such as being successful in school and in personal relationships. When we do things that bring happiness (e.g., excelling at work or play, making friends, being part of a team, helping the needy), dopamine is released, giving us a sense of pleasure and increasing the possibility that we will do those things again.

> Dopamine is a neurotransmitter important in aspects of happiness and closely associated with moving toward some sort of goal, such as being successful in school and in personal relationships.

Happiness is transitory. Generating positive school and class climates takes *purposeful* action. Our genetic makeup is such that happiness, though designed to materialize under lots of circumstances, is also designed to evaporate. If the pleasure that comes from a particular achievement never ended, then we would not need to do it again. Back in the hunter-gatherer days of our development, if impressing others with a display of skill or courage left you permanently high, your stature would slowly fall as more restless rivals outdid you. Thus, among natural selection's mottoes is, "Stay hungry," or in other words, "Don't stay happy." Happiness is transitory because it relies on neurochemistry that is designed to make reward fleeting.

Educators, then, need to be purposefully involved in nurturing school and classroom climates, ensuring that those elements leading to success in all aspects of school life are consistently present. What

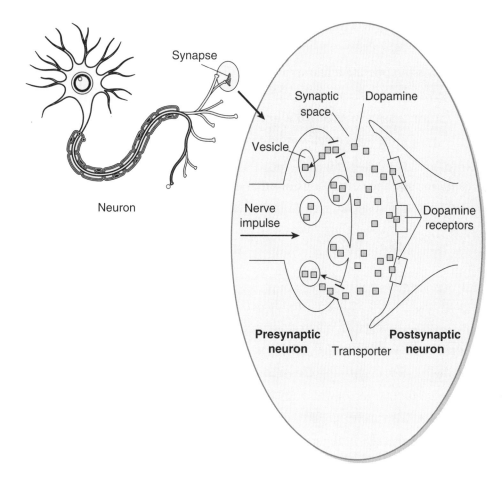

Figure 9.2   The diagram shows the activity occurring at the synaptic space. An electrical nerve impulse traveling along the (presynaptic) neuron on the left causes the release of neurotransmitters from sacs (vesicles). In this example, the neurotransmitter is dopamine and it flows across the space to dopamine receptors in the receiving (postsynaptic) neuron. After binding to the receptors, the dopamine molecules are usually taken back up into the presynaptic neuron through the transporter areas for the next impulse.

follows are some suggestions for how to assess classroom climate and a few strategies that teachers should consider for successfully managing student behavior in a positive and caring environment.

SUCCESSFUL BEHAVIOR MANAGEMENT IN THE CLASSROOM

Classroom climate is an important consideration in the management of every class. Notably, the climate within the classroom largely determines the types of relationships that may be fostered in that class and, as we discussed in previous chapters, positive relationships are the key to effective discipline. Classrooms that students perceive to be predominately punitive in nature will not facilitate the development of positive, respectful relationships, as was explained in Chapter 7 during the discussion of countercontrol. In such classrooms, students will not enjoy their experiences and teachers will be more likely to burn out than in a classroom where everyone feels valued and where the various attention needs of all students are being met.

Assessing Classroom Climate

Teachers who wish to operate a harmonious classroom and more effectively address the needs of students with behavior problems must consider the climate in their class. To do so, it is important to use a variety of informal assessments that allow the teacher to gauge the classroom climate from the various perspectives of those who dwell within that setting. There are three distinct types of measures that teachers may wish to consider in assessing the classroom climate for their class: self-perceptions, students' perceptions, and the perceptions of others, including other teachers and parents.

Self-Perceptions of Classroom Climate

Teachers may initially wish to take stock of how they feel, sense, and experience their own classrooms. Although some experts on classroom climate do not address this type of self-assessment, it is very important. When teachers complete a checklist on how they perceive the classroom, factors often emerge that teachers may have only vaguely considered beforehand. Abrams (2005), while not discussing classroom climate directly, suggested that teachers consider how they experience their interactions with their students, as well as examine their belief systems about those students. Townsend (2000) likewise recommended that teachers self-examine their attitudes and beliefs, particularly regarding minority students in the classroom.

The informal self-examination questions in Figure 9.3 may be used for such a self-examination. We recommend that teachers consider using this form as a precursor to other informal assessments when investigating the climate in their classroom. Teachers may then reflectively consider their own perceptions in relation to the perceptions of others.

Students' Perceptions of School Climate

Perhaps the most fundamental question concerning class climate is, "How do students experience their time in this classroom?" If limited time allows only one informal assessment, teachers should opt to investigate the students' sense of class climate. A brief informal student survey measure developed by Bender (2003) is shown in Figure 9.4 on page 186.

Teachers might want to use this form with all of their students around the beginning of the school year. It could provide valuable information for planning specific instructional modifications or behavioral interventions. Most students will not have major concerns and, therefore, most of the indicators will be marked 1 or 2. However, for students who are worried about specific indicators, some instructional ideas can be recommended. For example, students concerned with "Other students liking me" could benefit from cooperative learning opportunities (e.g., cooperative group work on a major project) that may assist students in building positive relationships with peers. Alternatively, the teacher could select a potential friend with similar social characteristics as the target student and match them up for various activities. Even if teachers do not plan specific

---

Teacher's Self-Assessment: My Experience in My Classroom

Directions: Circle the number that best represents the extent to which you agree with each of the following statements, based on your initial response and without much reflection. Because this is an informal evaluation, there are no scoring guidelines. However, after completing the form, examine the answers individually, and reflectively consider how these answers affect how you manage your class.

Do Not Agree	Agree Somewhat	Mostly Agree	Totally Agree
1	2	3	4

I believe all students can learn.	1	2	3	4
I try to teach to student strengths.	1	2	3	4
I enjoy some classes more than others.	1	2	3	4
I vary assessments to get a true picture of students' abilities and skills.	1	2	3	4
Some minority students may be challenged by hard work.	1	2	3	4
I make a special effort to recognize the dignity of each and every student.	1	2	3	4
I promote tolerance in my class.	1	2	3	4
I care less for some students than for others.	1	2	3	4
I try to get to know every student as a person.	1	2	3	4
I sometimes let my anger show in the class.	1	2	3	4
I actively listen to every student's problem.	1	2	3	4
I model self-control at all times in my class.	1	2	3	4
I observe students in non-class environments to know and understand them.	1	2	3	4
Students with disabilities may slow down the class.	1	2	3	4
There are some students I really don't like because of their behavior in class.	1	2	3	4
My class is characterized by use of humor.	1	2	3	4
I try to reach every child in a personal way.	1	2	3	4
I believe that the students generally enjoy my class.	1	2	3	4
I generally enjoy my class each day.	1	2	3	4
I communicate my faith in my students' abilities daily in my class.	1	2	3	4
I believe the overall class climate in my class is excellent.	1	2	3	4

Figure 9.3   This self-assessment may help teachers reflect on the type of classroom climate they establish in their class. See the Appendix for a black-line master of this form.

instructional modifications or activities from these assessments, they will still benefit from a deeper understanding of how various students experience their classroom.

We should also note that the emerging insights on the role of the brain and central nervous system in aggression and classroom misbehavior emphasize the importance of a safe, secure learning environment for the students (Sousa, 2007; Sylwester, 2000). Remember that when an individual feels insecure or threatened, the brain will become preoccupied with the stressful situation. Student security and happiness, then, are perhaps the most important factors in classroom climate overall, and a number of indicators in Figure 9.4 touch on these aspects of classroom climate (e.g., Do students seem friendly toward each other? Do the students feel like there is a bully in the class?).

Assessing Student Relationships

Directions: On this sheet, circle the number that represents the extent to which you agree with each of the following statements. Then answer the questions below.

	Not Worried About This	Hardly Worried About This	Worried About This	Very Worried About This
	1	2	3	4
Other students liking me	1	2	3	4
Being different	1	2	3	4
Having a teacher angry at me	1	2	3	4
Changing classes and meeting new people	1	2	3	4
Giving a presentation in front of others	1	2	3	4
Being picked on	1	2	3	4
Who to sit by in the cafeteria	1	2	3	4
Being sent to the principal	1	2	3	4
Dating	1	2	3	4
Unkind people	1	2	3	4
Walking past others in the hallways	1	2	3	4
Making friends	1	2	3	4
Not having an adult who listens	1	2	3	4
Not knowing what is expected by the teacher	1	2	3	4
New teachers	1	2	3	4
Club activities with other students	1	2	3	4
Opportunities for after-school activity	1	2	3	4

1. Tell your teacher here the thing that worries you the most. _____

2. Is there some class activity that you really don't want to do? _____

3. Can you recommend how the teacher can help make you more comfortable in class?_____

4. Are there things that make you nervous that you'd like to discuss with the teacher and principal? _____
_____

Thank you for sharing your thoughts. Although the teacher cannot always do the things students recommend, these ideas and concerns will be considered, and your input into our class is appreciated!

Figure 9.4   This is a sample assessment for getting student comments on how they feel about their relationships in school and in the classroom. See the Appendix for a black-line master of this form.

Perceptions of Classroom Climate by Other Adults

Generally, other teachers and parents perceive one's classroom in a fashion similar to one another. Although there are exceptions to this, adults who are looking at a school classroom look for several specific things as marks of high-quality instruction. These typically include:

- An orderly classroom environment in which learning is clearly taking place
- A variety of instructional contexts and activities
- The overall sense that the students and teachers are generally happy

With these three things in mind, Bender (2003) identified a number of indicators of what adults would typically look for as indicators of a successful, enjoyable learning environment. The checklist in Figure 9.5 may be used by teachers, or even modified for use by parents, as an informal evaluation of the classroom climate of the child's class. Order in the classroom and structured learning assignments are the basic components for a successful classroom and most adults recognize this. In particular, most parents realize that students with behavioral problems do need more structure

---

Checklist for Assessing Overall Classroom Climate

Directions: Answer each question with a yes or no. Answer immediately, without long reflection.

_____ 1. Is the teacher smiling?

_____ 2. Are the students working on their assigned tasks?

_____ 3. Are the students quietly whispering?

_____ 4. Do students usually raise their hands before answering?

_____ 5. Would you like to have your own child in this class?

_____ 6. Do students seem friendly toward each other?

_____ 7. Does the teacher speak respectfully to students?

_____ 8. Do the students feel like there is a bully in the class?

_____ 9. Are various disciplinary options in evidence (e.g., rules posted, behavior charts)?

_____ 10. Are students of different races working together?

_____ 11. Do the students often pick on one particular person?

_____ 12. Do parents often visit or help with projects?

_____ 13. Are an array of instructional activities used?

_____ 14. Do the students seem to get along, in general?

_____ 15. Are most homework assignments handed in?

_____ 16. Does the teacher use a signal to get the students' attention?

_____ 17. Are there displays of student work in the class?

_____ 18. Do the students seek out the teacher for help with a problem?

_____ 19. Are learning centers set up around the classroom?

_____ 20. Is the classroom generally pleasing to look at?

Figure 9.5 Here is an example of a checklist that can be used by another teacher or a parent to assess overall classroom climate. See the Appendix for a black-line master.

overall. Thus, an ordered classroom will tend to alleviate some behavior problems. Several indicators on the checklist in Figure 9.5 are intended to specify the signs of an ordered classroom (e.g., Are the kids working on their assigned tasks?). Other indicators target the variety of educational tasks in the classroom (e.g., Are an array of instructional activities used? Are there displays of student work in the class?).

Most adults will want to see a variety of learning options, rather than a highly traditional classroom in which lecture or teacher presentation seems to be the main teaching approach. Displays of students' work also add greatly to the classroom environment. Most importantly, when adults look at the classroom, they want to see happiness in the learning environment. They want to perceive that the students are comfortable in their relationships with the teacher, with other adults in the class, and with their peers. Students, too, want to feel valued, safe, and secure in their learning environment, and their demeanor in the classroom will often indicate whether they are having positive experiences.

A teacher might want a colleague to evaluate classroom climate. The form may be used at any point in the school year, after the students have become familiar with the class routine. A teacher seeking information on classroom climate would then invite another teacher to come observe the class and complete this form.

We should emphasize that this informal instrument should never be used to critique a teacher's class. No scoring norms or reliability and validity data are available for this informal measure. It is intended as a self-evaluation tool that may be completed by other educators to assist a teacher in self-reflection. Teachers, of course, should feel free to use the form in Figure 9.5 in a formative evaluation of their own classroom, perhaps as one component of their self-improvement goals.

CLASSROOM MANAGEMENT AND CULTURAL DIVERSITY

When considering classroom management issues, teachers should examine the factors that we have discussed in prior chapters, such as flexibility in rule application, childhood temperament, differences in parenting to which students have been exposed, and classroom climate. One additional consideration that we have not previously addressed involves working with various sub-cultural groups and minority students in the class. Most classes today involve students from a variety of minority groups and sub-cultures, including African-American, Hispanic, Native American, Islamic, Asian, and a growing mix of other groups. The U.S. Census Bureau (2003) states that 18 percent of the U.S. population (about 47 million people) speak a language other than English in the home. For almost 60 percent of those people, Spanish is the primary language. Just over 20 percent speak other Indo-European languages and nearly 15 percent speak Asian and Pacific island languages. This provides some indication of the cultural diversity in today's communities and classrooms.

Even these commonly used group labels are not very accurate because each group actually involves a variety of sub-groups. For example, the term "Hispanic" in southern Florida may mean

Americans of Cuban heritage who have been in this country for several generations. Alternatively, it may also include recent refugees from Honduras, Bolivia, Panama, Guatemala, and Columbia (Violand-Sánchez & Hainer-Violand, 2006). In southern Texas or Arizona, however, the term "Hispanic" frequently refers to immigrants from Mexico rather than other areas. Moreover, these groups are vastly different from each other in cultural heritage, political outlook, and religious beliefs. For example, the Spanish-speaking population in southern Texas tends to be highly religious, politically conservative, and strongly supportive of education. These individuals prefer the term Mexican-American rather than Hispanic, and they believe that they are vastly different from many of the Hispanic immigrants in other regions, such as in south Florida and California. Asian minorities, likewise, comprise a variety of subgroups—Japanese, Korean, Chinese, Vietnamese—just to name a few. Again, these broad terms for various sub-cultural groups mask significant differences within these groups.

Teachers now must consider these cultural variations when planning management strategies for their classes. Of course, there are no hard and fast rules governing how teachers should discipline students in various sub-groups, but there are considerations that teachers must be aware of, and we would be remiss if we did not offer some broad guidelines for working with and respecting students from diverse cultures, religions, races, and sub-groups.

Guidelines for Managing Diverse Classes

Research in this area supports several guidelines that can help you successfully manage classes with a culturally and ethnically diverse student population.

- **Build positive relationships.** You will be more effective when you build positive relationships with students in all the sub-groups in your classes (McKinley, 2006; Violand-Sánchez & Hainer-Violand, 2006). McKinley (2006) studied a group of teachers who were able to close the achievement gap between black and white students in their classes. Using data from schools in Seattle, Washington, he looked at teachers who had a minimum of five students from each of several different sub-groups in their class. He then examined the philosophies of those teachers where no achievement gap existed and found that teachers who attended to the social context for learning and behavior, and who sought cultural proficiency in their dealings with minority students were able to close the achievement gap between the races. In short, the data revealed that teachers who strived to build positive relationships with minority students were much more effective than others in working with minority students and helping those students achieve in school.

  Students often know little about the various cultures represented in their class. When possible, teach specifics about various cultures represented in the class and celebrate holiday traditions from various cultures. Discuss cultural differences frequently and point out that diverse cultures are typically stronger cultures historically.

- **Study and value the cultures represented in the class.** Study and value not only the students you teach, but also the culture from which those students come. Frequent reflection on the cultural meaning and context of behaviors, such as classroom participation and disruptive behavior is essential. For example, students in many Asian, Native American, and some Spanish-speaking cultures are specifically taught not to look directly at authority figures. For these students, avoiding eye contact with figures in authority is a sign of respect. However, in most Western cultures, a student looking at the floor during a discussion of inappropriate behavior may be interpreted by some educators as a sign of disrespect. Clearly teachers must understand these cultural differences in order to effectively manage student behavior (McKinley, 2006; Violand-Sánchez & Hainer-Violand, 2006).

  Other cultural differences may also be important. For instance, Townsend (2000) indicated that in many African-American homes children are accustomed to engaging in multitasking, involving participating in multiple conversations while eating, studying, or watching television. These students may be more comfortable with activities in the classroom that allow them to socialize while doing school work. Further, these students may even be penalized in classrooms that stress only one individual activity at a time. Violand-Sánchez and Hainer-Violand (2006) indicated that many Latino students experience U.S. culture as a bombardment of materialism, television, pop culture, and technology, and consequently, these students may be very uncomfortable in a classroom where they are in the minority. In such cases, you will have to strive to make these students more comfortable with their surroundings in order to help them achieve their potential. A careful study of the primary cultures of these students allows you to better interpret student behavior, leading to more effective class management and less potential conflict overall.

- **Modify instruction to support cultural differences.** Perhaps as important as studying students' cultures is teaching in a way that reflects respect for those cultural differences. McKinley (2006) indicated that effective teaching for African-American students might require some modifications in instruction. He recommended that teachers use instructional activities that provide students opportunities for learning together, such as cooperative learning groups, reciprocal teaching, and sharing of instructional duties with students. In this approach, students support each other while they hear and reflect on various ideas and concepts presented by someone from their own sub-cultural group. These peer-to-peer interactions can often make the difference between casual exposure to an idea versus a deeper understanding of the concept.

- **Implement school-wide class management interventions.** Consistency of behavioral expectations is critical for all students. However, students who sense that their own background may be different from the predominate school culture will typically require clearer guidelines for the behavioral expectations of the class and the school. Thus, school-wide disciplinary plans, coupled with school-wide consistent reinforcement options for appropriate behavior are highly recommended as supports for students from diverse cultures (Sobel, Taylor, & Wortman, 2006).

- **Use problem solving strategies and peer norms to modify behavior.** Students in various sub-groups respond more favorably to behavioral interventions when they see that their inappropriate behavior has a negative impact on others like them in the class. Strategies that couple problem solving and peer influence (such as the peer confrontation procedure we discussed in Chapter 6) are likely to be effective for many minority students (Sobel, Taylor, & Wortman, 2006).

- **Use special codes that are culturally relevant to signal behavioral expectations.** A special code is any indicator, sign, or word that you and the students jointly select to signal the need to immediately change behavior. Many teachers develop such codes for gaining the attention of their classes (e.g., some teachers raise their own hand to signal for quiet). However, in certain cases, you may wish to develop a special code that only a specific group of students recognize. This strategy may elicit higher levels of participation in honoring that code (Sobel, Taylor, & Wortman, 2006; Townsend, 2000).

- **Build class cohesion.** For minority students in certain situations (e.g., an Asian child in a class of white students), the sense that they do not "belong" can be overwhelming. In this instance, you should seek to build class cohesion by directly emphasizing that "We are all in our class together, and we need to be concerned for and care for each other." With older students, open discussions of how it may feel to be a minority student may be appropriate, and you should talk with the minority students about these feelings.

- **Use student-to-student support programs.** Students from different cultural or linguistic backgrounds can greatly benefit from peer tutors and other student-to-student support programs. For example, in the Arlington, Virginia, public schools, 44 percent of the school population come from homes where English is not the primary language, and implementation of peer tutoring programs resulted in better behavior and improved academic scores. Some of these programs were "tutoring assistance" drop-in programs located at various schools, while others were more formal peer-tutoring programs. Such student support programs can be a significant benefit for minority students (Violand-Sánchez & Hainer-Violand, 2006).

POSITIVE BEHAVIORAL SUPPORTS IN THE CLASSROOM

What Are Positive Behavioral Supports?

After describing throughout this book the neurological basis for various classroom behavior problems and suggesting a variety of approaches for management of those problems, we also have a responsibility to place these strategies in the context of the disciplinary procedures currently used in schools. This

Positive behavioral supports have been successful in helping teachers assess why students misbehave the way they do and in developing an effective plan for addressing the misbehavior in the context of a productive classroom climate.

chapter has already provided several class-wide considerations, including suggestions for improving overall class climate and reflections on cultural diversity issues within the class. Now we offer some suggestions on how to fit these considerations, along with all of the previously described intervention strategies, into the context of positive behavioral supports (PBS) (Harlacher, Roberts, & Merrell, 2006; Zuna & McDougall, 2004).

PBS is a problem-solving model, similar to Response to Intervention, that offers a range of interventions that are systematically applied to students based on their level of need. The process is comprised of three tiers. Tier 1 (the universal level) is the practice of teaching and reinforcing students for displaying the school-wide expectations and is delivered to every student in every setting. This proactive approach increases the likelihood that most students will act according to the expectations. It is only after academic and behavior instruction and evidence-based interventions are established at both the school-wide and classroom levels that educators should conclude that a student has a need for additional services.

When a student has been identified as needing additional support, school personnel use evidence-based interventions that require resources appropriate to the student's level of need, then monitor the progress of students receiving those interventions. This Tier 2 (targeted group level) phase provides interventions that are easy to administer to small groups of students, and which require limited time and staff involvement. In schools that are using PBS, a check-in/check-out program such as the Behavior Education Program meets these criteria and provides a way to focus at-risk students' attention on the school-wide expectations (Todd, Campbell, Meyer, & Horner, 2008). Other Tier 2 interventions include group counseling, social skills groups, and mentoring programs.

Students whose problem behavior continues after Tier 2 interventions are implemented are candidates for Tier 3 (individual student level). At Tier 3, the school team conducts a more in-depth analysis of the student's data. This includes all of the information examined at Tier 1, as well as the student's response to the Tier 2 interventions. Classroom teachers have a larger role at this stage of the process because more in-depth information is collected through one-on-one consultation. Tier 3 consultations regarding persistent behavior problems include a *Functional Behavior Assessment* (FBA) and the completion of a behavioral or mental health rating scale. A simple *Behavior Improvement Plan* (BIP) that includes evidence-based interventions and is based on the results of the FBA is used early in Tier 3, and the student's response to the BIP is closely monitored. If a student continues to show a poor response to the BIP, school personnel discuss a more structured problem-solving process and develop a more detailed plan.

Many teachers in today's classrooms have had the experience of completing a functional assessment of behavior and in developing behavior improvement plans. Although these aspects of behavioral management have been discussed in individual case studies presented throughout this text, we discuss here a complete positive behavioral support process for a single student to show how these strategies may work together in the context of the general education classroom.

The Functional Assessment of Behavior

In addition to keeping a baseline record of misbehavior (as we have emphasized in previous chapters), teachers today are often asked to undertake a Functional Behavioral Assessment (FBA) of inappropriate behaviors (Harlacher, Roberts, & Merrell, 2006; Zuna & McDougall, 2004). The FBA emerged from a large body of behavioral research and recent studies have shown the FBA procedures to be effective in developing interventions in general education settings. Usually, the FBA process involves developing a preliminary hypothesis statement about the function of a student's behavior through interviews and a review of records, then confirming the statement through direct observation.

Several case studies in earlier chapters have involved considering the function of a student's problem behavior. For example, in the discussion of the dialogue journals in Chapter 5, the teacher, Mr. Fuller, reflected on the function of Cynthia's behavior in determining which behavioral intervention to use. You may recall that Mr. Fuller suspected that Cynthia made inappropriate comments to peers in order to get attention and to show her dislike for the other students who had rejected her. In a case study in Chapter 7, Mr. Goff likewise reflected on Alfred's defiant behavior and determined that this behavior served the function of gaining attention for Alfred.

When developing a formal behavioral intervention plan for a student, teachers should collect baseline data on one or two specific, observable behavioral problems, and also reflect on what function those target behaviors serve for the child (Zuna & McDougall, 2004). Although this can be accomplished in narrative form (as in the previous examples), teachers may wish to use a more structured functional behavior analysis procedure. Figure 9.6 shows a sample Functional Behavioral Assessment form that can be applied in various classroom situations. Note that in addition to describing the misbehavior, the form encourages the teacher to analyze the misbehavior's triggers and delve deeper into reasons for the misbehavior. Coupled with a chart of baseline data, this completed form can often provide ideas concerning which strategies or interventions may be appropriate and more likely to work for certain students (March et al., 2000).

The Behavioral Improvement Plan

Once data has been collected on the target behavior, and the function of that behavior has been analyzed, teachers should prepare a Behavioral Improvement Plan, or BIP. In some cases, BIPs are required by law when behavioral problems interfere with providing education for children with disabilities in the general education class. Almost all school districts have a form for BIPs. Often they are one-page check-off sheets, indicating the type of interventions that general education teachers plan to use to alleviate the problem behavior. An example of such a planning sheet is shown in Figure 9.7.

Many schools have successfully implemented the BIP planning process by completing the BIP during the prereferral process. However, in some cases, that is the only step taken. Thus, one caution should be noted: Teachers should never confuse the BIP planning sheet with an actual BIP. For example, although the planning sheet in Figure 9.7 indicates what types of interventions the teacher will complete (or has previously undertaken), that planning sheet does not indicate the results of those interventions. Only one or more *measures of actual behavior* can demonstrate that a BIP was actually implemented and completed.

The actual BIP must include more than merely a checkoff planning sheet. Although many schools are implementing BIPs correctly, it is an unfortunate fact that many districts consider the process as finished once the planning sheet is completed, as if that were evidence that a behavioral improvement intervention was actually conducted. Of course, these districts often recognize that

---

Functional Behavioral Assessment Form

Student's Name: _____ Date _____ School _____

Teacher's Name: _____ Subject Taught _____

1. Identify at least three strengths or contributions the student brings to the school. _____ _____

2. Presenting Behavior Problem: Describe one or two instances of the problem behavior._____ _____

3. Co-occurring Behaviors: Describe any co-occurring behaviors. Note how these may be related to the presenting behavior problem. _____

4. Behavioral Antecedents: Note what happens immediately before the behavior problem. Does the problem occur at the same time, or in the same type of activity each day? _____

5. How long does the problem behavior last? _____

6. What is the level of danger of the problem behavior? _____

7. Who else is involved? Are others consistently involved in the misbehavior? _____

8. What does the student gain? What do you think the student seeks to accomplish with the misbehavior? _____

9. What is the payoff? Note how you or the student's peers respond to the misbehavior. _____

10. Based on these indicators, what function is served by the misbehavior? _____

11. What current efforts have been used to control the problem behavior? _____ _____

Figure 9.6 This is a sample form that helps teachers assess the reasons and results of a student's misbehavior. See the Appendix for a black-line master of this form.

A Behavioral Improvement Plan

Student's Name: _____ Date _____ School _____

Teacher's Name: _____ Subject Taught _____

1. Presenting Behavior Problem: Describe one or two instances of the problem behavior._____
   _____

2. How often does this occur? Attach a chart of baseline data or an ABC log. _____

3. Functional assessment of the misbehavior: Attach some notes or a completed FBA form. _____

4. What interventions will be used? Check the interventions you will undertake.

   _____ parent/student/teacher meeting   _____ more time on tests   _____ use cooperative groups

   _____ behavioral contract   _____ assign peer buddy   _____ assign study partner

   _____ use special seating   _____ self-monitoring   _____ provide para-professional

   _____ reinforce incompatible behavior   _____ other (describe below)

   _____

5. Second tier intervention: If the proposed intervention above does not work, what secondary intervention will you attempt? _____

6. Post-intervention data. Teachers must provide a chart for each intervention that includes baseline and intervention data (using an X/Y axis standard behavioral chart). These data must reflect a minimum of three weeks of intervention data. After the intervention, attach the chart to this form.

Figure 9.7   This form helps teachers decide on the behavioral intervention that is most appropriate for the target misbehavior being addressed. See the Appendix for a black-line master of this form.

error once they move into due process proceedings or legal action based on just a completed planning sheet. In short, a BIP, once implemented, must be documented not only with a plan but with actual behavioral data collected by any of the methods described in this text or in the behavioral measurement literature. This is why the interventions described in this book have emphasized daily collection of baseline and intervention data.

Multitiered Interventions and the Student Support Team

The final components of the positive behavior supports approach involves the activation of the student support team and the implementation of a multitiered set of behavioral interventions (Harlacher, Roberts, & Merrell, 2006; Zuna & McDougall, 2004). If one considers the various interventions discussed in this text as designed to prevent further behavioral problems, the rationale for multitiered interventions becomes clear: Rather than provide only one behavioral intervention, teachers should address behavioral problems by implementing a series of tiered interventions of increasing intensity, until the behavior problem improves (Harlacher, Roberts, & Merrell, 2006). When presented with a behavioral problem, the teacher should address the problem using an appropriate intervention. However, if the data collected over several weeks of intervention indicate that the first intervention is not working, teachers should implement a more intensive second-tier intervention to alleviate the behavior problem.

To facilitate such a multitiered intervention process, many schools have organized a team of educators to assist teachers in planning for educational interventions when the teacher's initial efforts at behavioral control are not successful. Different names are used for this team, such as the Prereferral team, the Child Study Team (CST), or the Student Support Team (SST). The purpose of this team is to provide support to students and teachers for a variety of educational concerns, both academic and behavioral. In every state, teachers are usually required to bring a student to the attention of this team prior to making a referral for special education testing, which explains why some states use the term "prereferral team." However, even for students where a referral for special education is not appropriate, these expert teams should be consulted to provide assistance, especially if the first BIP-based intervention that the teacher implemented was unsuccessful. The expertise of these teams can greatly assist a teacher in identifying the types of second-tier interventions that may successfully address the behavioral problems.

Thus, the FBA, the BIP, the Student Support Team, and multitiered interventions fit together to form the basis for providing positive behavior supports in the classroom. See the **Resources** section in this book for a listing of Web sites that offer suggestions for various behavioral interventions and for implementing the positive behavior support process. Of course, any of the interventions presented in this text would be appropriate for this positive behavior support process. Here is an example of the entire process for one student.

A Case Study: Multitiered Positive Behavior Support to Curb Shouting in Class

Vanessa was a sixth-grade student who often shouted out her answers in class. She talked loudly to the teacher and others and shouted comments that were not related to the subject being discussed. Vanessa did pay attention to her work and avoided shouting whenever she was doing work she considered "fun," such as working out problems on the computer or watching a video. However, in class discussions, she would revert to shouting out answers and irrelevant comments. Her previous teachers confirmed that she was a consistent behavior problem although she had never been identified as a special education student. Ms. Cummins was her sixth-grade teacher and she chose to collect some baseline data on Vanessa's shouting in class.

The First Tier of Intervention. Because most of Vanessa's shouting occurred before the morning break, Ms. Cummins initiated a frequency count of Vanessa's shouting during the period from 8:15 a.m. until the break at 9:45 a.m. Over a period of three days, Ms. Cummins noted that

Vanessa shouted an average of 12 times each day. In addition to the data on the shouting behavior, Ms. Cummins also did a functional behavior assessment, using the FBA sheet represented in Figure 9.6. This is what the completed sheet looked like.

FBA of Vanessa's Shouting In Class

1. **Presenting Behavior Problem:** Shouting loudly in class during group discussions.

2. **Co-occurring Behaviors:** None noted.

3. **Behavioral Antecedents:** Only occurs during group work or classwide discussions, not during individual seat work, and never during computer work.

4. **Who else is involved?** Others in the class snicker when she does this, thereby reinforcing this behavior.

5. **What does the student gain?** Attention from the class.

6. **What is the payoff?** She has become the class clown by this behavior.

7. **What function does the misbehavior serve?** This behavior gets her attention that she craves from her peers.

Using the baseline data and the results of the completed FBA, Ms. Cummins developed a complete picture of the frequency of Vanessa's inappropriate behavior, as well as the function it served for her. At this point, Ms. Cummins was ready to move to the development of a BIP for Vanessa. Because Vanessa used her inappropriate behavior to gain attention, Ms. Cummins selected an intervention that would gain attention for Vanessa in a more appropriate fashion. She chose to use the "Shine My Light" strategy described in Chapter 8. Rather than begin with the entire "Shine My Light" planning sheet shown in Figure 8.6, Ms Cummins used three questions from that sheet along with a telephone call to Vanessa's parents to select a hobby that would allow Vanessa to gain positive attention from the class. The three questions she considered from that planning sheet were:

- *Does the student's interest show in his or her academic work in the class?* In Vanessa's case, she was so fond of working on the computer that Ms. Cummins was already using that as a reinforcer for her.
- *What do others (e.g., parents, peers) say about the student's interests?* Ms. Cummins telephoned the parents and confirmed that Vanessa indeed had a computer at home and was very active on one of the social networking Web sites, getting online almost daily from home.
- *What does the student identify as hobbies or areas of interest?* When offered free time in the classroom for any education task, Vanessa always chose computer time.

Armed with these insights into Vanessa's skills and hobbies, Ms. Cummins wrote out the following description of her behavioral improvement plan.

Based on the attached baseline data on Vanessa's inappropriate shouting in class, and a functional assessment of that behavior, it is clear that Vanessa desires attention from the class and that she is misbehaving to gain that attention. I've selected a "Shine My Light" intervention that will provide attention for Vanessa for an appropriate activity in the classroom. I will make five minutes of computer time available to her each day that she reduces the number of inappropriate shout outs. I will also co-teach with her a weekly lesson on computer skills and cautions about social networking sites, based on the school's policy and information sheet about use of such sites. Both the daily reinforcement (five minutes of computer time) and the weekly reinforcement (attention of the class that she gets while co-teaching a computer lesson with me) are contingent upon reduced shouting. I will continue to monitor and record the daily shout outs during this BIP intervention.

With this written plan in hand, Ms. Cummins chose not to use the BIP planning check-off sheet because that information would have been redundant. However, Ms. Cummins did shared this BIP with the principal. Next, she began the intervention by asking Vanessa to remain with her at the first part of the lunch period, and she initiated the following discussion.

Ms. Cummins:	Vanessa, I want your help in thinking through an idea for the class. I know that you participate on a number of social networking sites and have developed many computer skills by doing that. Is that right?
Vanessa:	Yeah. I get online almost every day and enjoy it a lot.
Ms. Cummins:	I'm so excited about this that I called your Mom to make sure that this idea was OK with her, and I've even talked with the principal. I want you to help me teach all the class about these social networking sites. Would you like to help me do that?
Vanessa:	What do you mean?
Ms. Cummins:	Well, we would plan what we wanted to teach to the class about the various sites and give the other students guidelines in using those sites. Which ones do you participate in?
Vanessa:	I'm on MySpace and most of my friends are, too.
Ms. Cummins:	Great, we'll start with that one. What I have in mind is teaching the class what the site looks like, the kind of information that people should post there, and the kind of information that should not be posted. You know about that, right?
Vanessa:	Yeah, I sure do! My dad told me to never give out anything that I didn't want everyone to know. He also said that I should never post information about others that might hurt their feelings.

Ms. Cummins:	That's right. It sounds like your dad is wise in his concerns. We certainly don't want to hurt anyone's feelings, right?
Vanessa:	I guess so.
Ms. Cummins:	Did your dad say to never set up meetings with anyone through MySpace?
Vanessa:	He sure did! He talked about men using this as a way to meet young girls or boys.
Ms. Cummins:	That's right. You should never set up meetings with anyone you don't know, and if you begin to feel like someone is asking personal questions, you should let your dad know immediately, right?
Vanessa:	That's what he said.
Ms. Cummins:	Well, it seems that you are just the expert we need to teach our whole class about these cautions. Here is what we'll do. I'll arrange for about five minutes of computer time for you each day so you can prepare for this lesson. Then, at least once a week, you and I will go to the computer and we'll get the class to look at your MySpace site. While we are doing that, they will see how smart you are. You'll be our class expert! Then, you and I can review with the class this list of guidelines from our school on how to use these sites without becoming a victim. How does that sound?
Vanessa:	So I'll be the class expert?
Ms. Cummins:	Yes, you will. And every week, the whole class will see you and me teach that short lesson together. How does that sound?
Vanessa:	That's sound great. When can we start?
Ms. Cummins:	We'll start this lesson next Monday, but I do want to mention one more thing. You realize that many times you shout out answers in class, or shout to others and call them names?
Vanessa:	Yeah. When I do, they all laugh.
Ms. Cummins:	I'm sure they do laugh, but we cannot let someone be an expert in this class when they misbehave that way, can we?
Vanessa:	Well . . .
Ms. Cummins:	Here's an idea. I'll count how many times you shout rudely to others or shout out answers. If that number is less than it was the day before—that is, if you can reduce the number of times you shout out—you earn your computer time each day. Also, if the weekly average goes down, we'll hold the lesson for the class on each Monday. How's that?
Vanessa:	I guess so.

Ms. Cummins: Tell you what. If you can reduce the number of times you shout this week, we'll even have our first lesson in just two days, this Friday. That way the class will know you are the expert much sooner, and they'll see you do another lesson the very next Monday too. How does that sound!

Vanessa: Great! I'd like that. I'll be the class expert!

In this case study, Ms. Cummins completed every major step in providing positive behavior support for Vanessa. She identified the target behavior (inappropriate shouting in class), collected baseline data, conducted a functional assessment of that behavior, and devised a behavior improvement plan for modifying that problem behavior. She also selected an intervention specifically targeted not only at the specific behavior problem, but also based on the function of that behavior for Vanessa.

Unfortunately, as every veteran teacher knows, even when everything is done right, things can still go wrong. The data over the next two weeks did not indicate a positive change in Vanessa's shouting behavior as shown in Figure 9.8. Although Vanessa did earn computer time on several days, (specifically, the first Thursday and Friday of the intervention period, and only on Wednesday of the following week), the behavior did not decrease after the first full week of intervention. Therefore, Vanessa was earning daily reinforcement only sporadically and no weekly reinforcement at all after the first week. Clearly, a second, more intensive, intervention was needed in this case.

The Second Tier of Intervention. At this point, Ms. Cummins wanted some ideas from her colleagues. Therefore, she shared the description of the BIP and the data in Figure 9.8 with the Student Support Team and sought their assistance in planning a second tier intervention. As discussed previously, the second tier intervention is intended to be more intensive in addressing the behavior problem if the initial intervention is unsuccessful.

The Student Support Team complimented Ms. Cummins on her BIP and intervention, and agreed that the function of Vanessa's behavior was to gain attention. Also, they liked the use of the "Shine My Light" strategy with Vanessa. However, in the team's discussion it became apparent that the intervention and reinforcement were not sufficiently intensive. One teacher on the team felt that Vanessa did not really understand the nature or frequency of her problem behavior and the degree to which it

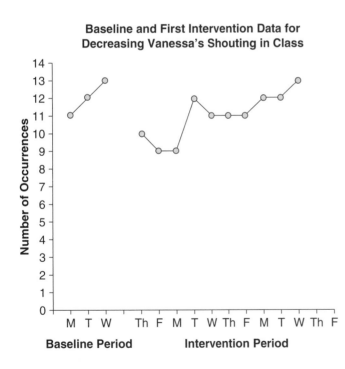

Figure 9.8   This chart shows the baseline data and the data collected during two weeks of the "Shine My Light" intervention. Vanessa's shouting in class was not reduced by the intervention.

disturbed the class. This led to the suggestion that Ms. Cummins begin a second tier of intervention, building upon the initial BIP plan but with an added overlay that involved self-monitoring. Thus, the team recommended that Ms. Cummins require Vanessa to self-monitor her own shouting in class in order to make her aware of how often she did it. Based on this recommendation, Ms. Cummins added a paragraph to the original BIP, noting the changes recommended by the Student Support Team. She then had the following conversation with Vanessa.

Ms. Cummins: Vanessa, I want to find a way for you to earn more time on the computer. Would you like that?

Vanessa: Yeah. I'm not getting much time right now, am I?

Ms. Cummins: Well, you haven't been able to earn any time on some days, but we can fix that. This idea is called self-monitoring, because it helps students monitor their own behavior. Would you like to learn how? You'll be the only one in class who knows how to do this.

Vanessa: What do you mean?

Ms. Cummins: Here is an index card with your name on it and the days of the week down the side. See? On each day of the week, I want you to count how many times you shout out in class during the morning. Every time you shout out, you will put a tally mark by that day of the week, and we'll just add up those marks each day.

Vanessa: Why? What good will that do?

Ms. Cummins: I think that if you count how many times you shout out, while I continue to keep my count, we can compare our counts and you'll become more aware of your shouting out in class. I'll even help you keep your count. If you shout out, I'll remind you to put a tally mark down so your count will be accurate.

Vanessa: Can I still get on MySpace?

Ms. Cummins: That's the great part. By keeping count I think you'll earn more computer time each week, then we can continue our computer lessons for the class every Monday like we planned.

Vanessa: So I can still get on the computer every day and teach a lesson each Monday?

Ms. Cummins: That's right. You'll be more aware of how many times you shouted in class on each day, so on the next day you can make certain you reduce that number. I think this will work nicely and get you more computer time. What do you think?

Vanessa: I guess so.

Ms. Cummins: Good. We'll start with this self-monitoring card tomorrow.

Ms. Cummins continued the "Shine My Light" strategy and the reinforcement plan, just as before. However, she also included this self-monitoring intervention. She made a point of talking with Vanessa each day after the morning period to compare Vanessa's shout outs that day with the previous days. In the meantime, Ms. Cummins continued to chart her own count of Vanessa's shout outs daily.

Figure 9.9 shows all of the data from the baseline period through the second intervention. As indicated, the self-monitoring was the appropriate additional intervention to help Vanessa reduce her shout outs in class, and by the end of this second tier intervention, shout outs were almost eliminated.

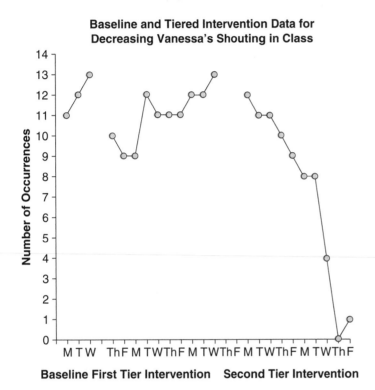

Baseline and Tiered Intervention Data for Decreasing Vanessa's Shouting in Class

Baseline   First Tier Intervention   Second Tier Intervention

Figure 9.9   This charts shows the baseline data and the data collected during the first and second tiers of intervention. The addition of the second tier intervention (self-monitoring) resulted in a significant decrease in Vanessa's shouting out in class.

Although most behavior problems do not warrant multiple interventions, or this degree of time from the teacher, certain behaviors can be persistent, and teachers should not expect that every intervention undertaken will work. That is why the positive behavior supports model emphasizes the concept of tiered interventions, with each intervention becoming more intensive than the previous one. In this example, Vanessa did not respond positively to the initial intervention, so a more intensive, involved intervention was necessary to curb her behavior problem.

For students who do not respond positively to several different interventions, it may be necessary to consult with other experts such as a school psychologist or social worker. In extreme cases, it may be necessary to refer a child for consideration for special education services. However, teachers should manage a variety of challenging behaviors in the classroom, and in most cases, the use of a second tier intervention will probably not be necessary.

SUMMARY

This chapter presents information on a variety of concerns that have an impact on class management. School and classroom climate are crucial components of an effective behavior management program. When students are in a positive educational environment, learning can occur more effectively and behavior problems are reduced. A part of the climate is happiness, now recognized in social neuroscience as an important contributor to attention and learning.

For those students who still exhibit behavior problems, assessing the function of the misbehavior and devising a workable behavior improvement plan can be successful approaches. A second tier strategy may be needed for those students who do not respond to the first intervention. Teachers today will need to implement their behavioral interventions in the context of positive behavioral supports, and our discussion here explains how that process works. The key here, though, is to initiate and carry out these strategies in a positive climate.

CONCLUSION

This book represents what we believe to be one of the first efforts at bringing together the results from recent neurological studies of the brain and the classroom management and disciplinary concerns of teachers. We are confident that the emerging research can and should inform practices in classrooms today, and we hope that presenting the current knowledge about how the brain influences behavior, coupled with descriptions of actual intervention tactics that teachers can readily use in the classroom, will benefit educators who struggle daily with disciplinary and classroom management issues.

We have intentionally included examples and strategies across the grade levels and related each instructional tactic to some area of scientific research. While other connections between specific strategies and certain areas of brain research would have been possible, we chose, for the sake of clarity, to make what we believe to be the most direct and clear connection between the two.

With that stated, this book is not primarily an introduction to classroom management. Many instructional suggestions and interventions that would have been presented in such a book are not found here. For example, we did not present a complete description of classroom organization (i.e., how a teacher arranges furniture, computers, worktables, and work spaces in the classroom), which is one element for effective class management. Rather, we have offered tactics and strategies that seemed most connected to current research on brain functioning. In this way we believe that this book can make a contribution by helping educators translate the emerging brain research into effective classroom management practices. Our hope is that, with the strategies contained here, teachers can spend less time disciplining and more time teaching.

> *Our hope is that, with the strategies contained here, teachers can spend less time disciplining and more time teaching.*

Finally, we recognize that dealing with a disruptive student can be emotionally upsetting. We suggest, though, that teachers should not take student misbehavior *personally,* and that they mentally separate the student from the behavior. More often, the student is rebelling for reasons that have nothing to do with the teacher. The teacher's responsibility is to remain calm and select an appropriate intervention to address the behavior while maintaining the dignity of the student.

Appendix

On the following pages are black-line masters of some of the instruments and data-collecting sheets that have been described throughout the book. They include:

- Graph for Charting Baseline and Intervention Data
- ABC Log of Anger Behavior
- Self-Monitoring Check Sheet
- Teacher Observation Check Sheet of Student On-Task Behavior
- Check Sheet of Class Preparedness Behavior
- The Anger Thermometer
- A Student Interview for Strength-Based Assessment
- A Teacher's and Parent's Planning Guide for the "Shine My Light" Strategy
- Teacher's Self-Assessment: My Experiences in My Classroom
- Assessing Student Relationships
- Checklist for Assessing Overall Classroom Climate
- Functional Behavioral Assessment Form
- A Behavioral Improvement Plan

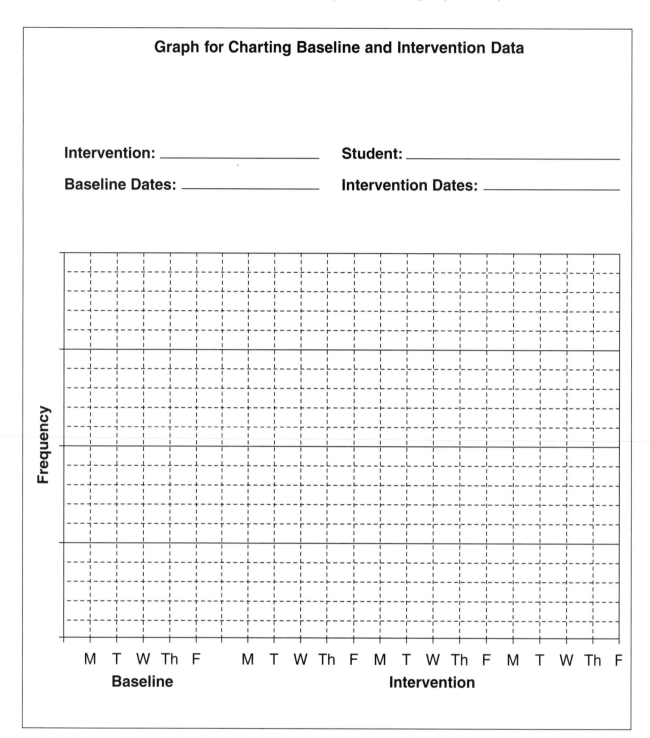

Graph for Charting Baseline and Intervention Data

Intervention: _____   Student: _____

Baseline Dates: _____   Intervention Dates: _____

Frequency

M T W Th F   M T W Th F M T W Th F M T W Th F

Baseline   **Intervention**

Directions: Insert numbers along the vertical axis, starting with zero (0) at the lower left-hand corner. Place a dot on the line representing the number of times the target behavior appears each day both before (baseline) and after the intervention. Connect the dots to see the trend in the frequency of the behavior.

ABC Log of _____ (Student) Anger Behavior			
Day/Date	Antecedent	Behavior	Consequences

Self-Monitoring Check Sheet

Name _____ Date _____ Period _____

Number of times I was paying attention today _____

WAS   I   PAYING   ATTENTION?

YES	NO
_____	_____
_____	_____
_____	_____
_____	_____
_____	_____
_____	_____
_____	_____
_____	_____
_____	_____
_____	_____
_____	_____
_____	_____
_____	_____
_____	_____
_____	_____

Directions: This self-monitoring check sheet is used with the cuing tape. This sheet reminds students of the self-questioning they should use to indicate if they were paying attention. The check sheet has lines on which students indicate if they were on- or off-task when the self-monitoring tone sounded on the audiotape. The value of this check sheet is that it can be used to self-monitor any behavior that the teacher and student agree to address.

Teacher Observation Check Sheet
of Student On-Task Behavior

Name _____ Date _____ Period _____

Percentage of on-task behavior _____
(On-task checks ÷ 60 = Percent of on-task time)

On task	Off task	On task	Off task	On task	Off task
_____	_____	_____	_____	_____	_____
_____	_____	_____	_____	_____	_____
_____	_____	_____	_____	_____	_____
_____	_____	_____	_____	_____	_____
_____	_____	_____	_____	_____	_____
_____	_____	_____	_____	_____	_____
_____	_____	_____	_____	_____	_____
_____	_____	_____	_____	_____	_____
_____	_____	_____	_____	_____	_____
_____	_____	_____	_____	_____	_____
_____	_____	_____	_____	_____	_____
_____	_____	_____	_____	_____	_____
_____	_____	_____	_____	_____	_____
_____	_____	_____	_____	_____	_____
_____	_____	_____	_____	_____	_____
_____	_____	_____	_____	_____	_____
_____	_____	_____	_____	_____	_____
_____	_____	_____	_____	_____	_____

Directions: To begin this intervention, collect baseline data on how well the target student is initially paying attention. Assign 15 minutes of individual practice work and observe the student every 10 seconds or so and check for on-task or off-task behavior for 10 minutes. At the end of the 10-minute period you have 60 indicators. Compute the student's percentage of on-task time by simply dividing the number of on-task checks by 60.

Check Sheet of Class Preparedness Behavior

Name _____   Date _____

Check off (✓) each period in which you were prepared for each indicator. At the end of the day, compute the percentage of "yes" answers by dividing the number of checks by 30. Discuss this with your homeroom teacher the following morning.

Class Preparedness   Classes/Subjects/Periods

_____ _____ _____ _____ _____ _____

1. I have my paper/pencils.   _____ _____ _____ _____ _____ _____

2. I have my textbook.   _____ _____ _____ _____ _____ _____

3. I have my homework.   _____ _____ _____ _____ _____ _____

4. I was in class when the bell rang. _____ _____ _____ _____ _____ _____

5. I took my seat before class.   _____ _____ _____ _____ _____ _____

6. Other behavior to be monitored   _____ _____ _____ _____ _____ _____

Directions: Students can use this check list to self-monitor their class preparedness behaviors. They should discuss their results with their teacher the next day.

The Anger Thermometer

How angry am I? Circle one set of words that describe how you feel and what you can do about it. If possible, please suggest how the teacher might help.

RED HOT! BURNING UP!

_____

_____

VERY HOT! TOUGH TO HANDLE!

_____

_____

Warm! Feeling some heat.

_____

_____

I noticed some anger.

_____

_____

Not really angry.

_____

_____

Directions: On this check sheet students identify their emotional intensity in any specific situation and perhaps identify some ways in which the teacher can help.

A Student Interview for Strength-Based Assessment

1. What are the best things about you? _____

   _____

2. Who are your closest friends? _____

   _____

3. What is your neighborhood like? _____

   _____

4. What do you like most about school, and about your neighborhood? _____

   _____

5. Do you feel you are doing well in school? _____

   _____

6. How do you feel about your grades, your friends in school, and your teachers? _____

   _____

7. Do you think it helps you to study and complete school assignments? _____

   _____

8. Other than your parents, who is your favorite adult friend? _____

   _____

9. How do you picture yourself five years from now? _____

   _____

10. Name three things that you really like to do? _____

    _____

A Teacher's and Parent's Planning Guide for the "Shine My Light" Strategy

I. The Student's Behavior and Interests

Identify a student who has demonstrated problem behaviors in the classroom. Consider first the types of behavior that have been demonstrated.

1. What behaviors suggest the student needs attention? Describe it here. _____

   _____

   _____

2. Has this student demonstrated this problem behavior before? If so, when? _____

   _____

3. What was the student's primary motivation for this behavior? Did this result in laughter from the rest of the class? _____

   _____

4. Does the misbehavior itself suggest a particular task or a particular type of attention the student would like?

   _____

   _____

5. Does the student's interest show in his or her academic work in the class (e.g., a student who always writes stories about bicycles)? _____

   _____

6. What do others (e.g., parents, peers, and other teachers) say about the student's interests? _____

   _____

   _____

7. What does the student identify as hobbies or areas of interest?

   _____

   _____

(Continued)

II. Exploration of Options

List below any possible hobbies/interest areas identified above.

_____   _____   _____

_____   _____   _____

1. Which of these options are the least expensive? _____

2. Are all of the options available, given the expense associated with almost any hobby? _____

_____

3. Which options take advantage of community resources (recreation leagues, ball fields, etc.)? ____

_____

_____

4. Which options, if any, parallel the interests of other siblings? _____

_____

5. Is some formal or informal training available to the student for any of these options (e.g., band training at school)? _____

_____

6. Can family or other students in the class provide informal training in this area at no cost? _____

_____

7. Do these options offer regular opportunities for this student to demonstrate the newly acquired skill?

_____

8. Based on this, which is the best option to explore? _____

_____

Teacher's Self-Assessment: My Experience in My Classroom

Directions: On this sheet, circle the number that best represents the extent to which you agree with each of the following statements, based on your initial response to the question and without much reflection. Because this is an informal evaluation, there are no scoring guidelines. However, after completing the entire form, examine your answers individually and reflectively consider how these answers affect how you manage your class.

Do Not Agree	Agree Somewhat	Mostly Agree	Totally Agree
1	2	3	4

I believe all students can learn.	1	2	3	4
I try to teach to student strengths.	1	2	3	4
I enjoy some classes more than others.	1	2	3	4
I vary assessments to get a true picture of students' abilities and skills.	1	2	3	4
Some minority students may be challenged by hard work.	1	2	3	4
I make a special effort to recognize the dignity of each and every student.	1	2	3	4
I promote tolerance in my class.	1	2	3	4
I care less for some students than for others.	1	2	3	4

(Continued)

(Continued)

I try to get to know every student as a person.	1	2	3	4
I sometimes let my anger show in the class.	1	2	3	4
I actively listen to every student's problem.	1	2	3	4
I model self-control at all times in my class.	1	2	3	4
I observe students in non-class environments to get to know and understand them.	1	2	3	4
Students with disabilities may slow down the class.	1	2	3	4
There are some students I really don't like because of their behavior in class.	1	2	3	4
My class is characterized by use of humor.	1	2	3	4
I try to reach every student in a personal way.	1	2	3	4
I believe that the students generally enjoy my class.	1	2	3	4
I generally enjoy my class each day.	1	2	3	4
I communicate my faith in my students' abilities daily in my class.	1	2	3	4
I believe the overall class climate in my classroom is excellent.	1	2	3	4

Assessing Student Relationships

Directions: On this sheet, circle the number that represents the extent to which you agree with each of the following statements. Then answer the questions below.

Not Worried About This	Hardly Worried About This	Worried About This	Very Worried About This
1	2	3	4

Other students liking me	1	2	3	4
Being different	1	2	3	4
Having a teacher angry at me	1	2	3	4
Changing classes and meeting new people	1	2	3	4
Giving a presentation in front of others	1	2	3	4
Being picked on	1	2	3	4
Who to sit by in the cafeteria	1	2	3	4
Being sent to the principal	1	2	3	4
Dating	1	2	3	4
Unkind people	1	2	3	4
Walking past others in the hallways	1	2	3	4

(Continued)

(Continued)

Making friends	1	2	3	4
Not having an adult who listens	1	2	3	4
Not knowing what is expected by the teacher	1	2	3	4
New teachers	1	2	3	4
Club activities with other students	1	2	3	4
Opportunities for after-school activity	1	2	3	4

1. Tell your teacher here the thing that worries you the most. _____

_____

2. Is there some class activity that you really don't want to do? _____

_____

3. Can you recommend how the teacher can help make you more comfortable in class?_____

_____

4. Are there things that make you nervous that you'd like to discuss with the teacher and principal? _____

_____

Checklist for Assessing Overall Classroom Climate

Directions: Answer each question with a *Yes* or *No.* Answer immediately, without long reflection.

_____ 1. Is the teacher smiling?

_____ 2. Are the students working on their assigned tasks?

_____ 3. Are the students quietly whispering?

_____ 4. Do students usually raise their hands before answering?

_____ 5. Would you like to have your own child in this class?

_____ 6. Do students seem friendly toward each other?

_____ 7. Does the teacher speak respectfully to students?

_____ 8. Do the students feel like there is a bully in the class?

_____ 9. Are various disciplinary options in evidence (e.g., rules posted, behavior charts)?

_____ 10. Are students of different races working together?

(Continued)

(Continued)

_____ 11. Do students often pick on one particular person?

_____ 12. Do parents often visit or help with projects?

_____ 13. Are an array of instructional activities used?

_____ 14. Do the students seem to get along, in general?

_____ 15. Are most homework assignments handed in?

_____ 16. Does the teacher use a signal to get the students' attention?

_____ 17. Are there displays of student work in the class?

_____ 18. Do the students seek out the teacher for help with a problem?

_____ 19. Are learning centers set up around the classroom?

_____ 20. Is the classroom generally pleasing to look at?

Functional Behavioral Assessment Form

Student's Name: _____ Date _____ School _____

Teacher's Name: _____ Subject Taught _____

1. Identify at least three strengths or contributions the student brings to the school. _____

   _____

2. Presenting Behavior Problem: Describe one or two instances of the problem behavior. _____

   _____

   _____

3. Co-occurring Behaviors: Describe any co-occurring behaviors. Note how these may be related to the presenting behavior problem. _____

   _____

4. Behavioral Antecedents: Note what happens immediately before the behavior problem. Does the problem occur at the same time, or in the same type of activity each day? _____

   _____

5. How long does the problem behavior last? _____

6. What is the level of danger of the problem behavior? _____

7. Who else is involved? Are others consistently involved in the misbehavior? _____

   _____

8. What does the student gain? What do you think the student seeks to accomplish with the misbehavior?

   _____

9. What is the payoff? Note how you or the student's peers respond to the misbehavior. _____

   _____

10. Based on these indicators, what function is served by the misbehavior? _____

    _____

11. What current efforts have been used to control the problem behavior? _____

    _____

A Behavioral Improvement Plan

Student's Name: _____ Date _____ School _____

Teacher's Name: _____ Subject Taught _____

1. Presenting Behavior Problem: Describe one or two instances of the problem behavior._____

   _____

   _____

2. How often does this occur? Attach a chart of baseline data or an ABC log. _____

   _____

3. Functional assessment of the misbehavior: Attach some notes or a completed FBA form. _____

   _____

4. What interventions will be used? Check the interventions you will undertake.

   _____ assign study partner   _____ more time on tests   _____ use cooperative groups

   _____ behavioral contract   _____ assign peer buddy   _____ parent/student/teacher meeting

   _____ use special seating   _____ self-monitoring   _____ provide para-professional

   _____ reinforce incompatible   _____ other (describe below)
              behavior

   _____

   _____

5. Second tier intervention: If the proposed intervention above does not work, what secondary intervention will you attempt? _____

6. Post intervention data. Teachers must provide a chart for each intervention that includes baseline and intervention data (using an X/Y axis standard behavioral chart). These data must reflect a minimum of three weeks of intervention data (attach a chart).

Glossary

Amygdala. The almond-shaped structure in the brain's limbic area that encodes emotional messages to long-term memory.

Anterior cingulate. The brain region located at the front end of the limbic area and just behind the center of the frontal lobe. It is involved in various executive functions such as monitoring responses, detecting errors, and attention.

Attribution theory. The basic principle, as it applies to motivation, that an individual's own perceptions or attributions for success or failure determine the amount of effort the individual will expend on that activity in the future.

Axon. The neuron's long and unbranched fiber that carries impulses from the cell to the next neuron.

Behavioral Improvement Plan (BIP). A BIP uses the observations from a Functional Behavioral Assessment (FBA) and turns them into a concrete plan of action for managing a student's behavior.

Cerebellum. One of the major parts of the brain, it coordinates muscle movement and is thought to play a role in long-term memory.

Cerebrum. The largest of the major parts of the brain, it controls sensory interpretation, thinking, and memory.

Cognitive-behavioral therapy (CBT). A psychotherapy, used individually or in groups, based on modifying thoughts, assumptions, beliefs, and behaviors, with the aim of positively influencing disturbed emotions.

Corpus callosum. The bridge of nerve fibers that connects the left and right cerebral hemispheres and allows communication between them.

Cortical pathway. The mechanism whereby sensory signals are routed from the thalamus to the frontal lobe for processing and then to the amygdala.

Countercontrol. The actions taken by a controllee to manipulate the behavior of the controller.

Fear conditioning. Learning in which a neutral stimulus acquires a negative response by virtue of being associated with an aversive event.

Frontal lobe. The front part of the brain that monitors higher-order thinking, directs problem solving, and controls the excesses of the emotional (limbic) area. Also referred to as the executive center.

Functional Behavioral Assessment (FBA). A comprehensive and individualized strategy to identify the purpose or function of a student's problem behavior.

Functional Magnetic Resonance Imaging (fMRI). An instrument that measures blood flow to the brain to record areas of high and low neuronal activity.

Hippocampus. A seahorse-shaped structure in the brain's limbic area involved in learning and memory.

Hypothalamus. A structure at the bottom of the limbic area important for the autonomic and endocrine systems, and for maintaining the body's internal stability (homeostasis).

Limbic area. The region within the center of the brain that generates and regulates emotions.

Mirror neurons. Clusters of neurons in the brain that fire not only when experiencing a task or emotion but also when seeing someone else experience that same task or emotion.

Movement-based instruction. Any classroom strategy that requires students to physically move their bodies to or from one place to another in order to complete the learning task.

Neuron. The basic cell making up the brain and nervous system, consisting of a globular cell body, a long fiber, called an axon, which transmits impulses, and many short fibers, called dendrites, which receive them.

Neurotransmitter. A chemical substance that transmits impulses from neuron to neuron across the synaptic gap.

Oppositional defiant disorder (ODD). A behavioral disorder evidenced in children by a persistent pattern of disobedience and hostility toward parents, teachers, or other adults, and their refusal to follow commands or requests by adults.

Orbitofrontal cortex. A brain area whose primary functions are related to the processing of emotions.

Responsibility strategy. A tactic that empowers students by providing them a way to earn positive attention for necessary and appropriate behaviors.

Responsiveness to Intervention (RTI). A method of determining whether students have learning difficulties by assessing their responses to the methods, strategies, curriculum, and interventions they encounter.

Self-concept. What we know about ourselves.

Self-esteem. How we feel about ourselves.

Strength-based assessment. The process of determining a student's areas of strength rather than weakness.

Thalamic pathway. The mechanism whereby sensory signals are routed from the thalamus to the amygdala for processing.

Thalamus. The part in the limbic area that receives all incoming sensory information, except smell, and shunts it to other areas of the brain for additional processing.

Working memory. The temporary memory where information is consciously processed.

References

Abrams, B. J. (2005). Becoming a therapeutic teacher for students with emotional and behavioral disorders. *Teaching Exceptional Children, 38,* 40–45.

Adolphs, R., Tranel, D., & Denburg, N. (2000). Impaired emotional declarative memory following unilateral amygdala damage. *Learning and Memory, 7,* 180–186.

Agassi, M. (2000). *Hands are not for hitting.* Minneapolis, MN: Free Spirit Publishing.

Agosta, E., Graetz, J. E., Mastropieri, M. A., & Scruggs, T. E. (2004). Teacher-researcher partnerships to improve social behavior through social stories. *Intervention in School and Clinic, 39,* 276–287.

Albert, L. (1996). *Cooperative discipline.* Circle Pines, MN: American Guidance Service.

Allen, J. (2006, September). My literary lunches with boys. *Educational Leadership, 64,* 67–70.

Allen, J. P., Porter, M. R., & McFarland, F. C. (2005). The two faces of adolescents' success with peers: Adolescent popularity, social adaptation, and deviant behavior. *Child Development, 76,* 747–760.

Anderson, A. K., & Phelps, E. A. (2002). Is the human amygdala critical for the subjective experience of emotion? Evidence of intact dispositional affect in patients with amygdala lesions. *Journal of Cognitive Neuroscience, 14,* 709–720.

Arntz, A. (2003, June). Cognitive therapy versus applied relaxation as treatment for generalized anxiety disorder. *Behaviour Research and Therapy, 41,* 633–646.

Aron, A. R., Behrens, T. E., Smith, S., Frank, M. J., & Poldrack, R. A. (2007, April). Triangulating a cognitive control network using diffusion-weighted magnetic resonance imaging (MRI) and functional MRI. *Journal of Neuroscience, 27,* 3743–3752.

Bang, M. (1999). *When Sophie gets angry—really, really, angry.* New York: Blue Sky/Scholastic.

Baron-Cohen, S. (2003). *The essential difference: The truth about the male and female brain.* New York: Basic Books.

Battin-Pearson, S., Newcomb, M. D., Abbott, R. D., Hill, K. G., Catalano, R. F., & Hawkins, J. (2000). Predictors of early high school dropout: A test of five theories. *Journal of Educational Psychology, 92,* 586–582.

Baumeister, R. F., Campbell, J. D., Krueger, J. I., & Vohs, K. D. (2005, January). Exploding the self-esteem myth. *Scientific American, 292,* 84–91.

Beale, A. V., & Hall, K. R. (2007, September/October). Cyberbullying: What school administrators (and parents) can do. *The Clearing House, 81,* 8–12.

Beaver, K. M., Wright, J. P., DeLisi, M., Walsh, A., Vaughn, M. G., Boisvert, D., & Vaske, J. (2007, June). A gene × gene interaction between DRD2 and DRD4 is associated with conduct disorder and antisocial behavior in males. *Behavioral and Brain Functions, 3,* 30.

Bender, W. N. (2003). *Relational discipline: Strategies for in-your-face kids.* Boston: Allyn & Bacon.

Bender, W. N. (2005). *Differentiating Math Instruction.* Thousand Oaks, CA: Corwin Press.

Bender, W. N. (2008). *Differentiating instruction for students with learning disabilities* (2nd ed.). Thousand Oaks, CA: Corwin Press.

Bendersky, M., Bennett, D., & Lewis, M. (2006). Aggression at age 5 as a function of prenatal exposure to cocaine, gender, and environmental risk. *Journal of Pediatric Psychology, 31,* 71–84.

Bendersky, M., Gambini, G., Lastella, A., Bennett, D. S., & Lewis, M. (2003, October). Inhibitory motor control at five years as a function of prenatal cocaine exposure. *Journal of Developmental and Behavioral Pediatrics, 24,* 345–351.

Bernard, B. (1992). *Mentoring programs for urban youth: Handle with care.* Portland, OR: Western Regional Center for Drug-Free Schools and Communities. Northwest Regional Educational Laboratory.

Bishop, K. M., & Wahlsten, D. (1997). Sex differences in the human corpus callosum: Myth or reality? *Neuroscience and Biobehavioral Reviews, 21,* 581–601.

Blankenship, T., & Bender, W. N. (2007, Winter). Widely used disciplinary options for aggressive kids: Are the current approaches effective? *The Journal of the American Academy of Special Education Professionals,* 1–38.

Book, A. S., Starzyk, K. B., & Quinsey, V. L. (2001, November-December). The relationship between testosterone and aggression: A meta-analysis. *Aggression and Violent Behavior, 6,* 579–599.

Booth, A., Granger, D. A., Mazur, A., & Kivlighan, K. T. (2006, September). Testosterone and social behavior. *Social Forces, 85,* 167–191.

Booth, A., Johnson, D. R., Granger, D. A., Crouter, A. C., & McHale, S. (2003). Testosterone and child and adolescent adjustment: The moderating role of parent-child relationships. *Developmental Psychology, 39,* 85–98.

Botvin, G. J., & Griffin, K. W. (2004). Life skills training: Empirical findings and future directions. *Journal of Primary Prevention, 25,* 211–232.

Boyd, J., Barnett, W. S., Bodrova, E., Leong, D. J., & Gomby, D. (2005). Promoting children's social and emotional development through preschool education. *Preschool Policy Brief,* National Institute for Early Education Research.

Brass, M., & Heyes, C. (2005, October). Imitation: Is cognitive neuroscience solving the correspondence problem? *Trends in Cognitive Sciences, 9,* 489–495.

Bryan, T. S. (1986). Self-concept and attributions of the learning disabled. *Learning Disabilities Focus, 1,* 82–88.

Buron, K. D., & Curtis, M. (2003). *The incredible 5–point scale: Assisting students with autism spectrum disorders in understanding social interactions and controlling their emotional responses.* Shawnee Mission, KS: Autism Asperger Publishing.

Bush, G., Luu, P., & Posner, M. I. (2000). Cognitive and emotional influences in anterior cingulate cortex. *Trends in Cognitive Sciences, 4,* 215–222.

Cahill, L. (2005, May). His brain, her brain. *Scientific American, 292,* 40–47.

Calvete, E., & Cardenoso, O. (2005, April). Gender differences in cognitive vulnerability to depression and behavior problems in adolescents. *Journal of Abnormal Child Psychology, 33,* 179–192.

Carey, T. A., (2002). *Countercontrol in schools: How often does it happen and what factors are associated with its occurrences?* Unpublished doctoral dissertation. The University of Queensland, St. Lucia, Brisbane, Queensland, Australia.

Carey, T. A., & Bourbon, W. T. (2004). Countercontrol: A new look at some old problems. *Intervention in School and Clinic, 40,* 3–9.

Carey, T. A., & Bourbon, W. T. (2006). Is countercontrol the key to understanding chronic behavior problems? *Intervention in School and Clinic, 42,* 5–13.

Caspi, A., McClay, J., Moffitt, T. E., Mill, J., Martin, J., Craig, I. W., Taylor, A., & Poulton, R. (2002, August). Role of genotype in the cycle of violence in maltreated children. *Science, 297,* 851–854.

Chapman, C. (2000). "Brain-compatible instruction." Paper presented on a nationwide telesatellite workshop. Found in *Tactics for brain-compatible instruction.* Bishop, GA: Teacher's Workshop.

Chibbaro, J. S. (2007, October). School counselors and the cyberbully: Interventions and implications. *Professional School Counseling, 11,* 65–68.

Choudhury, S., Blakemore, S-J., & Charman, T. (2006). Social cognitive development during adolescence. *Social Cognitive Affective Neuroscience, 1,* 165–174.

Clinton, G., & Miles, W. (1999). Mentoring programs: Fostering resilience in at-risk kids. In W. N. Bender, G. Clinton, & R. Bender (Eds.), *Violence prevention and reduction in school* (pp. 31–45). Austin, TX: ProEd.

Cohen, G. L., & Prinstein, M. J. (2006, July/August). Peer contagion of aggression and health risk behavior among adolescent males: An experimental investigation of effects on public conduct and private attitudes. *Child Development, 77,* 967–983.

Collins, B. C., Hall, M., Rankin, S. W., & Branson, T. A. (1999). Just say "no!" and walk away. *Teaching Exceptional Children, 31,* 48–52.

Collins, W. A., & Laursen, B. (2004). Changing relationships, changing youth: Interpersonal contexts of adolescent development. *Journal of Early Adolescence, 24,* 55–62.

Conrad, A., & Roth, W. T. (2007). Muscle relaxation therapy for anxiety disorders: It works but how? *Journal of Anxiety Disorders, 21,* 243–264.

Crawford, N. (2002). New ways to stop bullying. *Monitor on Psychology, 33,* 64.

Curtis, T., & Hansen-Schwoebel, K. (1999). *Big Brother Big Sisters school-based mentoring: Evaluation summary of five pilot programs.* Philadelphia: Big Brother Big Sisters of America.

Dabbs, J. M., & Dabbs, M. G. (2000). *Heroes, rogues, and lovers: Testosterone and behavior.* New York: McGraw-Hill

Damasio, A. (2003). *Looking for Spinoza: Joy, sorrow, and the feeling brain.* New York: Harcourt.

Damasio, A. R., Grabowski, T. J., Bechara, A., Damasio, H., Ponto, L. L., Parvizi, J., & Hichwa, R. D. (2000). Subcortical and cortical brain activity during the feeling of self-generated emotions. *Nature Neuroscience, 3,* 1049–1056.

Dappen, L. D., & Isernhagen, J. C. (2005, Spring). Developing a student mentoring program: Building connections for at-risk students. *Preventing School Failure, 49,* 21–25.

Davidson, M. C., Amso, D., Anderson, L. C., & Diamond, A. (2006). Development of cognitive control and executive functions from 4 to 13 years: Evidence from manipulations of memory, inhibition, and task switching. *Neuropsychologia, 44,* 2037–2078.

deBruyn, E. H., & Cillessen, A. H. N. (2006). Popularity in early adolescence: Prosocial and antisocial subtypes. *Journal of Adolescent Research, 21,* 607–627.

Diego, M. A., Field, T. M., & Sanders, C. E. (2003). Academic performance, popularity, and depression predict adolescent substance use. *Adolescence, 38,* 35–42.

Dinkes, R., Cataldi, E. F., Kena, G., & Baum, K. (2006). *Indicators of school crime and safety: 2006* (NCES2007–003/NCJ 214262). U.S. Departments of Education and Justice. Washington, DC: U.S. Government Printing Office.

Duckworth, A. L., & Seligman, M. E. P. (2006). Self-discipline gives girls the edge: Gender in self-discipline, grades, and achievement test scores. *Journal of Educational Psychology, 98,* 198–208.

Dunkley, D. M., & Grilo, C. M. (2007, January). Self-Criticism, low self-esteem, depressive symptoms, and over-evaluation of shape and weight in binge-eating disorder patients. *Behaviour Research and Therapy, 45,* 139–149.

Edwards, E. P., Eiden, R. D., Colder, C., & Leonard, K. E. (2006, June). The development of aggression in 18 to 48 month old children of alcoholic parents. *Journal of Abnormal Child Psychology, 34,* 409–423.

Eisenberg, D. T. A., MacKillop, J., Modi, M., Beauchemin, J., Dang, D., Lisman, S. A., Lum, J. K., & Wilson, D. S. (2007, January). Examining impulsivity as an endophenotype using a behavioral approach: a DRD2 TaqI A and DRD4 48-bp VNTR association study. *Behavioral and Brain Functions, 3.2.*

Eisenberg, N., Spinrad, T. L., Fabes, R. A., Reiser, M., Cumberland, A., Shepard, S. A., Valiente, C., Losoya, S. H., Guthrie, I. K., & Thompson, M. (2004). The relations of effortful control and impulsivity to children's resiliency and adjustment. *Child Development, 75,* 25–46.

Elias, M. J. (2004). The connection between social-emotional learning and learning disabilities: Implications for intervention. *Learning Disability Quarterly, 27,* 53–61.

Ellickson, P. L., McCaffrey, D. F., Ghosh-Dastidar, B., & Longshore, D. L. (2003). New inroads in preventing adolescent drug use: Results from a large-scale trial of Project ALERT in middle schools. *American Journal of Public Health, 93,* 1830–1836.

Emler, N. (2001). *Self-esteem: The costs and causes of low self-worth.* York, England: York Publishing Services.

Epstein, M. H. (1998). Assessing the emotional and behavioral strengths of children. *Reclaiming Children and Youth, 6,* 250–252.

Epstein, M. H. (1999). Development and validation of a scale to assess the emotional and behavioral strengths of children and adolescents. *Remedial and Special Education, 20,* 258–262.

Epstein, M. H. (2000). *Assessing the emotional and behavioral strengths of children and adolescents.* Paper presented at the annual meeting of the Council for Exceptional Children, Austin, TX: (October 21).

Fadiga, L., Craighero, L., & Olivier, E. (2005, March). Human motor cortex excitability during the perception of others' action. *Current Opinion in Neurobiology, 15,* 213–218.

Ferguson, R. (2002). *What doesn't meet the eye.* Naperville, IL: North Central Regional Educational Laboratory.

Fleming, C. B., Haggerty, K. P., Catalano, R. F., Harachi, T. W., Mazza, J. J., & Gruman, D. H. (2005, November). Do social and behavioral characteristics targeted by preventive interventions predict standardized test scores and grades? *Journal of School Health, 75,* 342–349.

Fleming, D. C., Ritchie, B., & Fleming, E. R. (1983). Fostering the social adjustment of disturbed students. *Teaching Exceptional Children, 15,* 172–175.

Foley, D. L., Eaves, L. J., Wormley, B., Silberg, J. L., Maes, H. H., Kuhn, J., & Riley, B. (2007, March). Childhood adversity, monoamine oxidase-a genotype, and risk for conduct disorder. *Archives of General Psychiatry, 64,* 377–378.

Freiberg, H. J. (1998, September). Measuring school climate: Let me count the ways. *Educational Leadership, 56,* 22–26.

Frith, C. D., & Frith, U. (2006). The neural basis of mentalizing. *Neuron, 50,* 531–534.

Gallup (2004). *In teens' own words: Which teachers motivate you?* Available online at http://www.gallup.com/poll/11848/Teens-Own-Words-Which-Teachers-Motivate-You.aspx.

Garcia, S. B., & Ortiz, A. A. (2006). Preventing disproportionate representation: Culturally and linguistically responsive prereferral interventions. *Teaching Exceptional Children, 38,* 64–68.

Gazzaniga, M. S., Ivry, R. B., & Mangun, G. R. (2002). *Cognitive neuroscience: The biology of the mind.* New York: Norton.

Ge, X., Conger, R. D., & Elder, G. H. (1995). Coming of age too early: Pubertal influences on girls' vulnerability to psychological distress. *Child Development, 67,* 3386–3400.

George, M. S., Ketter, T. A., Parekh, P. I., Horwitz, B., Herscovitch, P., & Post, R. M. (1995). Brain activity during transient sadness and happiness in healthy women. *American Journal of Psychiatry, 152,* 341–351.

Giedd, J. N., Blumenthal, J., Jeffries, N. O., Castellanos, F. X., Liu, H., Zijdenbos, A., Paus, T., Evans, A. C., & Rapoport, J. L. (1999). Brain development during childhood and adolescence: A longitudinal MRI study. *Nature Neuroscience, 2,* 861–863.

Gifford-Smith, M., Dodge, K. A., Dishion, T. J., & McCord, J. (2005, June). Peer influence in children and adolescents: Crossing the bridge from developmental to intervention science. *Journal of Abnormal Child Psychology, 33,* 255–265.

Ginsburg-Block, M. D., Rohrbeck, C. A., & Fantuzzo, J. W. (2006, November). A meta-analytic review of social, self-concept, and behavioral outcomes of peer-assisted learning. *Journal of Educational Psychology, 98,* 732–749.

Goldberg, E. (2001). *The executive brain: Frontal lobes and the civilized mind.* New York: Oxford University Press.

Goldberg, I. I., Harel, M., & Malach, R. (2006, April). When the brain loses its self: Prefrontal inactivation during sensorimotor processing. *Neuron, 50,* 329–339.

Goleman, D. (2006, September). The socially intelligent leader. *Educational Leadership, 64,* 76–81.

Gorenstein, E. E., Tager, F. A., Shapiro, P. A., Monk, C., & Sloan, R. P. (2007, May). Cognitive-behavior therapy for reduction of persistent anger. *Cognitive and Behavioral Practice, 14,* 168–184.

Granillo, T., Jones-Rodriguez, G., & Carvajal, S. C. (2005, March). Prevalence of eating disorders in Latina adolescents: Associations with substance use and other correlates. *Journal of Adolescent Health, 36,* 214–220.

Grosbras, M-H., Jansen, M., Leonard, G., McIntosh, A., Osswald, K., Poulsen, C., Steinberg, L., Toro, R., & Paus, T. (2007, July). Neural mechanisms of resistance to peer influence in early adolescence. *Journal of Neuroscience, 27,* 8040–8045.

Haberstick, B. C., Lessem, J. M., Hopfer, C. J., Smolen, A., Ehringer, M. A., Timberlake, D., & Hewitt, J. K. (2005). Monoamine oxidase A (MAOA) and antisocial behaviors in the presence of childhood and adolescent maltreatment. *American Journal of Medical Genetics Part B: Neuropsychiatric Genetics, 135B,* 59–64.

Haggerty, N. K., Black, R. S., & Smith, G. J. (2005). Increasing self-managed coping skills through social stories and apron storytelling. *Teaching Exceptional Children, 37,* 40–47.

Hall, N., Williams, J., & Hall, P. S. (2000). Fresh approaches with oppositional students. *Reclaiming Children and Youth, 8,* 219–236.

Hall P. S., & Hall, N. D. (2003, September). Building relationships with challenging children. *Educational Leadership, 61,* 60–63.

Hallahan, D. P., Lloyd, J. W., & Stoller, L. (1982). *Improving attention with self-monitoring: A manual for teachers.* Charlottesville, VA: Curry School of Education, University of Virginia.

Hannula, D. E., Simons, D. J., & Cohen, N. J. (2005). Imaging implicit perception: Promise and pitfalls. *Nature Reviews Neuroscience, 6,* 247–255.

Hansen, J. M., & Childs, J. (1998, September). Creating a school where people like to be. *Educational Leadership, 56,* 14–17.

Hänze, M., & Berger, R. (2007, February). Cooperative learning, motivational effects, and student characteristics: An experimental study comparing cooperative learning and direct instruction in 12th grade physics classes. *Learning and Instruction, 17,* 29–41.

Harlacher, J. E., Roberts, N. E., & Merrell, K. W. (2006). Classwide interventions for students with ADHD: A summary of teacher options beneficial for the whole class. *Teaching Exceptional Children, 39,* 6–12.

Harris, S. L., & Petrie, G. F. (2003). *Bullying: The bullies, the victims, the bystanders.* Lanham, MD: Scarecrow Press.

Hart, A. J., Whalen, P. J., Shin, L. M., McInerney, S. C., Fischer, H., & Rausch, S. L. (2000). Differential response in the human amygdala to racial outgroup vs. ingroup face stimuli. *NeuroReport, 11,* 2351–2355.

Heatherton, T. F., Wyland, C. L., Macrae, C. N., Demos, K. E., Denny, B. T., & Kelley, W. M. (2006). Medial prefrontal activity differentiates self from close others. *Social Cognitive and Affective Neuroscience, 1,* 18–25.

Herschell, A., Calzada, E., Eyberg, S.M., & McNeil, C.B. (2002). Parent-child interaction therapy: New directions in research. *Cognitive and Behavioral Practice, 9,* 9–16.

Hill, A., & Pallin, V. (1998). Dieting awareness and low self-worth: Related issues in 8–year-old girls. *International Journal of Eating Disorders, 24,* 405–413.

Hudziak, J. J., Derks, E. M., Althoff, R. R., Copeland, W., & Boomsma, D. I. (2005, September). The genetic and environmental contributions to oppositional defiant behavior: A multi-informant twin study. *Journal of the American Academy of Child and Adolescent Psychiatry, 44,* 907–914.

Huffman, L. C., Mehlinger, S. L., & Kerivan, A. S. (2001). Risk factors for academic and behavioral problems in the beginning of school. In *Off to a good start: Research on the risk factors for early school problems and selected federal policies affecting children's social and emotional development and their readiness for school.* Chapel Hill, NC: University of North Carolina, FPG Child Development Center.

Iacoboni, M. (2007). The quiet revolution of existential neuroscience. In E. Harmon-Jones & P. Winkielman, (Eds.). *Social neuroscience: Integrating biological and psychological explanations of social behavior* (pp. 439–453). New York: Guilford Press.

Iacoboni, M., Molnar-Szakacs, I., Gallese, V., Buccino, G., Mazziotta, J. C., & Rizzolatti, G. (2005). Grasping the intentions of others with one's own mirror neuron system. *PloS Biology, 3,* e79.

Jackson, D. A., & King, A. R. (2004, April). Gender differences in the effects of oppositional behavior on teacher ratings of ADHD symptoms. *Journal of Abnormal Psychology, 32,* 215–224.

Jaime, K., & Knowlton, E. (2007). Visual supports for students with behavior and cognitive challenges. *Intervention in School and Clinic, 42,* 259–270.

Jekielek, S. M., Moore, K. A., Hair, E. C., & Scarupa, H. J. (2002, February). Mentoring: A promising strategy for youth development. Research brief. *Child Trends.* Available at www.childtrends.org.

Jenson, W. R., & Reavis, H. K. (1999). Using group contingencies to improve academic achievement. *Best Practices, 1,* 77–84.

Johnson, D. D. P., McDermott, R., Barrett, E. S., Cowden, J., Wrangham, R., McIntyre, M. H., & Rosen, S. P. (2006, October). Overconfidence in war games: Experimental evidence on expectations, aggression, gender and testosterone. *Proceedings of the Royal Society: Biological Sciences, 273,* 2513–2520.

Johnson, M. H., Griffin, R., Csibra, G., Halit, H., Farroni, T., De Haan, M., Tucker, L. A., Baron–Cohen, S., & Richards, J. (2005). The emergence of the social brain network: Evidence from typical and atypical development. *Developmental Psychopathology, 17,* 599–619.

Johnstone, T., van Reekum, C. M., Oakes, T. R., & Davidson, R. J. (2006). The voice of emotion: an fMRI study of neural responses to angry and happy vocal expressions. *Social, Cognitive, & Affective Neuroscience, 1,* 242–249.

Jones, M., Boon, R. T., Fore, C., & Bender, W. N. (2008). Our mystery hero! A group contingency intervention for reducing verbally disrespectful behaviors. *Learning Disabilities: A Multidisciplinary Journal,* (in press).

Kellner, M. H., & Turtin, J. (1995). A school-based anger management program for developmentally and emotionally disturbed high school students. *Adolescence, 30,* 813–825.

Kern, L., & Dunlap, G. (1994). Use of a classwide self-management program to improve the behavior of students with emotional and behavioral disorders. *Education and Treatment of Children, 17,* 445–459.

King, K., & Gurian, M. (2006, September). Teaching to the minds of boys. *Educational Leadership, 64,* 56–61.

Konrad, M., Fowler, C. H., Walker, A. R., Test, D. W., & Wood, W. M. (2007). Effects of self-determination interventions on the academic skills of students with learning disabilities. *Learning Disability Quarterly, 30,* 89–114.

Kringelbach, M. L. (2005, September). The human orbitofrontal cortex: Linking reward to hedonic experience. *Nature Reviews Neuroscience, 6,* 691–702.

Kurzban, R., Tooby, J., & Cosmides, L. (2001). Can race be erased? Coalitional computation and social categorization. *Proceedings of the National Academy of Sciences, 98(26),* 15387–15392.

LaFontana, K. M., & Cillessen, A. H. N. (2002, September). Children's perceptions of popular and unpopular peers: A multimethod assessment. *Developmental Psychology, 38,* 635–647.

Lane, K. L., Givner, C. C., & Pierson, M. R. (2004). Teacher expectations of student behavior: Social skills necessary for success in elementary school classrooms. *Journal of Special Education, 38,* 104–110.

Lazerson, D. B., Foster, H. L., Brown, S. I., & Hummel, J. W. (1988). The effectiveness of cross-age tutoring with truant, junior high school students with learning disabilities. *Journal of Learning Disabilities, 21,* 253–255.

Li, Q. (2006). Cyberbullying in schools: A research of gender differences. *School Psychology International, 27,* 157–170.

Lochman, J. E., Lampron, L. B., Gemmer, T. C., Harris, S. R., & Wyckoff, G. M. (2006, February). Strategies in behavioral change: Teacher consultation and cognitive-behavioral interventions with aggressive boys. *Psychology in the Schools, 26,* 179–188.

Lopata, C. (2003). Progressive muscle relaxation and aggression among elementary students classified as emotionally disturbed. *Behavioral Disorders, 28,* 162–172.

Lopata, C., Nida, R. E., & Marable, M. A, (2006). Progressive muscle relaxation: Preventing aggression in students with EBD. *Teaching Exceptional Children, 38,* 20–25.

MacLean, P. D. (1952). Some psychiatric implications of physiological studies on frontotemporal portion of limbic system (visceral brain). *Electroencephalography and Clinical Neurophysiology, 4,* 407–418.

Maher, C. A. (1982). Behavioral effects of using conduct problem adolescents as cross-age tutors. *Psychology in the Schools, 19,* 360–364.

Maher, C. A. (1984). Handicapped adolescents as cross-age tutors. Program description and evaluation. *Exceptional Children, 51,* 56–63.

Mahoney, M. J. (1979). Cognitive skills and athletic performance. In P. C. Kendall & S. D. Hollon (Eds.), *Cognitive-behavioral interventions: Theory, research, and procedures* (pp. 423–443). New York: Academic Press.

March, R. E., Horner, R. H., Lewis-Palmer, T., Brown, D., Crone, D., Todd, A. W., et al. (2000). *Functional Assessment Checklist: Teachers and Staff (FACTS).* Eugene, OR: Educational and Community Supports.

Marzano, R. J. (2003). *Classroom management that works* (with J. S. Marzano & D. Pickering). Alexandria, VA: Association for Supervision and Curriculum Development.

Masood, A. F., Turner, L. A., & Baxter, A. (2007). Causal attributions and parental attitudes toward children with disabilities in the United States and Pakistan. *Exceptional Children, 73,* 475–487.

Massachusetts General Hospital (MGH) (2006). *Interventions in School.* Available online at www.school psychiatry.org.

Mathes, M. O., & Bender, W. N. (1996). Effects of self-monitoring on children with attention deficit disorders who are receiving medical interventions: Implications for inclusive instruction. *Remedial and Special Education, 18,* 121–128.

Mayes, L.C. (2002). A behavioral teratogenic model of the impact of prenatal cocaine exposure on arousal regulatory systems. *Neurotoxicology and Teratology, 24,* 385–395.

McCabe, K., Houser, D., Ryan, L., Smith, V., & Trouard, T. (2001). A functional imaging study of cooperation in two-person reciprocal exchange. *Proceedings of the National Academy of Sciences, 98,* 11832–11835.

McIntosh, K., Herman, K., Sanford, A., McGraw, K., & Florence, K. (2004). Teaching transitions: Techniques for promoting success between lessons. *Teaching Exceptional Children, 37,* 32–39.

McKinley, J. (2006, Fall). Winning methods of teachers who close the gap between black and white students. *The Journal of the National Staff Development Council, 27,* 43–47.

McNeal, R. B., Jr., Hansen, W. B., Harrington, N. G., & Giles, S. M. (2004, April). How All Stars works: an examination of program effects on mediating variables. *Health Education and Behavior, 31,* 165–178.

Mecca, A. M. (2001). *The mentoring revolution: Growing America one child at a time.* Part I. Tiburon, CA: California Mentor Foundation.

Meltzoff, A. N. (2007, January). The "like me" framework for recognizing and becoming an intentional agent. *Acta Psychologica, 124,* 26–43.

Mennuti, R. B., Freeman, A., & Christner, R. W. (Eds.). (2006). *Cognitive-behavioral interventions in educational settings: A handbook for practice.* New York, Routledge.

Meyer-Lindenberg, A., Buckholtz, J. W., Kolachana, B., Hariri, A. R., Pezawas, L., Blasi, G., Wabnitz, A., Honea, R., Verchinski, B., Callicott, J. H., Egan, M., Mattay, V., & Weinberger, D. R. (2006, April). Neural mechanisms of genetic risk for impulsivity and violence in humans. *Proceedings of the National Academy of Sciences USA, 103,* 6269–6274.

Minnesota Association for Children's Mental Health (MACMH). (2007). *Oppositional defiant disorder.* Available at http://macmh.org/publications/fact_sheets/ODD.pdf.

Mitchell, J. P., Banaji, M. R., & Macrae, C. N. (2005). The link between social cognition and self-referential thought in the medial prefrontal cortex. *Journal of Cognitive Neuroscience, 17,* 1306–1315.

Murphy, K. A., Theodore, L. A., Aloiso, D., Alric-Edwards, J. M., & Hughes, T. L. (2007). Interdependent group contingency and mystery motivators to reduce preschool disruptive behavior. *Psychology in the Schools, 44,* 53–63.

Musser, E. H., Bray, M. A., Kehle, T. J., & Jenson, W. R. (2001). Reducing disruptive behaviors in students with serious emotional disturbance. *School Psychology Review, 30,* 294–305.

Nelson-Gray, R. O., Keane, S. P., Hurst, R. M., Mitchell, J. T., Warburton, J. B., Chok, J. T., & Cobb, A. R. (2006, December). A modified DBT skills training program for oppositional defiant adolescents: Promising preliminary findings. *Behaviour Research and Therapy, 44,* 1811–1820.

Newcomb, M. D., Abbott, R. D., Catalano, R. F., Hawkins, J., Battin, S. R., & Hill, K. G. (2002). Mediational and deviance theories of late high school failure: Process roles of structural strains, academic competence, and general versus specific problem behavior. *Journal of Counseling Psychology, 49,* 172–186.

Newkirk, T. (2006, September). Media and Literacy: What's good? *Educational Leadership, 64,* 62–65.

Nixon, R. D., Sweeney, L., Erickson, D. B., & Touyz, S. W. (2004, June). Parent-Child Interaction Therapy: One- and two-year follow-up of standard and abbreviated treatments for oppositional preschoolers. *Journal of Abnormal Child Psychology, 32,* 263–271.

Ochsner, K. N. (2007). Social cognitive neuroscience: Historic development, core principles, and future promise. In A. W. Kruglanski & E. Tory (Eds.), *Social psychology: Handbook of basic principles* (2nd Ed.). (pp. 39–68). New York: Guilford Press.

Ochsner, K., & Lieberman, M. (2001). The emergence of social cognitive neuroscience. *American Psychologist, 56,* 717–734.

Olson, I. R., Plotzker, A., & Ezzyat, Y. (2007). The enigmatic temporal pole: A review of findings on social and emotional processing. *Brain, 130,* 1718–1731.

Parsons, L. D. (2006). Using video to teach social skills to secondary students with autism. *Teaching Exceptional Children, 39,* 32–39.

Patton, B., Jolivette, K., & Ramsey, M. (2006). Students with emotional and behavioral disorders can manage their own behavior. *Teaching Exceptional Children, 39,* 14–21.

Paus, T. (2005). Mapping brain maturation and cognitive development during adolescence. *Trends in Cognitive Sciences, 9,* 60–68.

Perrine, N. E., & Aloise-Young, P. A. (2004, December). The role of self-monitoring in adolescents' susceptibility to passive peer pressure. *Personality and Individual Differences, 37,* 1701–1716.

Peyton, J. K. (1997). Dialogue journals: Interactive writing to develop language and literacy. *Emergency Librarian, 24,* 46–48.

Phelps, E. A., O'Connor, K. J., Cunningham, W. A., Funayama, E. S., Gatenby, J. C., Gore, J. C., & Banaji, M. R. (2000). Performance on indirect measures of race evaluation predicts amygdala activation. *Journal of Cognitive Neuroscience, 12,* 729–738.

Phelps, E. A., & Thomas, L. A. (2003). Race, behavior, and the brain: The role of neuroimaging in understanding complex social behaviors. *Political Psychology, 24,* 747–758.

Presley, J. A., & Hughes, C. (2000). Peers as teachers of anger management to high school students with behavioral disorders. *Behavioral Disorders, 23,* 114–130.

Prudhomme, N. (2005, June). Early declarative memory and self-concept. *Infant Behavior and Development, 28,* 132–144.

Purkey, W. W. (2000). *What students say to themselves: Internal dialogue and school success.* Thousand Oaks, CA: Corwin Press.

Quiroz, H. C., Arnette, J. L., & Stephens, R. D. (2006). *Bullying in schools: Fighting the bully battle.* Westlake Village, CA: National School Safety Center. Available online at www.schoolsafety.us.

Ravner, C. C., & Knitzer, J. (2002). *Ready to enter: What research tells policymakers about strategies to promote social and emotional school readiness among three- and four-year-old children.* New York, NY: National Center for Children in Poverty, Mailman School of Public Health, Columbia University.

Redenbach, S. (2004). *Self-esteem and emotional intelligence: The necessary ingredients for success.* Davis, CA: ESP Wise Publications.

Regan, K. S. (2003). Using dialogue journals in the classroom: Forming relationships with students with emotional disturbance. *Teaching Exceptional Children, 36,* 39–40.

Restak, R. (2000). *Mysteries of the mind.* Washington, DC: National Geographic Society.

Ribble, M. S., & Bailey, G. D. (2006, March). Digital citizenship at all grade levels. *Learning and Leading With Technology, 33,* 26–28.

Robin, A., Schneider, M., & Dolnick, M. (1976). The turtle technique: An extended case study of self-control in the classroom. *Psychology in the Schools, 13,* 449–453.

Rodriguez, N. (2002). *Gender differences in disciplinary approaches* (ERIC Research Abstract: ED468259). Arlington, VA: Education Resources Information Center.

Rogers, M. F., & Myles, B. S. (2001). Using social stories and comic strip conversations to interpret social situations for an adolescent with Asperger syndrome. *Intervention In School and Clinic, 36,* 310–313.

Rolls, E. T. (1999). *The brain and emotion.* Oxford, UK: Oxford University Press.

Rudolph, S. H., & Epstein, M. H. (2000). Empowering children and families through strength-based assessment. *Reclaiming Children and Youth, 8,* 207–209.

Ryan, S., Whittaker, C. R., & Pinckney, J. (2002, Spring). A school-based elementary mentoring program. *Preventing School Failure, 46,* 133–138.

Salend, S. J., & Sylvestre, S. (2005). Understanding and addressing oppositional and defiant classroom behaviors. *Teaching Exceptional Children, 37,* 32–39.

Salend, S. J., Whittaker, C. R., & Reeder, E. (1992). Group evaluation: A collaborative, peer-mediated behavior management system. *Exceptional Children, 59,* 203–209.

Sandler, A. G., Arnold, L. B., Gable, R. A., & Strain, R. A. (1987). Effects of peer pressure on disruptive behavior of behavioral disordered classmates. *Behavioral Disorders, 12,* 104–110.

Savage, J., Brodsky, N. L., Malmud, E., Giannetta, J. M., & Hurt, H. (2005, February). Attentional functioning and impulse control in cocaine-exposed and control children at age ten years. *Journal of Developmental & Behavioral Pediatrics, 26,* 42–47.

Schneier, F. R. (2003, September). Social anxiety disorder: Is common, underdiagnosed, impairing, and treatable. *British Medical Journal, 327,* 515–516.

Shonkoff, J. P., & Phillips, D. A. (Eds.). (2000). *From neurons to neighborhoods: The science of early childhood development.* Washington, DC: National Academy Press.

Singer, T., Seymour, B., O'Doherty, J., Kaube, H., Dolan, R. J., & Frith, C. D. (2004). Empathy for pain involves the affective but not sensory components of pain. *Science, 303,* 1157–1162.

Skinner, B. F. (1953). *Science and human behavior.* New York: Free Press.

Smith, S. W., Lochman, J. E., & Daunic, A. P. (2005). Managing aggression using cognitive-behavioral interventions: State of the practice and future directions. *Behavioral Disorders, 30,* 227–240.

Smith, S. W., Siegel, E. M., O'Connor, A. M., & Thomas, S. B. (1994). Effects of cognitive-behavioral training on angry behavior and aggression of three elementary aged students. *Behavioral Disorders, 19,* 126–135.

Snoek, H., van Goozen, S. H. M., Matthys, W., Sigling, H. O., Koppeschaar, H. P. F., Westenberg, H. G. M., & van Engeland, H. (2002, February). Serotonergic functioning in children with oppositional defiant disorder: A sumatriptan challenge study. *Biological Psychiatry, 51,* 319–325.

Snyder, M. C., & Bambara, L. M. (1997). Teaching secondary students with learning disabilities to self-manage classroom survival skills. *Journal of Learning Disabilities, 30,* 534–543.

Sobel, D. M., Taylor, S. V., & Wortman, N. (2006, Winter). Positive behavior strategies that respond to students' diverse needs and backgrounds. *Beyond Behavior,* 20–26.

Sonsthagen, L. L., & Lee, S. (1996). America's most needed: Real life heroes and heroines. *Schools in the Middle, 5,* 37–42.

Sousa, D. A. (2006). *How the brain learns* (3rd ed.). Thousand Oaks, CA: Corwin Press.

Sousa, D. A. (2007). *How the special needs brain learns* (2nd ed.). Thousand Oaks, CA: Corwin Press.

Steinberg, L. (2005, February). Cognitive and affective development in adolescence. *Trends in Cognitive Sciences, 9,* 69–74.

Sterling, M. (1998, September). Building a community week by week. *Educational Leadership, 56,* 65–68.

Stipek, D. (2006, September). Relationships matter. *Educational Leadership, 64,* 46–49.

Suzuki, M., Hagino, H., Noharal, S., Zhou, S-Y., Kawasaki, Y., Takahashi, T., et al. (2005). Male-specific volume expansion of the human hippocampus during adolescence. *Cerebral Cortex, 15,* 187–193.

Swaggart, B. L. (1988). Implementing a cognitive behavior management program. *Intervention in School and Clinic, 33,* 235–238.

Sylwester, R. (2000). *A biological brain in a cultural classroom.* Thousand Oaks, CA: Corwin Press.

Tanaka, G., & Reid, K. (1997, October). Peer helpers: Encouraging kids to confide. *Educational Leadership, 55,* 29–32.

Tate, M. L. (2003). *Worksheets don't grow dendrites: Instructional strategies that engage the brain.* Thousand Oaks, CA: Corwin Press.

Tatum, A. W. (2006, February). Engaging African American males in reading. *Educational Leadership, 63,* 44–49.

Todd, A. W., Campbell, A. L., Meyer, G. G., & Horner, R. H. (2008, Winter). The effects of a targeted intervention to reduce problem behaviors: Elementary school implementation of check in-check out. *Journal of Positive Behavior Interventions, 10,* 46–55.

Torregrossa, M. M., Quinn, J. J., & Taylor, J. R. (2008, February). Impulsivity, compulsivity, and habit: The role of orbitofrontal cortex revisited. *Biological Psychiatry, 63,* 253–255.

Tournaki, N., & Criscitiello, E. (2003). Using peer tutoring as a successful part of behavior management. *Teaching Exceptional Children, 36,* 22–29.

Townsend, B. L. (2000). The disproportionate discipline of African-American learners: Reducing school suspensions and expulsions. *Exceptional Children, 66,* 381–391.

Tremblay, G., Saucier, J-F., & Tremblay, R. E. (2004, August). Identity and disruptiveness in boys: Longitudinal perspectives. *Child & Adolescent Social Work Journal, 21,* 387–406.

Twenge, J. M., & Campbell, W. K. (2002). Self-esteem and socioeconomic status: A meta-analytic review. *Personality and Social Psychology Review, 6,* 59–71.

U.S. Census Bureau (2003, October). *Language use and English speaking ability: 2000.* Washington, DC: U.S. Government Printing Office.

van Goozen, S. H. M., & Fairchild, G. (2006, November). Neuroendocrine and neurotransmitter correlates in children with antisocial behavior. *Hormones and Behavior, 50,* 647–654.

Verdick, E., & Heinlen, M. (2004). *Words are not for hurting.* Minneapolis, MN: Free Spirit Publishing.

Violand-Sánchez, E., & Hainer-Violand, J. (2006, September). The power of positive identity. *Educational Leadership, 64,* 36–40.

Walker, H. M., Colvin, G., & Ramsey, E. (1995). *Antisocial behavior in school: Strategies and best practices.* Pacific Grove, CA: Brooks/Cole.

Walker, H. W., & Sylwester, R. (1998). Reducing student refusal and resistance. *Teaching Exceptional Children, 30,* 52–58.

Walker, H. W., Todis, B., Holmes, D., & Horton, G. (1988). *The Walker social skills curriculum.* Austin, TX: ProEd.

Walker, R. (1998). Discipline without disruption. A presentation appearing in W. N. Bender and P. J. McLaughlin (Eds.). *The Tough Kid Professional Development Teleconference Series.* Athens, GA: Georgia Center for Continuing Education, University of Georgia.

Warshak, R. (1992). *The custody revolution.* New York: Poseidon Press.

West, J., Denton, J., & Reaney, L.M. (2001). *The kindergarten year: Findings from the Early Childhood Longitudinal Study Kindergarten class of 1998–1999.* Washington, DC: U.S. Department of Education, National Center for Education Statistics.

Wheatley, T., Milleville, S.C., & Martin, A. (2007). Understanding animate agents: Distinct roles for the social network and mirror system. *Psychological Science 18,* 6469–6474.

Willard, N. (2006). *Cyberbullying and cyberthreats: Responding to the challenge of online social cruelty, threats, and distress.* Eugene, OR: Center for Safe and Responsible Internet Use.

Williams, M. S., & Shellenberger, S. (1996). *How does your engine run: A leaders' guide to the Alert Program for self-regulation.* Albuquerque, NM: Therapy Works.

Winston, J. S., Strange, B. A., O'Doherty, J., & Dolan, R. J. (2002). Automatic and intentional brain responses during evaluation of trustworthiness of faces. *Nature Neuroscience, 5,* 277–283.

Yarkoni, T., Braver, T. S., Gray, J. R., & Green, L. (2005, November). Prefrontal brain activity predicts temporally extended decision-making behavior. *Journal of the Experimental Analysis of Behavior, 84,* 537–554.

Ybrandt, H. (2008, February). The relation between self-concept and social functioning in adolescence. *Journal of Adolescence, 31,* 1–16.

Young, S.E., Smolen, A., Hewitt, J. K., Haberstick, B. C., Stallings, M. C., Corley, R. P., & Crowley, T. J. (2006, June). Interaction between MAO-A genotype and maltreatment in the risk of conduct disorder: failure to confirm in adolescent patients. *American Journal of Psychiatry, 163,* 1019–1025.

Zahn, R., Moll, J., Krueger, F., Huey, E. D., Garrido, G., & Grafman, J. (2007, April). Social concepts are represented in the superior anterior temporal cortex. *Proceedings of the National Academy of Sciences, 104,* 6430–6435.

Zambo, D. M. (2007). What can you learn from Bambaloo? Using picture books to help young students with special needs regulate their emotions. *Teaching Exceptional Children, 39,* 32–39.

Zuna, N., & McDougall, D. (2004). Using positive behavioral support to manage avoidance of academic tasks. *Teaching Exceptional Children, 37,* 19–25.

Resources

Note: All Internet sites were active at time of publication

Association of Positive Behavior Support

P.O. Box 328

Bloomsburg, PA 17815

(570) 389-4081

Web: www.apbs.org

   This is an organization dedicated to the advancement of Positive Behavior Supports. Members of this organization receive newsletters, conference discounts, and subscriptions to *The Journal of Positive Behavior Interventions*.

Beach Center on Disability

University of Kansas

Haworth Hall, Room 3136

1200 Sunnyside Avenue

Lawrence, KS 66045-7534

(785) 864-7600

Web: www.beachcenter.org

   This is an organization devoted to improving the quality of life for families and individuals with disabilities. Current research topics include Positive Behavioral Support.

Big Brothers Big Sisters National Office

230 North 13th Street

Philadelphia, PA 19107

(215) 567-7000

Web: www.bbbs.org

   This site offers suggestions on how to establish a school-based mentoring program as well as information about successful programs already in place.

Cambridge Center for Behavioral Studies

Web: www.behavior.org

   This site can teach you how to help improve your child's language abilities. Also, specific information is available on autism, Applied Behavioral Analysis, and everyday behavior.

Center for Effective Collaboration and Practice

Web: http://cecp.air.org

This site includes sections on Functional Behavior Assessments, prevention strategies that work, prevention and early intervention, promising practices in children's mental health, and strength-based assessments.

Center for Evidence-Based Practice: Young Children with Challenging Behavior

Web: http://challengingbehavior.fmhi.usf.edu

This organization promotes the use of evidence-based practice to meet the needs of children who demonstrate problem behaviors. Here you will find effective intervention procedures, supporting research, presentation and workshop materials, training opportunities, and a variety of useful links.

Center for Safe and Responsible Internet Use

474 W 29th Avenue

Eugene, OR 97405

(541) 344-9125

Web: www.cyberbully.org

This site provides research and services regarding the safe and responsible use of the Internet. It provides guidance to educators, parents, librarians, policymakers, and others on effective strategies to assist young people in gaining the knowledge, skills, motivation, and self-control to use the Internet and other information technologies in a safe and responsible manner. A parents' guide to cyberbullying and cyber threats is available.

Council for Children with Behavioral Disorders

Web: www.ccbd.net

This professional organization is a division of the Council for Exceptional Children. It offers research syntheses, publications, message boards, an advocacy section, links to other sites, and a free online quarterly newsletter.

Council for Exceptional Children (CEC)

1110 North Glebe Road

Suite 300

Arlington, VA 22201

(703) 620-3660

Web: www.cec.sped.org

The CEC is dedicated to improving educational outcomes for individuals with exceptionalities, students with disabilities, and/or the gifted. The site offers strategies and resources for teachers and parents to help them with children who are exceptional.

Federal Office of Special Education Programs

National Technical Assistance Center on Positive Behavioral Interventions & Support

U.S. Department of Education

Web: www.pbis.org

This site provides assistance for administrators who are working to put a school-wide system in place for dealing with disciplinary issues. It includes a series of how-to-do-it guidelines and resources on conducting Functional Behavioral Assessments, collaborative teaming in positive behavior support, and group action planning.

The Gray Center for Social Learning and Understanding

4123 Embassy Dr. SE

Kentwood, MI 49546

(616) 954-9747

Web: www.thegraycenter.org

Although this non-profit is dedicated to individuals with autism spectrum disorders, it has numerous resources to address social issues, including suggestions for developing social stories.

Learning Disabilities Association of America

4156 Liberty Road

Pittsburgh, PA 15234-1349

(412) 341-1515

Web: www.ldanatl.org

Massachusetts General Hospital

Mood & Anxiety Disorders Institute Resource Center and School Psychiatry Program

Department of Psychiatry

55 Fruit Street

Boston, MA 02114

(617) 724-8318

Web: www.schoolpsychiatry.org

This Web site for parents, educators, and clinicians addresses the needs of children and teens who have mental health conditions.

Mental Health America

2000 N. Beauregard Street, 6th Floor

Alexandria, VA 22311

(800) 969-6642

Web: www.nmha.org

National Dissemination Center for Children with Disabilities (NICHCY)

P.O. Box 1492

Washington, DC 20013

(800) 695-0285

Web: www.nichcy.org

    This site includes a bibliography on Positive Behavior Support in schools.

National Association for Self-Esteem

P.O. Box 597

Fulton, MD 20759-0597

Web: www.self-esteem-nase.org

National Institute for Early Education Research

120 Albany Street, Suite 500

New Brunswick, NJ 08901

(732) 932-4350

Web: www.nieer.org

    This institute at Rutgers University supports early childhood education initiatives by providing objective, nonpartisan information based on research.

National Mental Health Information Center

P.O. Box 42557

Washington, DC 20015

(800) 789-2647

Web: http://mentalhealth.samhsa.gov

Project Alert

725 S. Figueroa Street, Suite 1825

Los Angeles, CA 90017

Phone: (213) 623-0580

Fax: (213) 623-0585

Toll-Free: 1-800-ALERT-10

Web: www.projectalert.com

    This site provides all the information about a nationally-recognized program for helping middle school students avoid substance abuse.

SchoolBehavior.com

Web: www.schoolbehavior.com/index.htm

This site is operated by a private psychologist who specializes in children and adolescents with Tourette syndrome. Here you will find overviews of different disorders, including Tourette syndrome, Asperger syndrome, attention deficit disorder, mood disorders, depression, sleep disorders, bipolar disorder, and obsessive compulsive disorder. The site also includes classroom tips on dealing with behavior problems.

Index

ABC log, 40
Abrams, B. J., 140, 184
Accepted Use Policy (AUP), 90
Adult mentoring, 104
  case study of, 112–114
  considerations on, 106–107
  initiating program on, 107–111
  self-esteem and, 175
All Stars Program, 17
Amygdala
  emotional processing and,
    10, 11–12, 70, 71
  impulsivity and, 32
  sadness and, 181
Anger thermometer, 65–66
Anterior cingulate, 46–47
Anterior temporal lobe, 96
Attention
  collecting data on, 59–60
  getting, 9–11
  nature of, 57–58
  self-talk and, 58–59
Attention-deficit hyperactivity disorder
  (ADHD), 76, 156
Attitudes
  adult mentoring and, 105, 111
  classroom climate and, 180, 184
  oppositional behavior and, 137–138
  peer influence and, 117–118
  self-esteem and, 162, 170
  social misbehavior and, 15–17

Attribution retraining, 36, 168–178
  case study in, 170–173
Attribution theory
  motivation research and, 168–170

Baxter, A., 169
Behavior
  gender differences in, 68–72
  peer management of, 119–135
  See also Oppositional behavior,
    Impulsive behavior
Behavioral improvement plan (BIP)
  example of, 195
  explanation of, 193–195
Bender, W. N., 81, 93, 184, 187
Bourbon, W. T., 141
Boy-friendly instruction, 77–81
Brain development
  emotional and rational areas, 8–10
  orbitofrontal cortex, 10–11
Brain imaging
  types of, 1–3
Bryan, T. S., 169

Carey, T. A., 141, 142
Cerebral lesions, 15, 33, 35
Chapter contents, 4–6
Classroom climate
  adults' perceptions of, 186–188
  assessing, 184–188
  behavior management and, 183

defined, 179–180

self-perceptions of, 184

students' perceptions of, 184

Climate. *See* Classroom climate, School climate

Cocaine

prenatal exposure to, 32–33

Cognitive-based interventions, 36

Cognitive-behavioral interventions, 36–37

Cognitive neuroscience, 94–97

Cooperative learning

building positive self–esteem and, 165

cultural differences and, 190

managing oppositional behavior and, 155

peer-mediated behavior management and, 119

school climate and, 184

Corpus callosum, 9, 14, 33, 70, 71

Correspondence training, 37

Cortical pathway, 14

Cortisol, 49, 149, 163, 164

Countercontrol, 141–142, 169, 183

Cultural diversity

classroom management and, 188–191

guidelines for managing classes

with, 189–191

Cyberbullying

dealing with, 90–91

versus bullying, 88–90

Damasio, A., 181

Dialogue journal, 100–104

Dielectical behavior therapy, 157

Dopamine

genetic variations and, 31–32

happiness and, 182

movement and, 74

Electroencephalography (EEG), 2, 46

Elias, M. J., 65

Emotional decision making, 11

Emotional intelligence, 16–17

Emotional processing, 8–13

Endorphins, 50, 163, 164, 182

Epstein, M., 165–166, 167

Explicit emotional learning, 12–13

Female brain

development of, 68–69

structural differences from male brain, 69–72

Females, controlling behavior of, 87–88

Ferguson, R., 93

Frontal lobe

controlling impulsive responses

and, 42, 43

cortical pathway and, 13–14, 36

description of, 8–9

gender differences, 70–71

genetic variations and, 32–33

happiness and, 181

maturation of, 11, 15, 35,

115, 116, 117

movement and, 73

self-control and, 46–47, 49

self-esteem and, 163

social development and, 96, 97

temperament and, 138

Functional behavioral assessment (FBA)

example of, 194, 197

explanation of, 193

Functional magnetic resonance imaging

(fMRI), 2, 115, 181

Gender differences

brain development and, 68–72

self-esteem and, 162

Goleman, D., 180

Group contingency interventions

cast study using, 133–134

description of, 131–135

Hainer-Violand, J., 190

Hallahan, D. P., 61, 62

Happiness
    biology of, 180–183
    sadness and, 180–181

Head Start Program, 46

Hippocampus
    emotional processing and, 8–9, 11–12, 14
    gender differences and, 70, 71

Hughes, C., 119

Humor
    classroom climate and, 185
    defusing oppositional behavior with, 145
    student use of, to gain attention, 128
    teacher use of, 50

100 Black Men of Atlanta, 106

Hypothalamus
    gender differences and, 70, 71–72
    oppositional behavior and, 138

Implicit emotional learning, 12

Impulsive behavior
    social context of, 38
    strategies for dealing with, 42–43
    using picture books to curb, 38–41

Inner speech, 36

Jamie, K., 65

Jenson, W. R., 132

Knowlton, E., 65

Life Skills Training Program, 17

Limbic area (system)
    description of, 8
    dopamine acting in, 32, 182
    emotional learning and, 11–13, 36, 47
    maturation of, 9–10, 46, 49
    sadness and, 181

Lloyd, J. W., 61, 62

Lopata, C., 154

MacLean, P., 8

Magnetoencephalography (MEG), 2

Maher, C., 83

Mahoney, M., 51

Male brain
    development of, 68
    structural differences from female brain, 69–72

Males
    tactics for motivating, 78–81

Marzano, R. J., 93

Masood, A. F., 169

McKinley, J., 190

Medial prefrontal cortex, 96

Mennuti, R. B., 37

Mirror neurons
    description of, 47–48
    self-control and, 48
    social behavior and, 94, 115–116, 117

Monoamine oxidase-A (MAOA), 31–32

Motivation
    attribution retraining and, 168–178
    behavior problems and, 176
    emotional intelligence and, 17
    responsibility strategy and, 81, 84
    self-esteem and, 161

Movement
    importance in learning, 50, 73–75
    ways of using, 75
    See also Movement-based instruction

Movement-based instruction, 73–77
    example of, 75–77

Multitiered interventions
    case study using, 196–202
    explanation of, 195–196

Mystery motivator/mystery character, 129–131

Neuron
activation in brain imaging, 2
effect of neurotransmitters on, 182–183
See also Mirror neurons
Neurotransmitters, 182

October Sky movie, 178
Oppositional behavior
case studies in managing, 146–148
causes of, 137–139
defusing techniques and, 144–146
power plays and, 144
teacher knowledge of, 140–141
See also Countercontrol, Turtle technique
Oppositional defiant disorder (ODD), 155–157
Orbitofrontal cortex, 10–11

Parent-child interaction therapy, 156
Parenting
class management issues and, 188
oppositional behavior and, 138, 139
self-esteem and, 161, 162
Parent management training, 156
Peer
populistic type, 118–119
prosocial-popular type, 118–119
Peer confrontation
case study using, 124–128
explanation of, 124–129
Peer influence
desire to be liked and, 118–119
research on, 117–118
Peer-mediated behavior management
explanation of, 119–135
factors to consider in, 120–121
Peer pressure, 56–57
Picture books, 38–41
Populistic peers, 118–119

Positive behavioral supports (PBS)
explanation of, 191–193
Positron emission tomography (PET)
explained, 2
happiness and, 180–181
Preoptic area, 71–72
Presley, J. A., 119
Project Alert, 17
Prosocial-popular peer, 118–119

Reavis, H. K., 132
Redenbach, S., 16
Relationships
developing teacher-student type, 98–114
neuroscience and, 94–97
Relaxation techniques, 149–154
Responsibility strategy
examples of, 82–84, 86–87
explanation of, 81–82
implementing, 84–86

"Say No and Walk Away," 56–57
School climate, 179, 180
Self-concept, 159
Self-control
brain structures involved in, 46–48
children and, 46
emotional intensity and, 65–66
explanation of, 45–46
helping student regain, 50–51
losing, 48–49
mirror neurons and, 48
self-talk and, 57–63
Self-esteem
biology and, 163
cautions about, 160
factors influencing, 161–162
guidelines for building, 164–165
power of, 160

research on, 161–163

Self-instruction, 36

Self-management

  explanation of, 36

  interventions using, 37–38

Self-monitoring

  check sheet for, 59

  example of, 63–65

  explanation of, 57

  script for introducing, 61

Self-reinforcement, 37

Self-talk, 51, 56, 58–59

Serotonin, 32, 182

Sex chromosomes, 31–32

"Shine My Light" strategy

  case study using, 197–202

  classroom use, 174–175

  planning activity for, 176–177

  recommend to parents, 177–178

  teacher's and parent's planning

    guide for, 176

Skinner, B. F., 141

Social anxieties

  dealing with, 18–19

  during adolescence, 97

Social cognition, 94

Social cognitive neuroscience

  description of, 95

  neuroscience research and, 96–97

  research on happiness and, 180

Social decision making, 10–11

Social problem solving, 36

Social responses, 13

Social stories

  creating, 22–25

  effectiveness of, 28

  guidelines for developing, 28

  intervening with, 25–26

  preparing, 20–22

using with angry students, 26–27

using with a verbally aggressive student, 22–26

why they work, 20

Socioeconomic status

  self-esteem and, 162

"So What" test, 143

Stereotyping, 15–16

Stoller, L., 61, 62

Strength-based assessment

  case study using, 166–168

  explanation of, 165–166

  student interview for, 166

Stressors, 139

Stress reduction, 36

Summary, 29, 43, 66, 91, 114, 135, 157, 178, 202

Suprachiasmatic nucleus, 71–72

Temperament, 138, 139

Testosterone

  gender differences and, 69

  impulsive behavior and, 34–35

Thalamic pathway, 14

Thalamus, 13–15

Townsend, B. L., 143, 184, 190

Triggers for misbehavior, avoiding, 147–149

Triple-A strategy, 119–120

  case study using, 121–124

  See also Peer-mediated

    behavior management

Turner, L. A., 169

Turtle technique

  grades K to 3, 150–153

  older students, 153–154

Vigilance, 13

Violand–Sánchez, E., 190

Walker, H. W., 144

ZIPPER strategy, 52–56

CORWIN PRESS